ESSENTIALS OF CORPORATE COMMUNICATION

This lively and engaging new book addresses a topical and important area of study. Helping readers not only to understand, but also to apply, the most important theoretical notions on identity, identification, reputation, and corporate branding, it illustrates how communicating with a company's key audience depends upon all of the company's internal and external communication. The authors, leading experts in this field, provide students of corporate communication with a research-based toolbox to be used for effective corporate communications and creating a positive reputation.

Essentials of Corporate Communication features original examples and vignettes, drawn from a variety of US, European, and Asian companies with a proven record of successful corporate communication, thus offering readers best practice examples. Illustrations are drawn from such global companies as Shell, Microsoft, Altria, and Johnson & Johnson. Presenting the most up-to-date content available it is a must-read for all those studying and working in this field.

Cees B.M. van Riel is Professor of Corporate Communication at the Rotterdam School of Management at Erasmus University in The Netherlands and Managing Director of the Reputation Institute, a privately held research and consultancy firm that he and Charles Fombrun created in 1999.

Charles J. Fombrun is Emeritus Professor of Management at New York University and Executive Director of the Reputation Institute.

ESSENTIALS OF CORPORATE COMMUNICATION

Implementing practices for effective reputation management

Cees B.M. van Riel
and Charles J. Fombrun

Routledge
Taylor & Francis Group

LONDON AND NEW YORK

ᴍᴸ

First published 2007
by Routledge
2 Park Square, Milton Park, Abingdon, Oxon OX14 4RN

Simultaneously published in the USA and Canada
by Routledge
270 Madison Ave, New York, NY 10016

Routledge is an imprint of the Taylor & Francis Group

© 2007 Cees B. M. van Riel and Charles J. Fombrun

Typeset in Akzidenz Grotesk
by Keystroke, 28 High Street, Tettenhall, Wolverhampton
Printed and bound in Great Britain
by Antony Rowe Ltd, Chippenham, Wiltshire

British Library Cataloguing in Publication Data
A catalogue record for this book is available from the British Library

Library of Congress Cataloging in Publication
A catalog record for this book has been requested

ISBN10: 0–415–32826–8 (hbk)
ISBN10: 0–203–39093–8 (ebk)

ISBN13: 978–0–415–32826–5 (hbk)
ISBN13: 978–0–203–39093–1 (ebk)

To the memory of our fathers
Stan van Riel and Marcel Fombrun
– who taught us a lot about character and reputation

CONTENTS

Illustrations   ix
Acknowledgments   xv

Introduction   The Communication System   1

Chapter 1   What is Corporate Communication?   13

Chapter 2   From Communication to Reputation   38

Chapter 3   Creating Identity and Identification   61

Chapter 4   Measuring Corporate Identity   80

Chapter 5   Communicating with the Corporate Brand   106

Chapter 6   Developing a Reputation Platform   131

Chapter 7   Expressing the Company   160

Chapter 8   Communicating with Key Stakeholders   181

Chapter 9   Assessing the Effectiveness of Corporate
              Communication   207

Chapter 10   Applied Reputation Research   228

Chapter 11   Organizing Corporate Communication   260

Bibliography   284
Index   302

ILLUSTRATIONS

Figures

I.1	Is this effective communication by Boeing in *The Economist* (September 13, 2003)?	5
I.2	Framework for the book	10
1.5	Examples of professional associations in marketing communications	19
1.2	The Reputation Institute (www.reputationinstitute.com)	21
1.3	Microsoft print advertising campaign (2005): "Your Potential, Our Passion"	32
1.4	Four visions of communication	33
1.5	Directing communications through "common starting points"	35
2.1	The relationship between image and reputation	43
2.2	An example of the relationship between reputation levels for Microsoft	45
2.3	Individual information processing	51
2.4	The workings of human memory	52
2.5	Linking communication and reputation to the business	60
3.1	Influence of identity mix on corporate image	68
3.2	Marks & Spencer's identity: trust, quality, and service	71
3.3	Identity types: four approaches for assessing organizational identity	72
3.4	DaimlerChrysler: communicating global integration	73
3.5	Linking identity and identification	75
3.6	The process of identity management	78

4.1	A consensus profile for describing a company's desired identity	83
4.2	Core dimensions of the personality profile	85
4.3	Sample results of a content analysis of a company's communications	91
4.4	The key dimensions of a company's expressiveness	92
4.5	Dimensions for classifying types of organizational climate	93
4.6	SOCIPO results for a medium-sized company compared to ideal type	95
4.7	Measuring organizational identification using ROIT	96
4.8	Testing effective and ineffective recall of logos	104
5.1	Altria group highlighting its role as parent company	108
5.2	The drivers of corporate branding	111
5.3	The search for synergy in the auto industry: repositioning DaimlerChysler, Ford Motor Company, and General Motors	113
5.4	Employee identification with corporate and business levels	116
5.5	The moderating effect of corporate brand dominance, fit, and involvement on the degree to which capability and responsibility associations influence purchase intentions	120
5.6	Typology of corporate branding strategies	123
5.7	Levels of corporate endorsement	125
5.8	Corporate advertising for Accenture	127
6.1	Nomenclature of some of the world's most visible corporate brands	133
6.2	Developing a nomenclature for the corporate brand	135
6.3	Virgin's Sir Richard Branson	138
6.4	An IKEA store	140
6.5	INVE's corporate story	142
6.6	LEGO's reputation platform	147
6.7	Creating a corporate story	149
6.8	Selecting the positioning elements to use in the corporate story	150
6.9	Using reputation drivers as starting points for story-telling	153
6.10	Building a cause–effect plot using the AAA model	154
6.11	An example of the AAA model in practice	156
6.12	Embedding the corporate story in multiple media	157
7.1	A seven-step model for implementing a corporate story	162
7.2	The stakeholder linkage model	163
7.3	Identifying key stakeholders	167

7.4	The domino principle	168
7.5	Defining perception gaps using the co-orientation model	169
7.6	Positioning HSBC as "The World's Local Bank"	172
7.7	Positioning Johnson & Johnson by emphasizing "nurturing" and "motherhood"	173
7.8	Johnson & Johnson's campaign: "Support Our Nurses"	174
7.9	The media balloon	176
7.10	Pre-testing a corporate communication campaign using the IMPACT model	178
7.11	The Reputational IMPACT model for assessing the expressiveness of a corporate communication campaign	179
8.1	Orchestrating corporate communication	182
8.2	Target audiences for investor relations	185
8.3	Investor relations: relationships between stakeholders	186
8.4	Employee relations: building organizational identification and performance	189
8.5	Effective employee relations: linking structure, flow, content, and climate	193
8.6	Overlap between marketing and organizational communication	196
8.7	Content analysis of press releases by a major US firm (2003–2004)	201
8.8	Which NGOs does the public trust?	202
8.9	Four issues management strategies	206
9.1	Results of a poll right before the 2000 and 2004 US presidential elections	208
9.2	EcQ™ The Strategic Alignment Monitor: linking internal communication to strategic alignment	210
9.3	Strategic alignment, expressiveness, and reputation	212
9.4	Questions to address in reputation research	214
9.5	Reputation objects created from natural grouping	217
9.6	A typical distribution of attributes obtained from Q-sort	218
9.7	Applying photo-sort to British Airways	220
10.1	How GM uses the J.D. Power & Associates #1 rating for publicity	229
10.2	The brand pillars measured in Y&Y's BrandAsset®Valuator	233
10.3	The power grid	234
10.4	Movement of a number of brands in the power grid	235
10.5	Linking financial value to brand health	236

10.6	The brand dynamics pyramid of BrandZ	238
10.7	Conceptual and empirical BrandZ maps	240
10.8	Different brand signatures for Marks & Spencer	241
10.9	EquiTrend's measure of brand equity	242
10.10	Brand power: drivers and effects	245
10.11	The six dimensions and 20 attributes of the Harris–Fombrun Reputation Quotien (RQ)	249
10.12	Using RQ dimensions as key performance indicators	252
10.13	The Reputation Institute's RepTrak® scorecard	255
10.14	The RepTrak® system	256
10.15	A RepTrak® driver analysis	258
11.1	The structure of the typical communication function	269
11.2	The reputation value cycle	271
11.3	The value chain of corporate communication	273
11.4	The process of communication planning	276
11.5	Coordinating corporate communication around the "carousel principle"	280
11.6	Building a coherent corporate communication system	281

Tables

2.1	Aaker's scale of corporate personality	41
2.2	Components of corporate personality	42
2.3	Multiple points of view on corporate reputation	50
4.1	Methods for measuring corporate identity	81
4.2	Dimensions for classifying types of organizational climate	94
4.3	The organizational communication scale	98
4.4	Comparing communication audits	102
5.1	Typology of corporate branding strategies	124
6.1	Results of a cobweb analysis of identity elements	152
7.1	Segmenting stakeholders	165
7.2	Types of target groups	166
9.1	Approaches to reputation management	213
9.2	Types of measurement methods applied in reputation measurement	215
9.3	The results of an attitude scaling of airlines	223
9.4	Evaluating methods of reputation measurement	226

10.1 Reputation dimensions across major research programs 231
10.2 Brand power of selected brands 244
10.3 The USA's most admired companies 248
10.4 How managers can impact reputation with corporate
communication 251
11.1 The principal activities of the communication function 267
11.2 Four models for managing corporate communication 269
11.3 Mechanisms for orchestrating corporate communication 274

Boxes

1.1 Integrated communication 29
2.1 Definitions of corporate communication 44
2.2 The value of a good reputation 48
3.1 Various definitions of organizational identity 66
4.1 Identity scales used to describe a university 87
5.1 Employee identification with corporate and business levels 116
8.1 Profiling the GR specialist 198
9.1 Questions to address in reputation research 214
11.1 Budgeting for corporate communication 277

Case studies

6.1 The Virgin corporate story: value for money 138
6.2 The IKEA corporate story: improving everyday life 140
6.3 The INVE corporate story: healthy feed for healthy food 142
6.4 The LEGO corporate story: imagination, learning, and play 147

ACKNOWLEDGMENTS

The book you are holding is the record of a unique partnership spanning ten years. At the start of our cooperation, one of the authors (Charles) worked as a professor at Stern Business School, New York University while Cees was professor at Rotterdam School of Management, Erasmus University, Rotterdam in The Netherlands. Both of us had just finished a book. Cees wrote *Principles of Corporate Communication* in 1995 (Prentice-Hall) and one year later Charles published his book, *Reputation: Realizing Value from the Corporate Image* (Harvard Business Press). We joined forces immediately after one intense session in New York in which we learned that our visions were rather comparable and at least complementary. The first action we jointly took was to organize a conference to which we invited a diverse group of academic colleagues interested in the topics of "Reputation, Identity and Competitiveness." In 2006 we celebrated the tenth anniversary of this conference. We also established a specialized journal, *Corporate Reputation Review*. Above all, we created a platform, the Reputation Institute, where practitioners and academics regularly meet and exchange ideas (www.reputationinstitute.com). The goal of the Reputation Institute is to advance knowledge about reputations and to improve the practice of reputation management. We sincerely hope that this book will contribute towards that goal. We have integrated our past research and consultancy work as the key building blocks for the 11 chapters that comprise this volume. This book intends to serve three main goals:

1. to present an overview of the main theoretical models from around the world into one integrated framework;

2. to provide a clear vision about the reputation management style that will be most successful in creating and/or maintaining a positive reputation;
3. to build a framework that can be used to teach the basics of corporate communication at higher levels of education in business schools and executive reputation management programs.

Various people in and around The Reputation Institute contributed extensively to the development of our ideas. We are particularly indebted to John Balmer (Bradford University), Garry Davies and Rosa Chun (Manchester Business School), Klaus-Peter Wiedmann (University of Hanover), Majken Schultz (Copenhagen Business School), Francesco Lurati (University of Lugano), Michael Pratt (University of Illinois), Kevin Corley (Arizona State University), Tom Brown (Oklohoma State University), and Davide Ravassi (Boconi University).

We would specifically like to thank those from our Corporate Communication Centre of RSM/Erasmus University: Majorie Dijkstra, Joke van Oost, Mirdita Elstak, Mignon van Halderen, Ahong Gu, Guido Berens, Sytske Seyffert, Edwin Santbergen, and Marianne Aalders. They all suffered, but never complained! It is great to have you as colleagues.

The same applies to all our colleagues at The Reputation Institute, in more than 20 countries around the world. We would especially like to express our gratitude to two colleagues who joined forces with us on a full-time basis since 2003, Kasper Nielsen and Nicolas Trad. We could not have done this job without the many initiatives implemented by the two of you during the last years.

Not to forget, we would also like to express our gratitude to our partners on the home front. Micheal Bevins and Hanneke Aarts kept supporting us all these years. Thanks a lot to both of you and may we be forgiven for the hours we missed while writing this book.

Last but not least, we like to thank our publishers Francesca Heslop and Emma Joyes of Routledge, who remained patient and kept stimulating us to finish this new book. In hindsight we do not regret it at all.

Thank you all.

Breda, The Netherlands, January 2007
New York, USA, January 2007

INTRODUCTION: THE COMMUNICATION SYSTEM

Do but take care to express yourself in a plain, easy Manner,
in well-chosen, significant and decent Terms,
and to give a harmonious and pleasing Turn to your Periods:
study to explain your Thoughts, and set them in the truest Light,
laboring as much as possible,
not to leave them dark nor intricate,
but clear and intelligible.
Miguel de Cervantes, Preface to Don Quixote

Communication is the lifeblood of all organizations: it is the medium through which companies large and small access the vital resources they need in order to operate. It is through communication that organizations acquire the *primary* resources they need (such as capital, labor, and raw materials) and build up valuable stocks of *secondary* resources (such as "legitimacy" and "reputation") that enable them to operate.

Organizations secure access to these resources in two ways: first, by directly negotiating the prices and terms on which a resource is purchased. This requires *direct* communication between buyers and sellers, and calls on familiar communication skills. Another way organizations gain control over valued resources is by influencing *indirectly* the context within which these exchanges occur (Pfeffer and Salancik, 1978). Through lobbying and collective action with other organizations, companies build entry barriers that can make it very difficult for rivals to enter their markets. Doing so creates a more hospitable environment in which to operate. Individually, through alliances, and by joining forces with other companies and forming collectives, managers can build up an image about how a particular issue or problem should be addressed. In democracies like the US and Australia, for instance, the public affairs departments of companies devote considerable time and energy in lobbying legislators to enact laws that will favor them over rivals. Often these departments get involved in building information campaigns designed to influence public opinion and pressure politicians to adopt preferred positions on contentious issues (Astley and Fombrun, 1983).

Activist groups can be equally skilful at influencing public images. For instance, Greenpeace is well known for its successful efforts to influence public opinion about the harmful effects of corporate initiatives on environmental pollution and climate change. The organization has been extremely effective at getting media organizations to publicize its controversial marches and protests. Among its more famous campaigns was its action against Shell in 1995 following the company's decision to dispose of the defunct Brent Spar oil platform. Greenpeace's efforts to prevent the sinking of the platform into the North Sea generated worldwide media attention on the issue of environmental pollution and vilified the Royal Dutch Shell Group in the minds of consumers for years to come. In similar ways, throughout the 1980s and 1990s the activist organization Act-Up was very effective in calling attention to the pharmaceutical industry's pricing and distribution policies for AIDS drugs. Act-Up successfully swayed public opinion against the pharmaceuticals by staging theatrical sit-ins at corporate facilities of targeted firms such as Pfizer, Merck, and GlaxoSmithKline and by developing mock ads, posters, and other incendiary communications which they distributed widely and which were re-diffused by the media.

Communication is therefore at the heart of organizational performance. The success of an organization's efforts to acquire resources and to influence the context within which it carries out its activities depends heavily on how well and how professionally a company communicates with its resource-holders.

We define an organization's *communication system* as the multiple tactical and strategic media it relies on to communicate with its stakeholders, as well as the message content it chooses to diffuse through those media. The communication system encompasses marketing communications, public relations, investor relations, and employee communications; it also includes the kinds of institutional communications an organization makes that are created to influence how issues are framed and the public debate that results about it. In its largest sense, it encompasses the initiatives that a company often undertakes to demonstrate "social responsibility" and "good citizenship" – most of these good deeds are important in helping a company to build a more favorable and welcome social environment for its routine operations.

From fragmentation to integration

In their efforts to exert control over the acquisition of these valuable physical and symbolic resources, organizations have proliferated a multiplicity of specialized groups whose responsibilities are to communicate with targeted stakeholders. The modern organization typically operates through departments charged with community relations, government relations, customer relations, labor relations, human resources – both at the corporate and at the business-unit levels. This kind of specialization has fostered a fragmentation of the organization's communication system that has severely limited its effectiveness over the years.

The presence of multiple specialized senders of information, when they are not explicitly and strategically coordinated, stands in the way of creating consistency of external and internal corporate communication. Managers in different geographical locations or working for different parts of the same firm find themselves frequently contradicting one another, and therefore conveying inconsistent impressions about the company and its products to resource-holders.

Faced with a growing variety of challenges to their operations, in recent years organizations have grown increasingly aware of the need to overcome fragmentation and to reduce the volume of inconsistent communications that they convey. They seek ways to improve coordination among the many different specialists involved in communication activities for the organization. The expression used to describe this trend is "integrated communication" – a systematic process for building a fully coordinated communication system inside the organization.

When orchestration of communications is limited, an organization's image and reputation are put at risk. For example, it's clearly not a good thing when two entirely contradictory messages about a company appear in the same medium on the same day. Yet it happens very frequently. Consider British American Tobacco. On the very same day that the UK manufacturer placed a costly advertisement touting its superior financial performance in a Dutch newspaper, the front page of the same paper announced the lay-off of 123 employees in its Amsterdam branch. A similar inconsistency did significant damage to AT&T's image when in January 1996, the company famously announced plans for a record downsizing of 50,000 employees *at the same time* that the financial pages announced record earnings for investors. The public lynching these companies received as a result damaged their image and points to a systemic failure of integration across these companies' communication systems.

Boeing, the mammoth maker of airliners, provides yet another example. The company chose to place a full page advertisement for the company on the back cover of *The Economist* precisely on the day of the two-year anniversary of the 9/11 attacks on NY – the fateful day on which hijacked Boeing planes had been used as missiles by Al Qaeda terrorists (Figure I.1). The move was probably unwise and suggests that someone at Boeing was simply not paying close attention to integration – they failed to anticipate the actions and reactions that stakeholders would have to those simultaneous but contradictory messages.

Incidents like these happen to all organizations. One cannot control everything, everywhere. Nonetheless, we suggest here that it is feasible to put in place a more coherent process for orchestrating the different communication specialties and help to limit their negative effects. If AT&T, British American Tobacco, and Boeing had sought to apply such an explicit process for coordinating investor relations with media relations, these contradictions might have been avoided.

And that is the subject of this book.

Corporate branding and communication

The revived interest in integrated communication results not only from visible inconsistencies in the communication system, but also from a rising understanding that economic value can be created by strengthening *corporate brands* – the features of a company that employees, investors, customers, and the public associate with an organization as a whole. Whereas much of our past interest in questions of integration can be traced to the mass-marketing of product brands, the current emphasis in major companies is principally in the communication system that surrounds the corporate brand.

The purpose of a corporate brand is to personalize the company as a whole in order to create value from the company's strategic position, institutional activities, organization, employees, and portfolio of products and services. The corporate brand is increasingly being used to cast a favorable halo over everything the organization does or says – and capitalize on its reputation.

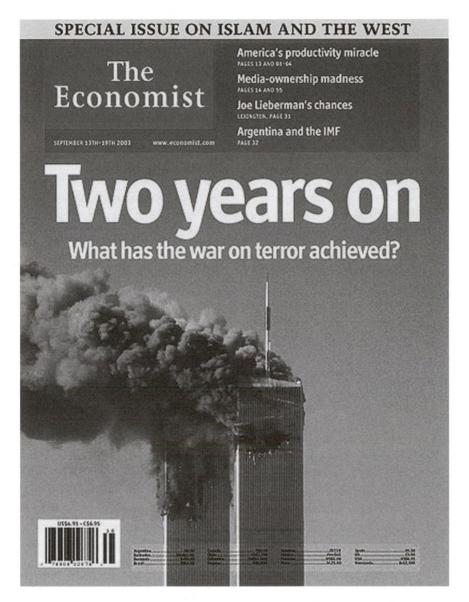

Figure I.1 Is this effective communication by Boeing in *The Economist* (September 13, 2003)?

An organization that wants to compete using its corporate brand is therefore challenged as never before to develop a coherent communication system.

Various trends are making corporate brands more relevant around the world, and so are encouraging the visible push towards more integrative communication in organizations.

- *Information availability*: The proliferation of information sources and instantaneous transmission of information has created an environment in which people find it difficult to trust the products and services that are available to them. In these circumstances, customers, investors, and potential employees seek a better understanding of the organization that stands behind those products. Companies are increasingly using their corporate brands to infuse attractive mental and emotional associations into stakeholder transactions with the organization.
- *Media mania*: In recent years, companies and their top executives now perform in the media spotlight, making corporate brands – and the reputation of the company behind the company's product brands – a major source of distinctiveness and value.
- *Advertising saturation*: From banners to billboards to radio and television commercials, we are mentally assaulted with product messaging. As overloaded publics pay less attention to these messages, purchased advertising space has lost some of its historical effectiveness. Broader corporate brand-building strategies rooted in public relations, sponsorship, and corporate citizenship have grown in importance in the media-mix for influencing perceptions and cutting through the crowded media marketplace to position the company behind the products (Ries and Ries, 2002).
- *Product commoditization*: International expansion has fostered increasing homogeneity in the kinds of products and services companies are selling across geographical markets. You cannot escape the proliferation of franchises around the world, whether in purchasing fast foods, beverages, or other consumer products. When product and service differences between offerings are slight, companies are using their corporate brands as a source of distinctiveness and differentiation.
- *Globalization*: Rivalry is on the rise due to the blurring of national boundaries and to the multi-market operations that companies develop to capitalize on regional differences in labor and to minimize logistical costs. When L'Oreal, Siemens, Ericsson, Shell, or Philips enter a new market, their reputational halos are a major force in attracting consumers, and in negotiating attractive deals with local suppliers and regulators. Foreign companies are finding

it beneficial to use their corporate brands to establish themselves internationally and to out-compete local rivals. Global corporate brands always attract attention, and research suggests that the attention they get is overwhelmingly favorable and endowed with prestige.

For these reasons, communicating about the corporate brand has become more important in recent years, and is having a growing effect on how we assess a company's communication system.

What makes for effective communication?

Assessing systematically the effectiveness of a company's communication structure and its communication activities has dogged practitioners for years. Schultz (1994) suggested calculating a "return on investment" (ROI) as a way to measure the results of an integrated marketing communication (IMC) initiative. Katz and Lendrevie (1996) proposed measuring effectiveness by examining different kinds of consumer exposure: media coverage, product impressions, and personal contacts. Baldinger (1996) suggested using the last three stages of the Advertising Research Foundation's model (ARF) – recall, communication, and persuasion – to develop a measure of the impact of an IMC campaign.

One way to measure communication results is through its net effect on the company's "brand equity." From a consumer point of view, brand equity is "the differential effect that brand knowledge has on a consumer's response to the marketing of the brand" (Keller, 1996, p. 104). Brand equity measures the strength of the consumer's associations with the brand, and has two components: brand awareness (brand recall and brand recognition) and brand image (the strength, favorability, and uniqueness of consumer associations).

Whereas brand equity describes the added economic value that a brand brings to the organization, brand image consists of the cluster of attributes and associations that consumers connect with the brand itself (Biel, 1992). Keller (1991, p. 7) defined brand image as "consumer perceptions about a brand as reflected by the brand associations that consumers hold in memory." Park *et al.* (1986) added that brand image is not a perceptual phenomenon affected by marketer's communication activities alone. They propose that [brand image] "is the understanding consumers derive from the total set of brand-related activities engaged in by the firm" (1986, p. 135).

From a branding perspective, the role of an integrated communication system is therefore to enhance brand equity: (1) by establishing the brand in the observer's memory, (2) by linking strong, favorable, and unique associations to the brand, and (3) by creating stakeholder motivation, ability, and opportunity to process persuasive messages and retrieve brand information from memory when making a brand choice or recommendation.

Brand-related communications influence the meanings associated with the brand and create an image for the brand. Advertising and public relations increase brand awareness and thereby increase the probability that a company's products and services, jobs, or shares will be evoked by resource-holders, affecting perceived brand value, and creating an image that influences how they view the company and its products (Cobb-Walgren et al., 1995).

An integrated communication system, particularly if it communicates corporate brand values, ultimately influences, not only brand equity, but overall evaluations of the company (Fombrun, 1996; Farquhar, 1989). If the corporate brand can be more immediately retrieved from memory, it shows a highly accessible association between the communication system and the corporate brand, and so demonstrates increased brand equity (Edell, 1993; Herr and Fazio, 1993) and improves overall reputation (Fombrun and van Riel, 2004). A global reputation measure, carried out with the resource holders of the organization, can therefore act as a powerful tool for measuring the effectiveness of an integrated communication program.

Although the communication system as a whole is generally viewed as a positive contributor to an organization's performance and reputation, specialized communications sub-functions often remain a weak link in the chain. In most organizations, communications specialists tend to lack influence with top management. Experience suggests that the powerlessness of these specialist communications functions largely results from: (1) a historical failure by communications specialists to take responsibility for their actions and demonstrate accountability for bottom-line indicators like sales, profits, awareness, recall, or reputation (a notable exception is for marketing specialists who often demonstrate that their communications activities are directly responsible for sales increases), (2) a lack of third-party verification of contributions that communications make to the company's results, and (3) a tendency to remain remote from the business objectives being fulfilled by specialized communications activities. As we have observed first hand, that makes a weak argument for including communications specialists as members of strategic decision-making committees or involving them in the dominant coalitions of organizations.

The framework of this book

The purpose of this book is to suggest that a strategic focus on what we call the *total communication system* is the only way to overcome the existing fragmentation of communications in most organizations. By developing an integrated communication system, an organization can flesh out a structure for *corporate communication* that can assist in the implementation of strategic objectives, build brand and reputation, and thereby create economic value.

The book proposes a simple framework for developing the corporate communication structure of any organization. As we have suggested, the effectiveness of an organization depends on its ability to attract key resources from stakeholders, be they capital, labor, or raw materials, as well as legitimacy and reputation. To succeed, organizations must therefore develop and maintain healthy interactive relationships with their stakeholders – and the purpose of a company's communication system is to facilitate that engagement. Creating a *system for corporate communication* is therefore a vital component of every company's strategy-setting and execution.

The central question that we address in this book is: how can organizations best develop and manage an integrated communication system? As we have learned, no universal solutions apply. Readers should therefore not expect to find here a panacea that will apply easily to all organizations. However, since the 1980s, a rich collection of insights has developed from the study of management, marketing, and organizational communications in both theory and practice that make it possible for senior managers today to be better prepared to build an effective corporate communication system. The purpose of this book is to capture these insights succinctly, and we do so by applying the integrative model of Figure I.2.

The model takes as its point of departure that the communication system is a key tool for guiding and executing corporate strategy. Strategy guides the selection of businesses in which the company competes and how the company wants to position itself in those businesses – as a market-leading innovator, follower, cost-cutter, or premium-focused niche player. The company's relative strategic position defines key attributes and features the organization must be perceived to have by major stakeholders in order to be competitive and effective. In turn, these attributes have to be consistent with the organization's identity in order to be credible to observers. Credibility itself is judged on the basis of the company's existing reputation.

Strategy, identity, brand, and reputation therefore jointly define the "starting points" for building the corporate communication system. The corporate brand

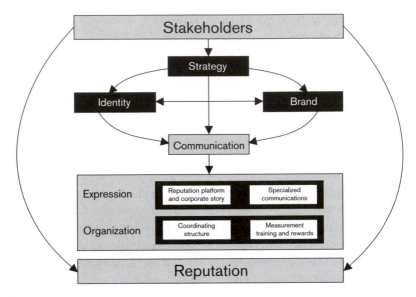

Figure I.2   Framework for the book

is *expressed* by creating a *sustainable corporate story* that serves as a frame around which to hang the full array of communications the organization disseminates (van Riel, 2001). The sustainable corporate story sets the stage for all expressions of the company's identity to stakeholders – and constitutes its "reputation platform" (Fombrun and van Riel, 2004). Although every organization has multiple stakeholders, we focus in this book on four primary resource-holders and the specialized forms of communication in which they are involved: Financial audiences (investor relations), employees (internal communications), customers (experience marketing), and the public (issues management).

Ultimately, the model of Figure I.2 suggests that a coherent focus on the organization's communication system positively contributes to the favorable image that each specialized component of the communication system develops, which in turn affects the development of positive stakeholder perceptions about the organization, improves its performance, and so increases its ability to acquire additional resources and succeed. As we suggest, a favorable corporate reputation is not an isolated objective, but a vital means through which the success of the organization develops. Recent studies we have reviewed elsewhere validate the empirical relationship between organizational performance and corporate reputation (Fombrun and van Riel, 2004). Orlitzky *et al.* (2003) provide a detailed comparative analysis of 52 studies that verifies a systematic and robust empirical relationship between social and economic indicators of organizational performance.

The rest of the book is divided into 11 chapters corresponding to key components of the model. Chapter 1 defines the perspective of "corporate communication" and its growing importance. Chapter 2 examines the link between corporate communication and corporate reputation – the perceptions that stakeholders have of an organization. Chapter 3 looks more closely at the roots of corporate reputation in the process of generating identity, identification, and support. Chapter 4 examines different methodologies for uncovering identity elements in an organization.

Chapters 5–8 examine in more detail how companies express themselves to targeted stakeholders. Chapter 5 begins by describing the rationale and processes that organizations can use to develop strong corporate brands. Chapter 6 focuses on the creation of sustainable corporate stories. Chapter 7 deepens the implementation of those corporate stories through corporate campaigns targeted to four primary audiences: financial, employee, government, and public. Chapter 8 shows how five types of specialized communications can be used to carry out a corporate communication campaign. In Chapters 9 and 10, we turn to assessment. Chapter 9 suggests that the effectiveness of the corporate communication system can be assessed by measuring corporate reputation systematically using appropriate measurement methods. Chapter 10 reviews important applied reputation research programs now in use by companies around the world.

We conclude the book in Chapter 11, by examining the organization of the communication function and exploring how internal and external communications can be orchestrated in practice. We end each chapter with short discussion questions designed to stimulate readers to think about how they might apply some of the issues raised.

Discussion Questions

Pick a company with which you are very familiar.
1.　Describe the company's communication system.
2.　Who is responsible for the communication about products and services?
3.　Who is responsible for the corporate brand?
4.　Who is responsible for communicating with financial audiences, regulators, legislators, and with potential employees?

5. Who is responsible for internal communication with employees?
6. How are communication efforts being coordinated across resource-holders, markets, and media?
7. How integrated are these communications?
8. In what way do communication methods applied in one company differ from those of the company's two most important competitors?

1

WHAT IS CORPORATE COMMUNICATION?

Speak out
Let us have some variation on the theme
Speak freely
Clear
Not thoughts you think we like to hear
But thoughts that sear and form and grow
To change
Change our cluttered cramped ideas
Speak out
For that is why you are here

Egal Bohen

Organizations are networks of people who communicate with each other. In all organizations, communications flow vertically and horizontally, internally and externally, formally and informally, linking employees internally to each other, to various layers of management, and to the many external resource-holders of the organization. Not all of the communications in an organization are work-related, nor are they necessarily relevant to fulfilling organizational objectives. All communications, however, influence to some extent the perceptions of participants and observers about the organization and its activities, and so affect the organization's image, brand, and reputation.

In this chapter, we focus specifically on the formal task-related communications that link internal and external audiences of the organization. After reviewing the three principal types of communications in organizations, we propose the concept of *corporate communication* as an integrative communication structure linking stakeholders to the organization. A corporate communication structure describes a vision of the ways in which an organization can strategically orchestrate all types of communication. In the rest of the book, we propose a coherent approach to the application of a corporate communication perspective to all organizations.

Types of communication

There are three principal clusters of task-related communication activity within organizations. They are typically classified as management communications, marketing communications, and organizational communications.

The most strategic cluster is "management communications", the communications that take place between the management level of the organization and its internal and external audiences. The management level consists of all employees with authority over the acquisition and retention of key resources in the company. In other words it includes, not only senior management, but also various levels of business-unit and department managers within the organization. Executive speeches, for instance, are among the strategic communications managers make whose targets are both internal and external. When senior managers speak at conferences, or when they lobby legislators about topics of interest, they are clearly presenting a personalized view of the organization to powerful constituencies, and so influencing the public debate about those issues as well as contributing to building an image and reputation for the organization.

To support management communications, organizations rely heavily on specialists in the areas of marketing communications and organizational communications. Marketing communications get the bulk of the budgets in most organizations, and consist of product advertising, direct mail, personal selling, and sponsorship activities. They are supported to a greater or lesser extent by "organizational communications" that generally emanate from specialists in public relations, public affairs, investor relations, environmental communication, corporate advertising, and employee communications.

Management communications are far more effective when marketing and organizational communications support them. This has two consequences. First, managers must realize the possibilities and limitations of their own roles in the communication process. Second, specialists in all areas of communication must understand how to support management in their communications.

Specialists have a responsibility to act as advisors to management and to contribute professionally and critically to the implementation of the organization's objectives.

In recent years, other groups and roles have become involved in marketing and organizational communication. In many organizations, internal and external affairs departments have lost their historical monopoly over communications. Whether this is desirable or not is a moot point. In practice, the playing field has changed, and both public relations and advertising are increasingly splintered into ever more specialized sub-groups and roles. In the area of marketing communications, for instance, the elements of the promotion mix generally remain under the responsibility of a marketing director, and so specialization has been less consequential. In contrast, growing fragmentation of the organizational communication cluster has had more far-reaching consequences in many organizations. Fragmented groups involved in organizational communication often report into different managers, and their activities are often inconsistent. Additionally, seldom are organizational communications linked directly to outcome measures such as exposure, brand equity or sales increases, making turf wars between groups difficult to arbitrate.

Management communications

Managers fulfil key functions in organizations. Management is often described as "accomplishing work through other people." Typically this includes functions such as planning, organizing, coordinating and controlling. Management is only possible with the consent of those being managed. In other words, it's difficult to manage anyone who does not want to be managed. As a consequence, one of the manager's roles is to continuously persuade individual subordinates that the goals of the organization are worth fighting for. Communication is therefore one of the most important skills a manager must have in order to gain acceptance for the organization's goals.

Management communication is not only a task that takes place at the top of the organization. All levels rely on communication in order to (Pincus *et al.*, 1991):

1. develop a shared vision of the company within the organization;
2. establish and maintain trust in the organization's leadership;
3. initiate and manage the change process;
4. strengthen the identification of employees with the organization.

Various authors are critical and even cynical in their description of the lack of effectiveness and skill managers have in communicating to their own staff and to external audiences. However, more and more people are convinced that the success of managers and organizations depends to a large extent on the degree to which managers effectively apply themselves well to the task of communicating.

Although all management layers do have to communicate, top management has a special role to play in representing the organization to internal and external audiences. In particular, the chief executive officer (CEO) plays an important symbolic role as the spiritual and emotional leader of the organization and is sometimes ascribed heroic characteristics. Even when top managers are very skilful in acting as figureheads of the organization, communication is too important to be left solely to their discretion. Communications specialists are needed to support managers in improving the effectiveness of their communications. In essence, the work of these specialists consists of preparing and executing projects that increase the involvement of internal stakeholders and improve the opinions external audiences have of the organization.

The supportive role of communication specialists should not be confused with the role played by occasional experts called in to cure specific organizational ailments.

> *Such a communication specialist quickly becomes the resident expert and a feeling seems to creep over the rest of the management team that they no longer need to worry about the problem. The danger is, of course, that it is patently absurd to expect one person (or department) operating out of one position, to solve a problem that is organizationally pervasive. This kind of lip service to remedy organizational ills will not relieve anyone in the organization of their own proper communication role, any more than the presence of a training executive relieves individual managers of their responsibility for training.*
>
> *(Allen, 1977)*

In the academic departments of leading business schools, management communication receives very little attention. Researchers are often journalists, skilled in case-writing and language, but lacking training in research methodology. Teaching activities revolve around skill-building in making presentations, delivering speeches, or preparing written reports. Core management courses relegate communication to support roles and mostly rely on them to help students improve their writing, make oral presentations, and develop listening skills.

Yet the field of communications involves far more than skill-building. The conceptual framework for communications is mostly found in journals such as *Speech Communication*, *Human Communication* and in journals providing technical information about organizational communication. Similarities in research and education, but especially their application to organizations, are larger than one would assume, and it is becoming ever more apparent that the different subsets of organizational communication, colored by the paradigms of their professional disciplines, are becoming more complementary to one another than competitive. It's therefore only logical that groups like the *Arthur Page Society* and the *International Association of Business Communicators* periodically call for initiatives that will integrate content about organizational and marketing communication into international business management curricula.

Marketing communications

Marketing communications consist primarily of those forms of communication that support sales of products, services, and brands. In marketing communications, a distinction is often made between the promotional mix and the public relations mix (Rossiter and Percy, 2000; Kitchen, 1999). Gusseklo (1985) similarly distinguishes between the corporate communication mix and the marketing communication mix.

Almost every author on the subject regards advertising as a vital and salient component of the communication mix. Franzen (1984) describes advertising as a process of relatively indirect persuasion, based on information about product benefits, designed to create favorable impressions that "turn the mind toward" purchase. Sales promotion is often regarded as "additional activities to above-the-line media advertising, which support sales representatives and distributors" (Jefkins, 1983). Direct mail is described by Knecht and Stoelinga (1988) as "any form of direct advertising distributed by addressed mail." The same authors describe sponsorship as "an activity in which an institution (the sponsor) gives material (usually financial) support to (a) an association or individual for the presentation of sporting or artistic performances, or other performances of a kind interesting to a particular public, or (b) the organizers of a cultural or sporting event, in exchange – as a minimum – for mention of its brand name."

Within the promotional mix, the greatest share of the budget goes to personal selling and sales management. Its distinguishing feature is the direct personal contact that takes place between the seller and the prospective buyer, which tends to facilitate responsiveness to the needs of the individual client. Personal selling involves "oral presentation in a conversation with one or more prospective purchasers for the purpose of making sales" (Kotler, 1988).

A number of authors regard marketing-oriented public relations – *publicity* – as an instrument of marketing communication. Publicity consists of "non-personal stimulation of demand for a product, service or business unit by planting commercially significant news about it in a published medium or obtaining favorable presentation of it upon radio, television or stage that is not paid for by the sponsor" (Kotler, 1988).

By far the largest share of a company's total communication budget, however, is devoted to marketing communication, and particularly to advertising. Global advertising expenditures in 2003 were estimated to be around $262 billion (*World Advertising Trends*, NTC, 2003). Considering the enormous sums of money involved, a great deal of information is available on both qualitative and quantitative aspects of marketing communication, including financial data (e.g. advertising expenditures), information on target groups (e.g. patterns of media consumption), and data about the relative performance of agents (e.g. advertising agencies).

Many large international organizations and important journals are devoted to the study or practice of marketing communication, and it is of direct interest to a variety of academic networks around the world, not so much as an independent discipline, but as a component of the marketing curriculum in accredited MBA programs. In economics and communication sciences, the field of marketing communication has been a part of the curriculum for many years.

Large numbers of researchers work in this field, so it should come as no surprise that marketing communication has adopted a positivistic paradigm. Indeed, articles published in such outlets as the *Journal of Advertising*, *Journal of Advertising Research*, *Journal of Brand Management*, *Journal of Marketing Communication* or the *Journal of Consumer Research* are often so specialized and technical that few of those engaged in the practice of marketing communication are able or willing to read them! Figure 1.1 illustrates some of these groups and publications.

EUROPEAN
MARKETING CONFEDERATION

AMERICAN ASSOCIATION
of ADVERTISING AGENCIES
www.aaaa.org

IABC INTERNATIONAL ASSOCIATION
OF BUSINESS COMMUNICATORS

Figure 1.1 **(opposite)** Examples of professional associations in marketing
communications

Source: EMC www.emc.be

Organizational communications

The third type of communications is organizational communications: they encompass public relations, public affairs, investor relations, corporate advertising, environmental communication, and internal communication. They denote a heterogeneous group of communication activities that have four characteristics in common:

▌ Organizational communications are aimed at corporate audiences, such as shareholders, financial journalists, investment analysts, regulators, and legislators.
▌ Organizational communications have a long-term perspective and do not directly aim at generating sales.
▌ Organizational communications apply a different style of communication compared with marketing communication; exaggeration and puffery are limited and messages are more formalistic.
▌ Organizational communications are generally initiated by external parties. External pressures generally compel the company to reveal information that would not have been shared otherwise. As Grunig (1992) points out, in organizational communications, stakeholders generally decide whether the organization should communicate with them, whereas in marketing communications, the organization chooses its target audiences and avoids communicating with those that are not "commercially interesting."

Companies differ greatly in the ways in which organizational communications are incorporated into their organizational structures. In many companies, most specialized organizational communications are governed by the external affairs department. But many organizational communications are also developed outside the external affairs department. This generally happens when needs arise in a particular functional area to address specific stakeholders – for which a special form of communication gets introduced.

Two pre-conditions are necessary to justify creating a new communication department outside the boundaries of the external affairs department. First, the particular corporate audience should be strategically important to the organization. Second, knowledge creation should be important. For example financial managers or human resource managers often claim that a specific modality of communication (like investor relations or employee communication) can be better exploited if it is anchored within their relevant (knowledge-generating) functional area.

In contrast to the state of affairs in marketing communication, however, we lack hard data about organizational communications. Budgets for organizational communications are not as clearly identified as those of marketing communications. It's often difficult to uncover what sponsorship funds and donations are spent on, nor are their results – successes and failures – easily explained.

There are many national and international associations for professional communicators. They include the International Association of Business Communicators, International Association for Public Relations, and American Association for Investor Relations. Most of these associations tend to focus on one aspect of organizational communication, and do not provide an integrated view of the field. In 1999, we created the Reputation Institute (RI) to foster synergy across related disciplines of communication and reputation (Figure 1.2). The RI is an alliance network of academics and practitioners interested in advancing knowledge about corporate communication and reputation management. The RI hosts an annual scientific and practitioner conference, as well as periodic forums internationally. The RI also publishes the quarterly *Corporate Reputation Review* and is involved in developing theoretical frameworks, standardized measurement instruments, and applied work methods to upgrade the field.

Today, the most influential journals in the field of corporate communication are *Corporate Reputation Review*, *Journal of Public Relations Research*, *Journal of Business Communications* and *Management Communication Quarterly*. Important articles also appear regularly in more general management journals such as: *Academy of Management Journal*, *Academy of Management Review*, *Strategic Management Journal*, *Long Range Planning*, *Journal of Business Strategy*, and *Sloan Management Review*.

Figure 1.2   The Reputation Institute (www.reputationinstitute.com)

The "corporate communication" perspective

"Corporate communication" encompasses marketing communications, organizational communications, and management communications. By "corporate communication", we mean a coherent approach to the development of communications in organizations, one that communication specialists can adopt to streamline their own communications activities by working from a centrally coordinated strategic framework.

Corporate communication adopts a "corporate" point of view. Derived from the latin "corpus" meaning "body" or "the whole", it invites communication specialists to focus, first and foremost, on the problems of the organization as a whole. Corporate communication therefore addresses the fulfilment of organizational objectives. Developing a corporate communication perspective does not require establishing a new function in organizations. Rather, it invites bringing down the traditional "Chinese Walls" that exist in most organizations between segmented communication functions.

Since the 1980s, the perspective of "corporate communication" has found a receptive ear at senior levels and among communication specialists. In the Netherlands, for instance, early proponents of corporate communication were inspired by consulting firms. They found an appreciative audience in large companies and large government institutions. Most of the time, they stimulated companies to launch corporate image campaigns, and recommended increased uniformity in communication policies. Corporate communication therefore became synonymous with strengthening corporate brands through corporate advertising and adopting a "monolithic identity" by endorsing all of a company's offerings with a single corporate name such as Shell or Philips (Chapter 3 examines these corporate branding approaches in depth).

Gradually, both consultants and clients gained insight into the antecedents of corporate brands, namely the nature of the corporate strategy, the corporate identity, and the heterogeneity of the context of the environment in which the organization operates. This soon led to a growing awareness that it is not always desirable nor is it practical to stimulate "uniformity" in overall communication policy.

Consultants ultimately fell victim to the persuasive power of their own arguments. As the walls crumbled between marketing and organizational communications, as steering committees were put in place to harmonize communication policies, companies began to take the lead in orchestrating their own communication system. This is entirely appropriate: in our experience, the activities involved in carrying out corporate communication should be vested in an ensemble of on-site specialists, not in outside agencies or consultancies.

Key tasks of corporate communication

Corporate communication requires an emphasis, not only on external image improvement, but on internally directed activities aptly described by Luscuere (1993) as creating a "diagnostic and alteration capability" to stimulate all employees to work together to support the company's overall objectives, rather than merely focusing on their functional tasks.

The responsibilities of corporate communication are therefore:

- to flesh out the profile of the "company behind the brand" (corporate branding);
- to develop initiatives that minimize discrepancies between the company's desired identity and brand features;
- to indicate who should perform which tasks in the field of communication;
- to formulate and execute effective procedures in order to facilitate decision-making about matters concerning communication;
- to mobilize internal and external support behind corporate objectives.

The holistic perspective of corporate communication makes it an area that can be meaningfully positioned within the interdisciplinary research and educational field of management. As we pointed out in the previous section, for decades training in "Business Administration" has given short shrift to communication topics, and addressed them under multiple names and with varying content. The differences we have observed lie mainly in the emphasis placed on:

1. *Skill building versus theory development*: skills are necessary to successfully execute communication tasks, but business education in communications over-emphasizes skills at the expense of research and theory.
2. *Holistic versus specialist training*: specialist perspectives are over-emphasized in communication research, fostering fragmentation of the field and a lack of coherence, thereby contributing to further fragmentation of the function in organizations.

In our view, academic departments addressing "corporate communication" should be holistic rather than specialized, and oriented to theory-building and testing rather than to skill-building.

Some examples drawn from many studies of the communications area should illuminate this point. One of the first was Johanson's (1971) study of the link between company image and product image. Birkigt and Stadler (1986) released an influential analysis of the relationship between identity and image. These authors had a considerable impact, not only in the Netherlands, but in their native German-speaking regions. Their publications have been valuable resources for scholars in Germany (Wiedmann, 1988; Kammerer, 1988; Tanneberger, 1987; Merkle, 1992), Austria (Hinterhuber, 1989), and Switzerland (Fenkart and Widmer, 1987; Tafertshofer, 1982), particularly with regard to establishing a link between corporate strategy and corporate communication. French researchers such as Ramanasoa (1988), Reitter (1991), and Kapferer (1992), as well as Italian researchers such as Gagliardi (1990) also had significant impact on the development of the field of corporate communication.

Other international academics have intentionally or unintentionally influenced our understanding of corporate communication. They include Selznick (1957), Kennedy (1977), Dowling (1986), Abratt's (1989) discussion of image measurement, Higgens and Diffenbach (1989), Sobol and Farrelly's (1989) work on the image effects of corporate strategy disclosure, and Fombrun and Shanley's (1990) analysis of the antecedents of corporate reputation. Poiesz (1988), Verhallen (1988), Pruyn (1990), and Scholten (1993) contributed valuable research describing how images form. In the Netherlands, van Rekom *et al.* (2006) proposed a pragmatic method for establishing the identity of a company through a laddering/means–end analysis (we review it in Chapter 8). Van Riel *et al.* (1994) measured communication effects on employee identification with the organization. Finally, van Ruler (2003), Cornelissen (2001), and Kleijneijenhuis (2001) have all provided useful insights about corporate communication, with a particular focus on how it is carried out in Dutch companies.

Much progress has also been made in exploring the organization of the communication function. Studies by Knapper (1987), Verbeke *et al.* (1988), and Adema *et al.* (1993) examined the relative effectiveness of various organizational structures. However, in comparison to the many rigorous empirical studies of "identity" and "reputation", studies of the communication function have been principally exploratory, and focused heavily on describing the activities carried out in selected companies that may not generalize to other countries.

Corporate communication and related concepts

The following definition, formulated by Jackson, was among the first to appear in the international literature:

> *Corporate communication is the total communication activity generated by a company to achieve its planned objectives.*
>
> *(Jackson, 1987)*

Blauw (1986) describes corporate communication as:

> *The integrated approach to all communication produced by an organization, directed at all relevant target groups. Each item of communication must convey and emphasise the corporate identity.*

Thomas and Kleyn (1989) also advanced two early descriptions of corporate communication as:

- all communication of an organization whereby coordination, based on a strategic plan, exists between the different communication disciplines and the resources they use;
- all communication of an organization whereby the organization or the elements of it are central instead of the products and/or services.

Definition

We define *corporate communication* as the set of activities involved in managing and orchestrating all internal and external communications aimed at creating favorable starting points with stakeholders on which the company depends. Corporate communication consists of the dissemination of information by a variety of specialists and generalists in an organization, with the common goal of enhancing the organization's ability to retain its license to operate.

We follow Jackson's example in using "corporate communication" in the singular. In the plural form, it implies a proliferation of methods. In the singular form, it refers directly to the integrated communication function. As Jackson remarks:

> *Note that it is corporate communication – without a final "s." Tired of being called on to fix the company switchboard, recommend an answering machine or meet a computer salesman, I long ago adopted this form as being more accurate and left communications to the telecommunications specialists. It's a small point but another attempt to bring clarity out of confusion.*
>
> *(Jackson, 1987)*

A disadvantage of adopting "corporate communication" to refer to the total communication activity of the organization is the impression created that corporate communication is only relevant to business corporations. As with terms such as "corporate culture" and "corporate strategy", the use of the word "corporate" in "corporate communication" should not be taken as the adjective corresponding to "corporation". Rather, it should be interpreted in relation to the Latin word "corpus", meaning "body", or, in a more figurative sense, "relating to the whole".

Ideas about corporate communication are relevant to both private and public companies, to businesses and to not-for-profit organizations. Because they operate in competitive environments, businesses have been aware for some time of the value of developing attractive images. Corporate communication has therefore been more heavily associated with business than with other organizations. In recent years, however, pressure has been increasing on subsidised institutions and government agencies as well to give a good accounting of themselves to their audiences. We therefore see growing attention to these matters in the not-for-profit sector.

A corporate image is like a mirror: it reflects the identity of the organization. Having a favorable or unfavorable image is determined in part by the signals that an organization broadcasts about itself. These signals are interpretations by stakeholders based on the company's actions and self-expressions (Fombrun and Shanley, 1990; Fombrun, 1996; Schultz *et al.*, 2000). No matter how frank, open, and appealing the content of these signals, however, there is no guarantee that they will create a positive image in the minds of all members of the target group. Earning a top rating for diligence, for instance, does not automatically lead to a positive image.

Various other factors also influence the image an organization develops, including the conduct of employees and managers, the dissemination of rumours, and, most of all, the rational and seemingly irrational ways in which members of targeted groups *interpret* the signals they receive. As Bauer (1964) points out, the public often turns out to be far more obstinate in its views than managers expect.

Tools of corporate communication

Integrated communication can be achieved in various ways. We highlight four practices here:

1. application of visual identity systems (sometimes referred to as "house style");
2. use of integrated marketing communications;
3. reliance on coordinating teams;
4. adoption of a centralized planning system.

These four mechanisms are tools of *expression* (Hatch, Schultz, and Larsen, 2001). Insofar as organizational expressions and integrative communications rely on "common starting points" that express the organization's distinctive identity, brand, and strategy, they will be instrumental in generating identification by stakeholders, and so in building the reputation of the organization. As we emphasize throughout this book, coordination and integration are the hallmarks of an effective system for corporate communication.

Visual identity systems

Organizations express themselves through their communications. Visual communications are an important tool for integrating communications across the organization. As early as the turn of the twentieth century, industrial design specialists began emphasizing the application of consistent themes on products and services through the use of common names, trademarked graphics and logos (the Nike "swoosh"), sounds (the Harley-Davidson engine, the Steinway piano), and even smells (Chanel). Since then, a specialized industry of "identity firms" has emerged that helps organizations develop a uniform set of symbols, and put together house-style manuals that provide employees with guidelines for creating a uniform image for the organization through the application of signature themes in logos, clothing, furniture, and architecture.

In the 1950s, the rapid growth of mass marketing throughout the United States created enormous interest in packaging. The rise of supermarkets and department stores called for a substitute voice for the salesman who used to stand behind the counter and interface with the customer. Packaging design fulfilled that role, and what was once a sideline that printers had dreamed up to sell boxes and containers quickly became a full-fledged business.

Today, all major companies rely on elaborate handbooks that specify appropriate language, style, and nomenclature that help to guide integration across their communication systems. Even small companies find it advisable to do the same in order to build recognition and reputation and attract more investors and customers.

Integrated marketing communications

Attempts to achieve an "integration of effort" in communications have been made since the 1950s. The pursuit of integration is rooted in the marketing literature and involves not only the familiar elements of the marketing mix (price, product, place, and promotion – the so-called 4-Ps), but also the elements of the communication mix *within* each of the 4-Ps. Central to the concept of marketing is the need to operate in a customer-centric mode. This is only possible if each specialized function within the organization makes a valuable contribution to the communication system as a whole.

Initially, "integration" meant coordination across the marketing functions and specialty disciplines. However, the notion of integration was subsequently extended to encompass complementary activities performed by all functional departments, integrated around the customer in order to increase loyalty. Schultz and his colleagues were among the first to specify key elements of integrated programs in marketing (Schultz, 1993; Schultz and Barnes, 1995; Schultz *et al.*, 1993). As they proposed, integration should always develop from the top down, and be carried out from the stakeholder's point of view. Finally, they suggest that marketing and communications should develop shared objectives, allowing communications to lead all marketing activities when the company is responding to stakeholder demands.

Although integration was initially understood as a call for uniformity – the need to "become one", it was quickly softened to a requirement that brand messages be consistent and free of internal contradictions (Nowak and Phelps, 1994). Consistency could result only if all communication instruments were fine-tuned to each other during preparatory planning. By implication, specialists responsible for developing each of the brand communication instruments were advised to engage in intense dialogue early on in the process to diminish the chance of subsequent inconsistencies and contradictions. Unison gave way to a more apt metaphor of singing in "harmony".

In process terms, Moore and Thorson (1996) suggest that integrated marketing communications should start by: (1) identifying all target audiences relevant to achieving marketing objectives, (2) segmenting audiences on the basis of stage in the purchase decision cycle, (3) determining messages and communications tools to reach each segment, and (4) allocating appropriate levels of resources.

Although integrated marketing programs were originally introduced in the 1950s, they have not been fully endorsed by all practitioners. For instance, in the late 1980s the Dutch marketing specialist Knecht carried out a study of integrated communication on behalf of the Union of Advertisers and the Dutch Association of Recognised Advertising Agencies. He distinguished five stages in the evolution towards integrated communication. A synopsis of Knecht's five stages is provided in Box 1.1. His study demonstrated that very few agencies or companies have actually ever progressed beyond stage three.

Box 1.1 Integrated communication

1. Integrated media advertising

The mix of media used to transmit the message.

2. Integrated advertising

Coordinated application of media advertising, direct advertising, and packaging.

3. Integrated media communication

Coordinating media advertising, direct advertising, editorial publicity, product placement, and promotion of the brand or product name by means of sponsorship.

4. Integrated marketing communication

Coordinating all elements of the marketing mix beyond those described in stage 3. A vital element is personal selling, although price and distribution are also crucial.

continued

5. Integrated communication

Application of communication elements primarily developed for marketing but extended to other functions of the enterprise. Communication is coordinated across enterprise functions and target groups so as to prevent the emergence of contradictions that could harm the organization's image.

Source: Knecht (1989)

Coordinating teams

Another tool for facilitating integration is the use of coordinating teams – work groups or steering committees in which representatives of specialized communication departments that are active throughout the organization jointly develop a common policy and evaluate its execution. Chapter 11 pays specific attention to the coordination of the total communication function via coordinating teams.

Communication planning system

A communication planning system (CPS) is an automated tool for preparing and executing communication projects targeted to internal and external audiences. A CPS can be used to execute a project requiring an entire communication program for the organization. It can also be used to manage simpler projects such as are involved in corporate sponsorship activities, developing annual reports, or creating internal newsletters.

Use of a CPS offers an organization a few concrete advantages:

1. Per project a certain degree of planning is stimulated because an array of protocols (based on research) have to be followed.
2. It is possible to manage and control at a general level because one can "force" employees to absorb certain information such as the common starting points, budgetary constrictions, time-limits etc.
3. CPS also works as an orchestrating instrument through the level of overview it offers of plans, market research (such as image research, information about competitors, clients, etc.), and communication items (text, pictures,

and even films). The overview that this offers of all the possibilities has an implicit character. By being aware of all the efforts that are taken by the different communication functionaries, one makes sure there is a minimum of repetition or conflicting messages.

4. CPS functions as a form of knowledge base that retains knowledge even after employees depart.

5. CPS offers efficiency advantages, for example by delivering standard structures of reports that can be used in various situations.

When is corporate communication successful?

Organizations spend large sums of money on communicating with their stakeholders. Companies like Microsoft, Shell, and DaimlerChrysler are among the major corporate advertisers in the world, but are also very active in all areas of communication. Figure 1.3 shows a Microsoft advertisement that highlights the company's commitment to education. It is supported by multiple communications, donations, and events supporting the "education" theme that the company favors. The theme is manifested in the company's widely promoted corporate campaign "Your Potential, Our Passion".

In contrast, some companies are large corporate advertisers but are less active in other communication domains. For instance, hotel groups like the Mandarin Oriental or Accor advertise a great deal, but do little else. Similarly with airlines, utilities, and many consumer goods companies. Among nongovernmental organizations (NGOs), Greenpeace is one of the most visible in generating both free publicity and in carrying out co-sponsored advertising. Few other NGOs have the slack resources needed to carry out any advertising at all.

Despite the different approaches to communication used by companies, NGOs, and governments, they all allocate significant resources to communication activities. The question therefore arises – how do we know when communications are successful? What makes for effective communication?

When communication provokes changes in knowledge, attitudes and behaviors

Communications are successful when they generate changes in knowledge, attitude and behaviour (KAB). Many researchers in marketing communications

Our mission is not just to unlock the potential of today's new technologies. It is to help unleash the potential in every person, family and business. We want to help you do the things you do every day – express your ideas, manage your finances, build your business – faster, easier, and better. At Microsoft, we see the world not as it is, but as it might someday become.

Factory
We see a comeback.

Assembly
We see nothing small about them.

Ovation
We see a standing ovation.

King of the Skies
We see the king of the skies.

Hat
We see a label with your name on it.

World of inventions
We see new skills, tomorrow's inventions.

Figure 1.3   Microsoft print advertising campaign (2005): "Your Potential, Our Passion"

have underscored this principle, but found that the order is irrelevant. In many cases, for example, people are known to buy cars first (change in behavior) but only subsequently to confirm their choice psychologically by paying attention to selected advertising or communications about the car. Studies show that some customers only become aware of salient features of their cars *after* they have purchased it.

The simplified analysis of the KAB model is problematic in practice as well. Almost all communication activities aim to change people's behavior. In practice, it is hardly ever possible to affect all three simultaneously. Generating a change in knowledge implies an entirely different communication approach than aiming at changes in attitude or behavior. In our experience, many communication activities fail when companies try to do all three at once. We will discuss this topic at greater length in Chapter 8.

When communications are honest and symmetrical

Grunig (1992) proposed a two-dimensional framework from which he distinguished four perspectives on communication: on one axis, an organization chooses whether to engage in a one-way or two-way information exchange with its stakeholders; on the other axis, the organization decides whether it is prepared to reveal the complete truth about its operations and objectives, or to be only partially truthful. The four perspectives on communication are summarized in Figure 1.4.

	One-way communication	Two-way communication
Entirely true	Public information	Two-way symmetrical communication
Complete truth not essential	Press agentry communication (propaganda)	Two-way asymmetrical communication

Figure 1.4 Four visions of communication
Source: Grunig (1992)

In Grunig's view, press agentry or propaganda is the least desirable form of communication because it involves a one-way flow of information where the organization is less than truthful about its activities and justifies its deception on the basis of lofty goals. Propaganda often results, for instance, when a company communicates about externalities in its production processes: managers avoid revealing the complete effects of the company's operations on communities and the environment, and often also resist efforts to establish a dialogue about it with constituencies.

The second model, public information, also involves a one-way flow of communication, but one in which the organization attempts to communicate the truth. Instructions given to employees about safety and health procedures in companies are a typical example of this type of communication.

The third model involves two-way-asymmetric communication. Communication is imperfect because, although the organization is revealing accurate information, the organization does not invite much dialogue. This occurs, for instance, when companies use scientific evidence to convey information to audiences. Recent advertisements by pharmaceutical organizations touting the health benefits of their drugs are a case in point. Audiences are not expected to raise refuting arguments that could change the message.

The fourth model describes Grunig's ideal type of communication. It involves a company in two-way symmetric communication. Under this model, both parties are open and truthful about each other's point of view, and exchange information with reciprocal respect so as to arrive at a common understanding of the situation. Grunig's model encourages organizations to think carefully about their intentions in communicating with a target group.

When communications are accountable and adopt measurable success criteria

Success of corporate communication results when companies demonstrate their accountability on three levels: *overall accountability*, *specialist accountability*, and *coordinated accountability*.

Corporate accountability involves demonstrating the effects of corporate communication on building a favorable reputation for the entire organization. It allows the communication structure to enforce authenticity and consistency across all functional management areas. A precondition for corporate accountability is being part of the dominant coalition and systematically illustrating the added value of corporate communication for the company. Having quantitative information about the organization's reputation demonstrates overall accountability.

Specialist accountability involves creating protocols describing both the procedures applied and the success criteria used at the functional level. Use of specialist scorecards to gauge their success in delivering quantitative and qualitative results with targeted audiences helps spur overall success of corporate communication.

Finally, companies want to demonstrate accountability around the coordination of their activities. Coordination results when all communication specialists draw on the same core elements to implement their specialized communications. It involves ensuring that the organization's communications policies are derived from the core strategy–identity–brand (SIB) triangle described in the Introduction to this book. Managers who rely on the SIB triangle to develop a set of "common starting points" that are the basis for creating functional communication plans can help create coordinated accountability. Figure 1.5 diagrams the link between the SIB and the corporate communication system.

Starting points are specific to a company and should be developed jointly by all specialists in communication, not dictated by senior managers from a corporate head office. Starting points provide a sound basis for carrying out communication policy objectives, even within individual specialized areas of communication. Starting points create a bandwidth around which communication specialists can work, but do not imply absolute conformity or uniformity.

Another way to put it is that starting points act as guidelines for all of the organization's communications. They clarify the priorities inherent in a

Figure 1.5 Directing communications through "common starting points"

communication policy and accountability system. To work effectively with common starting points, we recommend paying attention to two sets of considerations:

1. Translate the corporate strategy into common starting points that can be used for communication at both the *corporate level* and the *business level* by applying the PPT model as follows: indicate what the organization wants to *P*romise to its most important internal and external stakeholders; indicate how it expects to *P*rove it; and identify what *T*one of voice it wants to use to communicate messages to those audiences.
2. Make plans more specific by applying the KAB model: specify what the organization wants target groups to know (*K*nowledge), to feel (*A*ttitude) and to do (*B*ehaviour), both with respect to the entire company and with respect to the individual business unit.

Chapters 3–8 flesh out the process through which corporate communication can thus be created and accountability developed. Chapters 9 and 10 specify the criteria against which corporate communication should be evaluated, namely corporate reputation.

The communication agenda: to build reputation

Corporate communication helps an organization to create distinctive and appealing images with its stakeholder groups, build a strong corporate brand, and develop reputation capital (Dowling, 1994; van Riel, 1995; Fombrun, 1996). To achieve those ends, all forms of communication must be orchestrated into a coherent whole (van Riel, 1992; Bronn and Simcic, 2002), and success criteria developed that enable measuring the effects of the organization's communications on its reputation and value (Fombrun and van Riel, 2004).

In the next chapter, we turn to the literature on corporate reputations, and identify the role that corporate communication can play in building an organization's reputation. In particular, we suggest that reputation is the most meaningful outcome through which we can evaluate the successful development of a corporate communication system. Reputation therefore belongs at the top of the corporate communication agenda.

Discussion Questions

1. Pick an organization. Prepare an organization chart of the organization and identify conceptually the principal types of communication in which it engages.
2. Gather messages emanating from your chosen company and classify them as management communications (e.g. a CEO speech), marketing communications (e.g. a product advertisement), or organizational communications (e.g. an annual report, press release, etc.). Can you identify common themes across these communications?
3. How can organizations limit fragmentation in their communications?
4. Find published articles in the principal journals of the field that focus on management communication. Compare them to articles in journals focused on marketing communication, and in journals focused on organizational communication. Do you observe any similarities or differences?

2

FROM COMMUNICATION TO REPUTATION

Reputation is only a candle,
of wavering and uncertain flame,
and easily blown out,
but it is the light by which the world looks
for and finds merit.
James Russell Lowell[1]

Corporate communication affects the perceptions of stakeholders about the organization's prospects, and so influences the resources that are made available to the organization. Stakeholder perceptions about organizations are described by different terms across disciplines. By far the most popular are the constructs of "brand", "image", and "reputation." Differences between them are relevant, not for reasons of academic purity, but because they represent different points of view and their pragmatic implications vary. Communication specialists should understand how their colleagues in different departments think about these matters since they are called upon to interface directly on strategic issues. Understanding one another is crucial if an effective dialogue is to result, and if a consistent form of corporate communication is to develop in the organization.

This chapter focuses on conceptualizations of brand, image, and reputation, and proposes that "corporate reputation" is a multi-stakeholder construct that is particularly appropriate for measuring the effectiveness of an organization's communication system. We indicate that the concept of corporate reputation, both in theory and practice, owes a large debt to the academic marketing literature (Dichter, 1964) as well as to prominent practitioners from the 1950s. We also recognize that the study of corporate reputations has been complemented more recently by contributions from other disciplines. In this chapter, we therefore add to the marketing mix a variety of perspectives that are anchored in psychology, strategic management, sociology, organizational science, and accounting. Chapter 2 sets the stage for the development of the corporate communication perspective that is articulated in the rest of the book.

Brand, image, and reputation

What is a brand? According to practitioners "a brand is a mixture of attributes, tangible and intangible, symbolized in a trademark, which, if managed properly, creates value and influence" (see www.brandchannel.com). The *Dictionary of Business and Management* similarly defines a brand as "a name, sign or symbol used to identify items or services of the seller(s) and to differentiate them from goods of competitors." Advertising guru David Ogilvy positioned a brand more expansively as "the intangible sum of a product's attributes: its name, packaging, and price, its history, its reputation, and the way it's advertised." More recently, David Aaker (1996) described a brand as a "mental box," and indicated that "brand equity" consists of "a set of assets (or liabilities) linked to a brand's name and symbol that adds to (or subtracts from) the value provided by a product or service." Al Ries (2002) asserts that "if you want to build a brand, you must focus your branding efforts on establishing a word in the prospect's mind – a word that nobody else owns."

Common to all of these definitions is the idea that brands create images in the minds of observers. They do so by communicating a combination of verbal, visual, and emotional cues that encourage targeted observers to identify with the brand. Historically, the branding literature has concentrated its efforts on explaining how organizations can create positive product perceptions with consumers. More recently, researchers have extended the brand concept and argued that the same branding principles can be used to create positive perceptions of the organization as a whole with targeted groups such as employees, communities, or environmental groups. It is part and parcel of a growing interest in "corporate branding" – the degree of endorsement a company chooses to put on all of its products and services. Chapter 4 addresses this issue at length.

The related term "image" is more commonly used to describe the specific configuration of perceptions that take root in the minds of observers. These images can be described in many ways. We dwell here on the content of the "corporate image" – the features of the company that stakeholders come to perceive. According to Dowling (1986), "an image is the set of meanings by which an object is known and through which people describe, remember and relate to it. That is it is the net result of the interaction of a person's beliefs, ideas, feelings and impressions about an object."

In fact, corporate image research can be traced to industrial design. As Tom Brown (1998) indicates:

> The notion of a "corporate identity system" was established during the 1930s, chiefly by such companies as Lord & Taylor, Steuben Glass, and the Container Corporation of America. In 1933, Lord & Taylor began to coordinate the manner in which the retailer would be presented to its publics through the design and consistent use of the Lord & Taylor signature in long-hand as the corporate logo. At the Container Corporation of America, total design integration was introduced so that the company as a whole could be promoted through all media reaching the consumer. Through the coordination of design and careful attention to the identity presented to important audiences, the notion of a corporate personality began to develop.

A number of researchers have sought to describe corporate images in terms of human personality. Jennifer Aaker (1997) proposed a typology based on the work of human psychologists who believe that personality can be described using words to label the way people act or react in certain contexts. Aaker's (1997) quantitative scale of corporate personality is shown in Table 2.1 and consists of 42 items organized around five dimensions: sincerity, sophistication, competence, excitement, and ruggedness.

More recently, Davies *et al.* (2003) developed an empirical measurement instrument for calibrating "corporate personality" that identifies seven central dimensions of corporate image: agreeableness, enterprise, competence, chic, ruthlessness, machismo, and informality. Table 2.2 provides a breakdown of those dimensions and the 49 items they encompass.

In our view, the concept of "corporate reputation" has gained attention recently because it captures *the effects* that brands and images have on the overall *evaluations* which stakeholders make of companies. Brand and image attributes are more or less appreciated by stakeholders. Organizations with particular brands and image attributes therefore develop greater or lesser *reputations*. "Reputation" can therefore serve a useful function by gauging the overall estimation in which the organization is held by its constituents

Table 2.1 Aaker's scale of corporate personality

Sincerity	Excitement	Competence	Sophistication	Ruggedness
Down-to-earth	Daring	Reliable	Upper class	Outdoorsy
Family-oriented	Trendy	Hard-working	Glamorous	Masculine
Small town	Exciting	Secure	Good looking	Western
Honest	Spirited	Intelligent	Charming	Tough
Sincere	Cool	Technical	Feminine	Rugged
Real	Young	Corporate	Smooth	
Wholesome	Imaginative	Successful		
Original	Unique	Leader		
Cheerful	Up-to-date	Confident		
Sentimental	Independent			
Friendly	Contemporary			

Source: Aaker (1997)

– and so measure the effectiveness of the organization's communications with those stakeholders (Fombrun, 1996). Figure 2.1 suggests that reputations evolve from the images that organizations develop in each of four domains: the product domain, the social domain, the financial domain, and the employment domain.

The popularity of the concept of "corporate reputation" owes much to the publication in 1982 by *Fortune* magazine of its first list of *America's Most Admired Companies*, a rating of the largest companies in the US that was developed from a quantitative opinion survey of top industry executives and analysts. The attention it received ensured that it would become an annual event, and it has since been widely imitated in other countries and regions.

A number of theoretical and empirical developments also explain the growing interest in corporate reputation analysis. Fombrun and Shanley (1990) presented one of the first and most influential empirical studies of the *Fortune* ratings. Their analysis explained corporate reputations on the basis of the communication halo that surrounds companies – created from a combination of signals broadcast by companies themselves, by financial analysts, and by the media. Grahame Dowling (1994) looked at reputations as extensions of the corporate brand. Van Riel's (1995) *Principles of Corporate Communication* presented a broad overview of the multiple disciplines contributing to the study of corporate communication in organizations. Fombrun (1996) proposed the broadest business framework for examining corporate reputations. He

Table 2.2 Components of corporate personality

Agreeableness	Enterprise	Competence	Chic	Ruthlessness	Machismo	Informality
Friendly	Cool	Reliable	Charming	Arrogant	Masculine	Casual
Pleasant	Trendy	Secure	Stylish	Aggressive	Tough	Simple
Open	Young	Hardworking	Elegant	Selfish	Rugged	Easy going
Straightforward	Imaginative	Ambitious	Prestigious	Inward looking		
Concerned	Up to date	Achievement oriented	Exclusive	Authoritarian		
Reassuring	Exciting	Leading	Refined	Controlling		
Supportive	Innovative	Technical	Snobby			
Agreeable	Extrovert	Corporate	Elitist			
Honest	Daring					
Sincere						
Trustworthy						
Socially responsible						

Source: Davies *et al.* (2003)

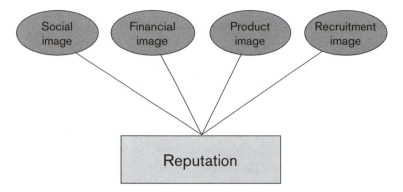

Figure 2.1 The relationship between image and reputation
Source: Fombrun (1996)

described a corporate reputation as a multi-stakeholder social construction that resulted from strategic communications created by an organization and refracted by the media and by analysts.

Despite the negative connotation of the word "reputation" in various European languages, the concept of "corporate reputation" has gained wide-spread acceptance around the world. Some of that resonance can be attributed to growing research in the US and around the world, a good deal of which has been featured at conferences organized by the Reputation Institute (RI) and in the RI's quarterly journal *Corporate Reputation Review* since 1997. Some of it is also due to multi-country measurements of visible companies initiated by the Reputation Institute with various research partners since 1999 that has relied on the standardized Harris–Fombrun "Reputation Quotient" (RQ) measurement instrument developed by Charles Fombrun and Harris Interactive. Schultz *et al.*'s (2000) edition of *The Expressive Organization* brought together many RI authors around an integrative view of the corporate brand.

What are corporate reputations?

Reputations are overall assessments of organizations by their stakeholders. They are aggregate perceptions by stakeholders of an organization's ability to fulfil their expectations, whether these stakeholders are interested in buying the company's products, working for the company, or investing in the company's shares. Box 2.1 illustrates a variety of definitions that have been proposed for the construct "corporate reputation" since 1984.

Box 2.1 Definitions of corporate communication

"Corporate reputation refers to the expectations, attitudes and feelings that consumers have about the nature and underlying reality of the company as represented by its corporate identity" (Topalian, 1984).

"A reputation is the set of meanings by which a company is known and through which people describe, remember and relate to it. It is the net result of the interaction of a person's beliefs, ideas, feelings and impressions about the company. A company will not have an reputation - people hold reputations of the company" (Dowling, 1986).

"Reputation refers to a holistic and vivid impression held by a particular group towards a corporation, partly as a result of information processing (sense-making) carried out by the group's members and partly by the aggregated communication of the corporation in question concerning its nature, i.e. the fabricated and projected picture of itself" (Alvesson, 1990).

"Corporate reputation is the overall estimation in which a company is held by its constituents. A corporate reputation represents the 'net' affective or emotional reaction - good-bad, weak or strong - of customers, investors, employees, and general public to the company's name" (Fombrun, 1996, of contradictions that could harm the organization's image).

As Box 2.1 suggests, an organization's reputation can be described in many ways. One way to describe it is to distinguish "levels" of analysis. Knecht (1986) proposed seven levels of analysis to which the notion of "reputation" could be applied: a product class, a brand, a company, a sector, a shop, a country, and a user. So we could examine the reputation of a product class such as "beer", for instance. We could also examine the reputation of a particular beer brand such as Heineken. The reputation of an organization as a whole should be distinguished from the reputation of an operating unit or subsidiary, and from the reputation of the industry in which it operates. Finally, a country-of-origin effect can be identified, such as the reputation that attaches to being a Dutch company. Viewed in this way, the reputation of any single organization derives partly from reputations that exist at other levels in which the organization is involved.

Country-of-origin effects are especially important for international organizations, and have a powerful effect on international trade. For instance, the high-quality reputation of Germany has historically had a favorable influence on German products such as cars and appliances. Nagashima (1977) defines the country-of-origin effect as "the picture, the reputation, the stereotype that businessmen and consumers attach to products of a specific country."

Country of residence also influences the degree of stereotyping. People tend to judge a country based on similarities: the closer one is to a country both physically and psychologically, the more favorable their opinion of that country. Some Japanese companies have applied this idea by moving selected manufacturing or assembly plants to high-reputation countries in the belief that "a company can improve its brand reputation significantly by building cars in a higher status country" (Johansson and Nebenzahl, 1986).

The expression "corporate reputation" is increasingly used to refer solely to the reputation of the organization as a whole and not to sub-brands. In order to indicate the reputation of an industrial sector, the term "industry reputation" is appropriate. The reputation of Microsoft is thus a corporate reputation, while the reputation of the information technology industry is the industry reputation. Its US country of origin doubtless affects the company's reputation as a global leader in software, and helps to raise the reputation of Microsoft's Game Studios. All three set a context for the company's ability to generate reputation for its X-Box product or brand. Figure 2.2 describes a simplified hierarchy of reputation levels in which the company is involved.

Figure 2.2   An example of the relationship between reputation levels for Microsoft

How do reputations form?

A reputation forms from networks of cognitive associations that develop over time from a group's cumulative exposure to sensory stimuli. The mosaic of associations comes together to create an overall impression.

Holzauer (1991) suggests that reputations develop from:

> the knowledge which we have of a company as a result of being confronted by forms of advertising. We know nothing about the company that owns the Marlboro cigarette brand. However, we should not be surprised if the company strongly resembled the cigarettes. We often develop a company reputation on the basis of the reputation we have of its products, i.e. the brand reputation. The brand reputation is formed on the basis of the only information we have about the company, namely, brand advertising. In other words, brand advertising can determine the reputation of the company. Conversely, the picture we have of a company (Woolworth, Philips, Braun) can determine what we think of the products of that company.

In reflecting on this example, it's important to point out that the reputation of the company (in this case Altria, parent of Philip Morris, itself parent of the Marlboro brand) does not come about solely because of advertising. In fact, there are three levels of information processing that affect people's impressions of the company (Bromley, 2000):

1. information processing at a primary level (based on personal experience);
2. information processing at a secondary level (based on what friends and colleagues have to say about an organization or product);
3. information processing at a tertiary level (based on mass media information, including paid advertising and unpaid publicity).

The largest influence on reputation takes place at the primary level – from direct personal experience. But people only assimilate a limited amount of direct information. Most of the information people absorb comes indirectly from friends and colleagues and through the amplificatory power of the mass media. In other words, although primary level influences have the greatest effect on individual perceptions, there are far fewer of them. The reputations of Altria and Philip Morris are therefore colored by the direct experience that people have from smoking its Marlboro cigarettes. But they are probably more affected by the ubiquitous cowboy imagery in the brand's secondary marketing communications. Most recently, many people's impressions of the company will also have been heavily colored by tertiary information revealed during the widely publicized anti-trust and health-care lawsuits brought by the US federal and state regulators against the tobacco industry in the 1990s (to which Altria/Philip Morris was a party).

A positive reputation works like a magnet. It strengthens the attractiveness of an organization, simplifying the realization of a broad range of activities. From the research literature, we know that companies with a positive reputation can more easily attract and retain employees and can ask a higher price for its products. They more easily attract new sources of financial capital and are less likely to find themselves at risk. The importance of reputation is recognized by most managers, and is visible in the increased attention paid to empirical measurement of corporate reputation – a topic we develop more fully in Chapter 9. The search for a standardized measure of brands and reputation, in particular, is clearly visible in the growing appreciation shown for measurement tools like Young & Rubicam's "Brand Asset Valuator", *Fortune*'s "Most Admired Company" measures, and the Harris–Fombrun "Reputation Quotient".

Reputations are important both for the owners of the reputation and for the subjects that have stored its reputation in their long-term memory. When a company owns a favorable reputation, it considers the transmission of its positive reputation an essential precondition for establishing a commercial relationship with its stakeholders. The company's reputation provides easy access to the "evoked set" of stimuli with the target group. Similarly, for the targeted subject, the company's reputation summarizes their perceptions of the company in terms of global assessments of effectiveness (good/bad, strong/weak, high/low). The more stakeholders rely on a company's reputation to make purchasing or investment decisions, the more important it is for the company to have a strong reputation. Box 2.2 summarizes some of the main arguments used to describe the importance of reputations.

Poiesz (1988) suggests that reputations are especially helpful when:

▮ the kind of information stakeholders need to make decisions is complex, conflicting or incomplete;
▮ the amount of information available to stakeholders is insufficient or too abundant to make a sound judgment;
▮ people have too low a degree of involvement with the product or the company to go through a complex information analysing process;
▮ there are external conditions that pressure stakeholders to make more rapid decisions.

Box 2.2   The value of a good reputation

A good reputation helps a company attract the people necessary for its success analysts, investors, customers, partners, and employees. Identity management can secure that good reputation (Chajet, 1989).

Reputation is a representation in the mind. It affects attitudes, which in turn affect behavior. No company can afford to ignore reputation. The impression it creates – consciously or unconsciously, whether it wishes to or not – inevitable affects people who do business with it (Bernstein, 1986).

Research has found 9 out of 10 consumers reporting that when choosing between products that are similar in quality and price, the reputation of the company determines which product or service they buy (Mackiewicz, 1993).

A good reputation can serve to buffer a corporation from economic loss in specific types of crises (Jones, 2000).

A good reputation acts like a magnet: It attracts us to those who have it (Fombrun and van Riel, 2004).

Poiesz (1988) adds that if consumers did not draw on reputation, they would have difficulty deciding which products to buy. Day-by-day, consumers are losing their ability to act as the economists' ideal-type "rational decision-makers": in judging a product, consumers are not familiar with all available alternatives; they are not aware of all the features of a particular product; they are unable to judge all of those features correctly prior to purchasing the product. Consumers also cannot make use of all their previous experience, because their memory is imperfect, and are not always able to process and store new experiences at all. Jointly, it means that consumers are unable to act in purely rational terms, and are more and more inclined to base decisions on earlier, imperfect, experiences, on hearsay, on emotions, on incomplete information, and on unconscious processes – and so are more likely to rely on "reputational data" (Poiesz, 1988).

Ultimately, reputation reduces the search for information by simplifying information processing (Lilli, 1983). Growing similarity among products and brands makes it more difficult for customers to distinguish between them.

Customers therefore look for simple ways to make distinctions between brands and companies and rely on subjective, non-observable features of the product. A corporate reputation provides a simple guideline for making decisions: if the customer's degree of involvement with the product is low, he or she should simply buy the product made by the company with the best reputation. Reputation creates a mental shortcut for stakeholders by providing them a global understanding that they can ascribe to a company and on which they can rely to justify relevant decisions (Pruyn, 1990).

Disciplinary contributions to analysis of corporate reputations

Concepts related to "reputation" have developed in various disciplines (Fombrun and van Riel, 1997). On one hand, diversity has enriched our theoretical understanding of the construct by incorporating insights from diverse literatures. On the other hand, it has also occasionally made the field resemble the proverbial Tower of Babble. In this section, we summarize key contributions from six disciplines to our understanding of corporate reputations: psychology, economics, strategic management, sociology, organizational science, and accounting. Table 2.3 previews the core themes from each perspective.

The influence of psychology

Insights from psychology regularly find their way into corporate reputation studies, explicitly or implicitly. The underlying framework for most discussions of reputation formation are information processing theories. The "Elaboration Likelihood" theory of Petty and Cacioppo (1986), for instance, suggests that a reputation is formed when a range of stimuli are presented to a subject by an object. The interpretation made by the subject, and the relative weight these stimuli attain in the mind of the subject, can be influenced by many factors. The process of evaluation that takes place is a function of how individuals process information. Figure 2.3 describes the five key phases involved in individual information processing.

Stimuli that are communicated to targeted individuals will only be retained when all stages of information processing are completed. A company seeking to influence a target audience must therefore ensure that its message meets three criteria: (1) generates appropriate awareness of the company, (2) gets

Table 2.3 Multiple points of view on corporate reputation

Psychology/ marketing	Economics	Strategic management	Sociology	Organizational science	Accounting
Reputations are cognitive associations about companies that predict stakeholder attachments and supportive behavior	Reputations are signals that are used by firms to convey the company's key strengths and build competitive advantage	Reputations are mobility barriers or mobility catalysts	Reputations are social constructions that are used or misused by companies to carry out impression management	Reputations are cognitive interpretations used by observers for sense-making and used by top managers to carry out sense-giving	Reputation is an intangible asset that measures the difference between a company's book value and its market value

Source: Fombrun and van Riel (1997)

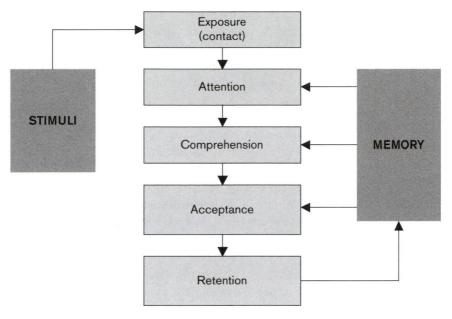

Figure 2.3   Individual information processing
Source: Engel *et al.* (1990)

the audience's attention, and (3) generates understanding. Traditional marketing communication typically falls short of addressing (3), and so often fails because it falls short of generating comprehension, acceptance, and retention.

By addressing comprehension, a company's communications can help audiences attach relevant meaning to the stimuli they are presented with. Meaning is created when individuals are able to classify stimuli into concepts already stored in their memory. Familiar concepts of salience, similarity, and difference derived from Gestalt theory are relevant here: individuals are more likely to create meaning from stimuli that are similar to others they have previously encountered – if they appear relevant. They are also more likely to attach meaning to stimuli that make the company stand out from others.

Acceptance centres on whether information stimuli produce the intended effects. This depends, amongst other things, on the extent to which the stimuli presented to the target audience can be integrated into each individual's existing conceptual system as a "script" – a kind of elaboration that Engel *et al.* (1990) define as "the amount of integration between the new information and existing knowledge stored in memory." The more favorable the reactions individuals have to the stimuli in the comprehension phase, the greater the probability of those stimuli being preserved in the retention phase – at which point individuals store the stimuli into their long-term memory.

Human memory has three components: sensory memory, short-term memory, and long-term memory. Figure 2.4 illustrates how they are interrelated. A stimulus enters sensory memory from available information about shape, color, and sound. At this stage, no meaning is attached to the stimulus – it simply generates awareness. Think of a logo (McDonald's golden arches), symbol (Nike's "Swoosh"), taste (Starbucks coffee), or sound (a Steinway piano).

Since human capacity in short-term memory is limited, these symbolic cues will only be transferred into short-term memory if they are attached to a meaning system. "Chunking" is the process through which information is broken down into bite-size, comprehensible units and organized in the human mind. Stimuli conveyed by an organization's communications, for instance, if it can be organized into chunks, will more easily enter into memory. When the Steinway "sound" is described by a well-known pianist playing the grand piano at La Scala in Milan, the information is organized as a "chunk" in people's minds – and creates a reputation for Steinway that makes it stand out from other rival piano-makers.

In this way, reputations are themselves chunks – they are meaning-systems or shorthand scripts that individuals use to organize impressions about an organization. They simplify reality. The process of reputation formation therefore consists of "chunking". When chunks appear repeatedly in an individual's short-term memory, they get transferred into long-term memory – and reputations crystallize. Long-term memory contains the lasting deposits

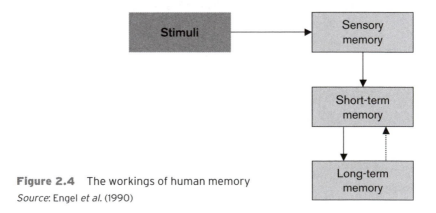

Figure 2.4   The workings of human memory
Source: Engel *et al.* (1990)

of our experiences and knowledge about an organization or its products. The diagram in Figure 2.4 summarizes the processes through which stimuli are retained in human memory.

The influence of communication depends on the degree of "elaboration" that occurs during information processing. In their Elaboration Likelihood Model (ELM), Petty and Cacioppo (1986) postulate that if the degree of elaboration is high, the subject is on the way to being convinced (see also Beijk and van Raaij, 1989). The only "signs" or "cues" that are important during information processing are those that shape *rational* understanding. Only the content and force of the arguments raised will influence opinion formation.

However, if the degree of elaboration is low, then the subject is less likely to be convinced. Message elements which are irrelevant to rational understanding become more important. Peripheral clues such as the attractiveness of the person conveying the message or the number of arguments contained in the message play a more important role in opinion formation (Wierenga and van Raaij, 1987). The path taken depends in large part on the degree to which people are motivated to process the information content in the messages communicated to them.

Important factors include the degree of involvement of subjects, their personal characteristics, and whether the message is consonant with their personal experience. For instance, if involvement with the company or product is high, the rational route will be taken; if involvement is low, the peripheral path will be taken. If the subject has a deep-seated "need for knowledge", it's likely that the level of involvement with the product or company will be high. Under time pressure, the peripheral path is more likely.

Most importantly for communication, when involvement is low, when audiences are not motivated to process information about the company or its products, and audiences embark on the more peripheral path, then corporate reputations will play an even more central role in influencing their behaviors.

The influence of economics

Economists view reputations as either traits or signals that organizations use to build a competitive advantage. Game theorists describe reputations as character traits that distinguish among "types" of firms and can explain their strategic behavior. Signaling theorists call our attention to the informational content of reputations. Both acknowledge that reputations are actually perceptions of firms held by external observers, a definition that is consistent with those proposed by psychologists.

In an influential article, two behavioral economists pointed out that "in game theory the reputation of a player is the perception others have of the player's values . . . which determine his/her choice of strategies" (Weigelt and Camerer, 1988). Information asymmetry forces external observers to rely on proxies to describe the preferences of rivals and their likely courses of action. Consumers rely on the reputations of organizations because they have less information than managers do about the commitment of those organizations to deliver desirable product features like quality or reliability (Grossman and Stiglitz, 1980; Stiglitz, 1989). Similarly, since outside investors in a company's securities are less informed than managers about the company's future actions, a good corporate reputation increases investor confidence that managers will act in ways that are reputation-consistent. For game theorists, then, reputations are functional: they generate perceptions among employees, customers, investors, competitors, and the general public about what a company is, what it does, what it stands for. These perceptions stabilize interactions between a firm and its publics.

Signaling theorists concur. A good reputation derives from the prior resource allocations managers make to first-order activities likely to create perceptions of reliability and predictability to outside observers (Myers and Majluf, 1984; Ross, 1977; Stigler, 1962). Since many features of a company and its products are hidden from view, reputations are information signals that increase an observer's confidence and trust in the company's products and services. Naturally, then, managers can make strategic use of a company's reputation to signal its attractiveness. When the quality of a company's products and services is not directly observable, high-quality producers are said to invest in reputation building in order to signal their quality (Shapiro, 1983). Their past investments in reputation-building allow them to charge premium prices, and may also earn them rents from the repeat purchases that their quality products will generate. In contrast, low quality producers avoid investing in reputation-building because they do not foresee repeat purchases (Allen, 1984; Bagwell, 1992; Milgrom and Roberts, 1986).

Similar dynamics operate in the capital and labor markets. For instance, managers routinely try to signal investors about their financial performance. Since investors are more favorably disposed to companies that demonstrate high and stable earnings, managers often try to smooth quarterly earnings and keep dividend payout ratios high and fixed, despite earnings fluctuations (Brealy and Myers, 1988). Sometimes companies pay a premium price to hire high-reputation auditors and outside counsel. They rent the reputations of their agents in order to signal investors, regulators, and other publics about their company's probity and credibility (Wilson, 1985).

The influence of strategic management

To strategists, reputations are both assets and mobility barriers (Caves and Porter, 1977). Established reputations impede mobility and produce returns to firms because they are difficult to imitate. By circumscribing firms' actions and rivals' reactions, reputations are therefore a distinct element of industry-level structure (Fombrun and Zajac, 1987). Reputations are difficult to duplicate because they derive from unique internal features of firms. By accumulating the history of firms' interactions with stakeholders they suggest to observers what companies stand for (Freeman, 1984; Dutton and Dukerich, 1991). Reputations are also externally perceived, and so are largely outside the direct control of firms' managers (Fombrun and Shanley, 1990). It takes time for a reputation to coalesce in observers' minds. Empirical studies show that even when confronted with negative information, observers resist changing their reputational assessments (Wartick, 1992). Therefore, reputations are valuable intangible assets because they are inert (Cramer and Ruefli, 1994).

Like economists, then, strategists call attention to the competitive benefits of acquiring favorable reputations (Rindova and Fombrun, 1999). They implicitly support a focus on the resource allocations that firms must make over time to create reputational barriers to the mobility of rivals (Barney, 1986). Since primary resource allocations also stand to improve organizational performance directly, however, it proves difficult to isolate their unique impact on performance and reputation. This explains why empirical studies have had difficulty untangling a causal ordering: both are produced by the same underlying initiatives (McGuire *et al.*,1988; Chakravarthy,1986).

The influence of sociology

Most economic and strategic models ignore the socio-cognitive process that actually generates reputation rankings (Granovetter, 1985; White, 1981). In contrast, organizational sociologists argue out that rankings are social constructions that come into being through the relationships that a focal firm has with its stakeholders in a shared institutional environment (Ashforth and

Gibbs, 1990). Firms have multiple evaluators, each of whom apply different criteria in assessing firms. However, these evaluators interact within a common organizational field and exchange information, including information about firms' actions in relation to prevailing norms and expectations. Thus, corporate reputations represent aggregated assessments of firms' institutional prestige and describe the stratification of the social system surrounding firms and industries (Shapiro, 1987; DiMaggio and Powell, 1983).

Faced with incomplete information about a company's likely actions, audiences not only interpret the signals that firms routinely broadcast, but also rely on the evaluations refracted by key intermediaries such as market analysts, professional investors, and reporters. Reporters and financial analysts are actors in an organizational field. They transmit and refract information among companies and their stakeholders (Abrahamson and Fombrun, 1992). An empirical study of firms involved in nuclear-waste disposal and photovoltaic cell development demonstrated how in both these industries reputational status depended not only on structural factors like company size and economic performance, but also on a firm's position in the interaction networks linking firms in each institutional field (Shrum and Wuthnow, 1988).

To sociologists, then, reputations are indicators of legitimacy: they are aggregate assessments of an organization's performance relative to expectations and norms in an institutional field. Sociologists point to the multiplicity of actors involved in the process of constructing reputations and their interconnectedness.

Consistent with the sociological approach, Alvesson (1990) suggests that a reputation consists of the picture that someone has of an organization (the sense reputation) and the impressions that the organization communicates (the communicated reputation). A reputation arises primarily out of information which is transmitted via the mass media and through interpersonal communication, and which is haphazard, infrequent, and superficial in nature. It does not arise from direct experiences with the "real" organization. At the heart of Alvesson's critique is the belief that Western society is flooded with reputational cues. Organizations are pressured to continually create signals that convey stronger reputations than they have to their audiences in order to stand out from rivals. Confusion results when discrepancies develop between people's personal experience with the company and the fabricated reputations conveyed by the media.

Alvesson's critique aligns with Daniel Boorstin's well-known 1961 book, *The Image, or What Happened to the American Dream*. Boorstin argued that American society had become overly dominated by an artificial reality that results from the wholesale manufacture of pseudo-events. As he suggests: "Initially, the reputation is the representation of reality, but ultimately reality becomes a representation of the reputation."

A more literary exposition of the view expressed by Alvesson and by Boorstin, can be found in the work of Milan Kundera (1990). He describes the pernicious effects of reputation in our society; the following is an amusing quotation from his section on "Reputationology":

> If as I write these pages everyone has decided to make Heidegger out to be a scatterbrain and a black sheep, this is not because his thinking has been overtaken by that of other philosophers, but because at that moment he has become the unlucky number in the reputationological roulette, the anti-ideal. The reputationologists create systems of ideals and anti-ideals, short-lived systems which follow each other in rapid succession, but which influence our behavior, our political opinions and aesthetic tastes, the color of carpets and the choice of books, just as strongly as ideological systems used to do.

The influence of organizational science

To organizational scholars, corporate reputations are rooted in the sense-making experiences of employees. A company's culture and identity shape an organization's business practices, as well as the kinds of relationships that its managers establish with key stakeholders.

Corporate culture influences managers' perceptions and motivations (Barney, 1986; Dutton and Penner, 1992). Corporate identity affects how managers both interpret and react to environmental circumstances (Meyer, 1982; Dutton and Dukerich, 1991). Shared cultural values and a strong sense of identity therefore guide managers, not only in defining what their firms stand for, but in justifying their strategies for interacting with key stakeholders (Miles and Cameron, 1982; Porac and Thomas, 1990).

Thick cultures homogenize perceptions inside an organization and so increase the likelihood that managers will make more consistent self-presentations to external observers. By creating focal principles, that is, general understanding of the right way of doing things in a firm, thick cultures contribute to the consistency of firms' reputations with stakeholders (Camerer and Vepsalainen, 1988).

Identity and culture are related. As we discuss in Chapter 3, identity describes the core, enduring, and distinctive features of an organization that produce shared interpretations among managers about how they should accommodate to external circumstances (Albert and Whetten, 1985). For instance, a comparative study of Bay Area hospitals showed how each institution responded differently to a strike because of their distinct self-reputations (Meyer, 1982). A case study of how the Port Authority coped with the problem of homelessness in New York demonstrated how an organization's self-reputation as a high-quality, first-class institution played a central role in constraining managers' actions to cope with the problem (Dutton and Dukerich, 1991). These reports suggest that organizations with strong, coherent cultures and identities are more likely to engage in systematic efforts to influence the perceptions of stakeholders. Managers in such firms will probably attend carefully to how their firms' key audiences feel about them (Albert and Whetten, 1985).

The influence of accounting

A vocal group of academic accountants has recently acknowledged the insufficiency of financial reporting standards in documenting the value of intangible assets like brands and reputations. They highlight the widening gap between factual earnings reported in annual statements and the market valuations of companies.

There are many reasons for this widening gap. Some of it is due to conservative accounting rules that prohibit capitalization of uncertain assets like goodwill, brands, and reputations. In most countries, goodwill is only recognized when assets are sold – the difference between the original price of the asset (its book value) and the market price paid for the asset is then capitalized. It is also subject to drastic depreciation schedules that invite quickly reducing its value to zero (generally over no longer than a ten-year term).

Standard accounting rules also require managers to fund research and development (R&D) activities, advertising, and training expenses activities, all of which contribute to enhancing actual and perceptual resource positions of a company (Scheutze, 1993; Lev and Sougiannis, 1996). As Deng and Lev (1997) suggest, current accounting practice induces a mismatch in the allocation of costs to revenues, and so misleads observers about the earning capabilities of firms and the true value of their assets. In regards to the valuation of R&D, they conclude that "hundreds of corporate executives, along with their auditors appear to be able to value R&D and technology in the development stage. This apparent inconsistency between the current regulatory environment which sanctions immediate expending of R&D and a fast developing business practice, obviously deserves a careful examination."

Instead, many accounting researchers have been calling for a broad-based effort to develop better measures for understanding how investments in branding, training, and research build important stocks of intangible assets not presently recorded in financial statements – assets that, not coincidentally, are said by strategists to build higher reputational assessments among observers (Rindova and Fombrun, 1997; Barney, 1986). Appropriate capitalization of these expenditures would better describe the value of a company's investments in what are fundamentally reputation-building activities.

In quantitative terms, accountants agree that the value of a public company's intangibles can be estimated using the market-to-book ratio. Fombrun (1996) described it as the company's "reputational capital" and made some cross-industry comparisons by subtracting the market value of a company (share price times number of shares in circulation) from the company's book value (assets minus liabilities), a quantitative estimate that provides a potentially useful benchmark for the hidden economic value of the company's intellectual, social, and institutional assets – the economic assets that effective corporate communication helps to defend.

Linking corporate communication to reputation

Although the analysis of reputation owes much to marketing, contributions to reputation studies are coming from far afield. Researchers and practitioners benefit from insights developed in psychology, economics, strategic management, organization science, and accountancy. Across disciplines, one can discern implications for how corporate communication influences reputation-building.

Figure 2.5 presents a framework for thinking strategically about the link between a company's strategic objectives, corporate communication, reputation, and financial performance. It describes two cycles that should complement each other. The "business cycle" is based on standard development of corporate strategies from which flow an array of business activities which, insofar as they are successfully implemented, build financial performance. Effective implementation calls for a parallel "communication cycle" that develops and executes an appropriate communication system for building reputation. If successfully carried out, corporate communication induces

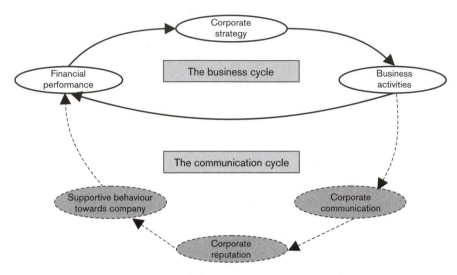

Figure 2.5 Linking communication and reputation to the business

stakeholder identification and stimulates supportive behaviors from the organization's stakeholders.

In the next chapter, we expand on the communication cycle and examine closely the process through which organizations build identity and identification with internal and external audiences.

Discussion Questions

1. Describe the differences between related constructs such as corporate reputation, corporate brand, and corporate image.
2. Explain the mnemonic process through which observers come to know a company. What role does advertising play?
3. How might a company's philanthropic activities contribute to strengthening its reputation with the public? Would it also apply to customers? To financial analysts? To journalists? Why or why not?

Notes

1 Source: ThinkExist.com Quotations. "James Russell Lowell quotes". *ThinkExist.com Quotations Online*, 1 March 2006. 4 April 2006.

3

CREATING IDENTITY AND IDENTIFICATION

Although the lie your voice may give,
Your actions do speak always true;
The manner in which your life you live,
Must show the truth, and you may rue;
The day you ever did dare to lie.

The moral, then, is thus as follows:

Be true to yourself;
And your words to your actions;
Honesty is good for your health,
And hypocrisy just a distraction.
Joshua Swanson

Companies regularly launch strategic changes in direction and structure to enhance their competitiveness. When companies embark on such radical changes, whether they are prompted by new CEO appointments or by related diversifications, mergers, asset sell-offs, or global expansion, managers are generally confronted with questions of organizational "identity" and "identi-fication" – questions that require addressing "who we are", "what we stand for", "what is our core purpose?", and "what does it mean to be involved in this company?"

Answers to these questions are fundamental to corporate communication and reputation management. They require probing closely how internal staffs and executives envision their involvement with the company. They force executives to juxtapose their own internal perceptions of the company against those of other employees, and demand a dialogue between *internal* views of the company – the claims the company makes about itself to outsiders – and the views that *external* parties hold about the company. Rarely do internal and external views coincide, nor is there a simple answer to the question of what a company should stand for. It begs asking: How long can a company hold itself up to outsiders in ways that do not match its own employees' sense of self? At a time when companies perform in the harsh glare of the media, how long can a company say one thing while being another without losing credibility and reputation internally and externally? How long can it do so before it loses credibility, authenticity, and trustworthiness to its own employees and other stakeholders?

Research suggests that perceptions of authenticity result when organizations take the time to explore core components of their identities (Fombrun and van Riel, 2004). It begins with a *process of discovery* designed to unearth the "beating heart" of the company – what the organization stands for at its core, what it really is. Discovery is an inside-out process initiated at the top of the organization and involves the organization in a broad dialogue about the company's "core purpose", its reason for being. Not all features of a company's identity are equally attractive, and so a "constructed identity" emerges that reflects those identity elements that the company wishes to endorse and emphasize. Often they are a reflection of historical accident; increasingly they are strategically selected by senior executives seeking to implement key business objectives. Gaining adherents to these shared identity elements requires a *process of internal expression* targeted, first, to employees, then to outside stakeholders. A company will never be perceived as authentic if its employees don't believe and express the company's shared values in their day-to-day interactions with customers and suppliers, investors, and the public. Employees must "sing in harmony", as it were. A company with a strong identity generates identification.

In this chapter, we examine the disparate literature on organizational identity in order to shed light on different approaches companies can adopt to improve their self-understandings. We distinguish different meanings of the term "identity" and reconcile the uses to which they can be put in applied situations. We then describe various methods for measuring "identity" internally and externally. We also distinguish from "identity" the key processes of "employee identification" and "stakeholder identification" that companies induce when they adopt an "identity mix" – the combination of behaviors, symbols, and corporate communication they use to crystallize their identities to internal and external audiences. The identity mix is the cognitive foundation on which companies can build their "constructed identities". To define the identity mix requires of a company a grounded understanding of how stake-holders perceive the company and the gap that exists with its "reality". This chapter provides managers with the necessary tools for conceptualizing, measuring, and overcoming the reality-perception gaps that often handicap their efforts to implement strategies. In subsequent chapters, we turn to detailed technologies for generating stakeholder identification with the constructed identity.

Conceptualizing identity: three major approaches

Most academic discussions about "organizational identity" observe that there is little agreement about the way the term is used. Hatch and Schultz (2000) speak of a "Tower of Babel". We suggest here three major approaches to scholarly and practitioner discussions of "identity".

Identity: rooted in design

A long tradition of work on organizational identity can be traced to the study of visual elements. According to Bernstein (1986), the word "identity" is derived from the Latin "idem" (meaning "same"). There is clearly a connection also to the Latin "identidem", meaning "repeatedly similar", or "the same each time". Early students of corporate identity often draw on such dictionary definitions to associate "identity" primarily with "design", e.g. logos, house style, and uniforms. Carter (1982) describes corporate identity as "the logo or brand image of a company, and all other visual manifestations of the identity of a company." The idea of generating agreement and similarity among employees, a unity of being, provided early design specialists with their core argument for developing and making consistent use of common symbols.

The emphasis on a suitable visual expression of the company recognizes the importance of first impressions on prospective and existing clients. In his influential 1978 book *The Corporate Personality*, Wally Olins called attention to these elements of the identity mix. The consulting firm he created (Wolff/Olins) received critical acclaim for creating the logos and branding systems for well established companies such as Akzo-Nobel, Renault, British Telecom, and Repsol. The visual expression he advocated was crystallized for these companies in house-style manuals and programs that enforce a consistent expression of the company. US Consultancies like Anspach Grossman, Landau, Lippincott–Mercer, or the Dutch firm Nykamp & Nyboer regularly assist companies in implementing and maintaining consistent visual expressions of their identities.

Choosing a logo or house style is not so arbitrary a process as it may seem. Members of the design school emphasize that visual expression is the culmination of a process of internal inquiry that asks fundamental questions about the organization's identity (*Who are we?*) in order to shape the selection and development of appropriate symbols and imagery.

Logos are only one element of a company's visual expression. More abstract presentations of a company's identity are also expressed in corporate architecture, art, the use of uniforms, reliance on dress codes, language, office layouts, and signage (Gagliardi, 1990; Kotha *et al.*, 2001). These identity expressions create a context for the logos and branding systems that are developed (Henderson and Cote, 1998). Visual symbols are a quick and penetrating way of conveying a simple idea about a company, and have considerable emotional value. Limiting identity to what Wathen (1986) calls "logomotion", however, underestimates the other factors that drive stakeholder identification with a company.

Identity: rooted in corporate culture

Students of organization behavior regard identity as far more than the visual elements of the design school. They suggest that identity comes not just from examining the visual and desired elements manifested in the constructed identity selected by a group of senior executives, but also from the shared beliefs and values of all organizational members. Identity is very much in the eye of the beholder: What you see depends very much on where you stand (Schultz *et al.*, 2000; Balmer, 1997; 1998; Balmer and Greyser, 2002). By implication, implementing strategic change in organizations requires a more sophisticated understanding of identity than the design view proposes (Pratt and Foreman, 2000).

Most of the research and analysis of identity in the "culture" tradition has relied on qualitative methodologies to reveal identity elements. Van Rekom (1997) and van Riel *et al.* (2006), Carroll and van Riel (2001), Davies *et al.* (2003), and Corley and Gioia (2000) are among those who have proposed the use of quantitative analysis to develop identity profiles. Their research suggests how positivistic analysis can help assess the antecedents and consequences of identity for various organizational outcomes such as "identification" and "morale".

Identity: rooted in communication

A third approach to the study of identity draws inspiration from academics and practitioners interested in messaging and communications. It examines how selected identity traits of a company can be "translated" through advertising and publicity (Rossiter and Percy, 1999; Aaker and Myers, 1991; Aaker and Keller, 1998; Kapferer, 1992, 2002; Grunig and Hunt, 1984; Grunig, 1992). Much of their work describes guidelines for communication programs built around a core identity and the telling of effective corporate stories (van Riel, 2000; Larsen, 2000). Many try to bridge the gap between conceptual development and pragmatic implementation (Jablin and Putnam, 2001).

Early proponents focused on creating symbol-intensive campaigns to convey long-range business goals and organizational strengths to stakeholders (Wathen, 1986). German researchers recognized the importance of the behavioral component in the identity-mix. Behaviour is the broadest possible form of communication. Communicating only through symbols is difficult because most stakeholders, whether consciously or unconsciously, rely on *all* of their senses to form an impression or judgment about a company. No company can generate and sustain perceptions of distinctiveness and authenticity solely through visual design (Tanneberger, 1987). Implementing strategy requires of managers a commitment to both symbolic and behavioral communication.

In both practice and research, these three approaches overlap. Consultants are often called upon to work with companies on a strategic repositioning of the company. This invariably leads to debate about branding implications and the appropriate visual consequences of change. When branding specialists develop new visual expressions for a client, they generally find it crucial to partner with change agents to induce employees to adopt the new branding elements. A steering committee is generally created to guide the integration of visual, behavioral, and symbolic elements of the identity mix.

Defining identity

Despite some recent convergence, considerable diversity remains in definitions of organizational identity. A small selection of the many definitions-in-use is provided in Box 3.1.

Box 3.1   Various definitions of organizational identity

"The corporate identity is the firm's visual statement to the world of who and what the company is – of how the company views itself – and therefore has a great deal to do with how the world views the company" (Selame and Selame, 1975).

"identity means the sum of all the ways a company chooses to identify itself to all its publics" (Margulies, 1977).

"Corporate identity is the tangible manifestation of the personality of a company. It is the identity which reflects and projects the real personality of the company" (Olins, 1978).

"Corporate identity is the strategy which helps to increase the economic performance and the efficiency of a company. It coordinates achievements, values and information, and leads to integration in the sense of cooperation" (Hannebohm/Blöcker, 1983).

"A series of interdependent characteristics of the organization from which it draws its specificity, stability and unity" (Larçon and Reitter, 1979, 1984).

"Organizational Identity is (a) what is taken by organizational members to be central to the organization, (b) what makes the organization distinctive from other organizations in the eyes of the beholding members, and (c) what is perceived by members to be enduring or continuing linking the present with the past and presumably the future" (Albert and Whetten, 1985).

"Corporate identity reflects the distinctive capability and the recognizable individual characteristics of the company. Identity in this sense also includes the distinction and recognition of parts of the whole company, and the attribution of those parts to the whole" (Tanneberger, 1987).

"Organizational identity is the strategically planned and operationally applied internal and external self-presentation and behavior of a company. It is based on an agreed company philosophy, long term company goals, and a particular desired image, combined with the will to utilise all instruments of the company as one unit, both internally and externally" (Birkigt and Stadler, 1988).

"What organizational members believe to be its [the organization's] central, enduring and distinctive character, the members' shared beliefs about what is distinctive, central, and enduring about their organization" (Dutton *et al.*, 1994).

"Corporate identity is the reality and uniqueness of an organization, which is integrally related to its external and internal image and reputation through corporate communication" (Gray and Balmer, 1998).

"Organizational identity comprises those characteristics of an organization that its members believe are central, distinctive and enduring. That is, organizational identity consists of those attributes that members feel are fundamental to (central) and uniquely descriptive of (distinctive) the organization and that persist within the organization over time (enduring)" (Pratt and Foreman, 2000).

"Identity is formed both from internal and external positions. Who we are cannot be completely separated from the perceptions others have of us and that we have of others. Multiple images of identity refer to the same organization. Identity is a text that is read in relation to cultural context. Tacit understandings sit alongside overt expressions of identity [and] identity involves the instrumental use of emergent cultural symbols" (Hatch and Schultz, 2000).

The identity mix

"Identity" consists of the collection of attributes that members use to describe an organization. For these attributes to be accepted internally and externally, an organization must have in place an identity mix that is appropriate to its target audiences. All self-expressions of a company can be classified into one of the following three forms:

1. *Communication*: Companies reveal their identities through verbal messaging. This is the most tactical tool managers can use to convey identity. Abstract signals are more easily conceived, modified, and transmitted to target groups.
2. *Behavior*: Companies reveal their identities through the initiatives they support and the behaviors they enact. Action is by far the most important medium through which identity is expressed. A company can easily claim to be "innovative"; it is far more difficult for a company to demonstrate innovativeness. Ultimately, target groups judge a company by its actions.
3. *Symbolism*: Companies also reveal their identities through the use of visual and audible symbols. Logos, signs, sounds, and taglines can be used to harmonize with other expressions of corporate identity, and create identifiers for what the organization wants to stand for.

Taken together, these forms of expression constitute the corporate identity mix – an expression we use to parallel the notion of "the marketing mix". They are the means through which a company manifests its "personality" to the world. In fact, corporate personality is "the manifestation of the company's self-perception" (Birkigt and Stadler, 1988). The identity-mix can therefore be seen as the outer expression of the company, and crystallizes the underlying personality of the organization. In this way, "corporate image" consists of the interpretations stakeholders make about the company. Figure 3.1 illustrates the relationship between corporate identity and corporate image.

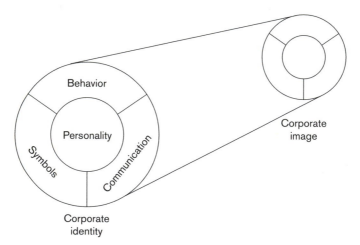

Figure 3.1   Influence of identity mix on corporate image
Source: Birkigt and Stadler (1986)

Although useful in linking image and identity, the model shown in Figure 3.1 is deficient because:

1. It fails to recognize that image is not just a reflection of identity, but is also influenced by contextual conditions.
2. It ignores the fact that image is never an end in itself, but a means to achieve improved legitimacy and effectiveness for the organization.
3. The model does not distinguish between static and dynamic identity elements. Static elements (such as culture) change slowly, whereas dynamic elements (such as communication and symbolism) can change quickly.
4. Finally, static and dynamic identity elements have an unequal impact on a company's image with target audiences. Static elements are likely to have a far greater impact than dynamic elements like communications and symbols.

Selecting identity elements

There are many ways to examine the identity of an organization. Some suggest that it ultimately comes down to the way in which senior executives choose to define and project the identity elements of the organization (Birkigt and Stadler, 1986). In a prophetic article, Larçon and Reitter (1979) proposed three criteria for selecting identity elements: continuity, centrality, and uniqueness. For instance, assuming "client-focused" were a core identity element, one could ask whether it was always present in the organization (continuity), whether it was widely shared across the organization (centrality), or whether the organization could effectively differentiate itself from others on this identity element (uniqueness). Albert and Whetten (1985) subsequently proposed similar criteria for describing organizational identity, and their formulation was widely adopted. As they advised, to assess the identity of an organization, one should use the viewpoint of its own members as a starting point, and define it against three criteria:

- *Centrality*: What characteristics are widely shared among members throughout the organization?
- *Continuity*: What characteristics of the organization are most used by members to link the past to its present and future?
- *Uniqueness*: What characteristics of the organization appear most unique to members in terms of their ability to differentiate the organization from other similar organizations?

The critical reader will quickly realize that these universal criteria are not easy to compile. For instance:

- How far back in time must one go to speak of adequate continuity?
- Can members of an organization effectively assess its uniqueness?
- To what extent are the most crucial characteristics of an organization widely understood by the entire organization, by managers, or by specialists?

Finally, identity elements can often appear general, yet still act as powerful reference points. Consider British retailing giant Marks & Spencer. The company regularly describes itself in terms of three core identity elements: *trust, quality, and service*. Although at first glance these traits appear very general and likely to be non-differentiating, they become differentiating elements when one learns that Marks & Spencer was among the first companies to issue a traceability certificate for its beef products (a guarantee of quality throughout the value chain) and it demonstrates it stays on top of other health issues as well (see Figure 3.2). These behavioral manifestations are identity-consistent actions for the retailer.

Conceiving organizational identity

There are diverse approaches to understanding organizational identity. To integrate these approaches, four types of identity can be distinguished (Balmer, 1997; Balmer and Wilson, 1998, 2002):

- *Perceived identity*: The collection of attributes that are seen as typical for the "continuity, centrality and uniqueness" of the organization in the eyes of its members.
- *Projected identity*: The self presentations of the organization's attributes manifested in the implicit and explicit signals which the organization broadcasts to internal and external target audiences through communications and symbols.
- *Desired identity* (also called "ideal" identity): The idealized picture that top managers hold of what the organization could evolve into under their leadership.
- *Applied identity*: The signals that an organization broadcasts both consciously and unconsciously through behaviors and initiatives at all levels within the organization.

Figure 3.2   Marks & Spencer's identity: trust, quality, and service

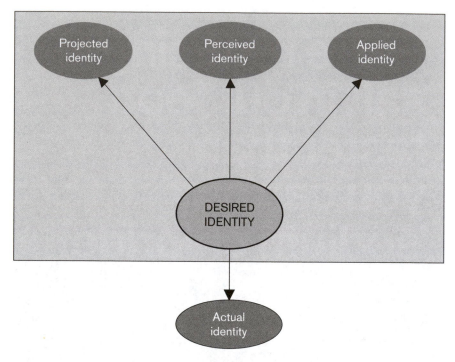

Figure 3.3 Identity types: four approaches for assessing organizational identity
Source: Adapted from Balmer and Greyser (2002)

Balmer's (Balmer and Greyser, 2002) AC^{2}ID model (depicted in Figure 3.3) suggests that a lack of correspondence between the four interpretations of identity leads to conflicting understandings about a company, such as becomes apparent when the inconsistency develops between a company's vision and strategy, or a gap develops between a company's behaviors and stakeholder expectations about what the company should be doing. In practice, the model is useful in evaluating identity programs, and can also be used to track identity elements in the organization.

In Chapter 4, we return to this typology of identities when discussing tools for measuring corporate identities.

The question of multiple and hybrid identities

The larger an organization becomes, the greater the chance that sub-identities will emerge that decrease identification with the corporate identity – or what is deemed to to be the corporate identity at the home office or headquarters. A company is frequently confronted with such questions of multiple and hybrid identities following a merger or acquisition. Consider DaimlerChrysler. Following the 2000 merger between Daimler-Benz and Chrysler, many employees continued to identify with the German or American sides of the merger. It has taken considerable effort by the company to establish a shared identity for the merged company. Figure 3.4 illustrates one of the ads DaimlerChrysler used to overcome its sub-identities and develop a unitary coherence between its two largest divisions. The ad is clearly targeted to both internal and external audiences.

Some organizations are more likely to develop multiple identities than others. Cooperatives (Foreman and Whetten, 1994), orchestras (Glynn, 2000), and hospitals (Pratt and Rafaeli, 1997) often develop multiple identities because of the multiplicity of specialists who come together to "make music"

Figure 3.4 DaimlerChrysler: communicating global integration

or "deliver health care." Multiple identities also develop in organizations that operate across very different regions (Gustafson and Reger, 1995), or that serve very distinct stakeholder groups (Cheney, 1991; Eisenberg, 1984; Ginzel *et al.*, 1993; Pratt and Foreman, 2000).

Although they can be a source of conflict, multiple identities are not necessarily problematic for an organization. Co-existence is possible, provided there are enough harmonizing elements in the overarching identity of the company as a whole. Problems generally arise when companies try to foster alignment among sub-identities that are fundamentally at odds. Albert and Whetten (1985) describe a hybrid identity as a set of characteristics that do not belong together, such as a "church" and a "business". Even this example, however, is far from universal since a number of well-known examples of cult-like or religious organizations such as the "Church of Scientology" have been observed to operate both as businesses and churches. They do so by developing more encompassing identity-elements and shared values that justify the union of objectives under a shared umbrella. Ron Hubbard's "scientific" philosophy is used to justify the unity of identity elements in the cultish organization, and to stimulate a unity of purpose among church members.

Pratt and Foreman (2000) underscore the presence of multiple identities in organizations. They ask how corporate leaders can deal with the multiplicity of concepts that emerge from addressing the question: "Who are we as an organization?" On the one hand, organizations with too many identities create confusion and are ineffective because of the contradictory demands that are placed on them. Organizations with too few identities, on the other hand, have great difficulty fulfilling the diverse demands of all their members. Identity-based tensions therefore develop in most large organizations; managers can pursue one of four strategies in addressing the "fragmented identity syndrome": compartmentalization, deletion, integration, and aggregation.

- *Compartmentalisation*: Applied when the organization and its members choose to preserve all current identities but do not seek to attain any synergy among them.
- *Deletion*: Applied when managers actually rid the organization of one or more of its identities.
- *Integration*: Applied when managers attempt to fuse multiple identities into a coherent whole.
- *Aggregation*: Applied when managers attempt to retain all of the company's identities while forging links between them.

From identity to identification

Ultimately, a company's identity matters because it creates *identification*. Employees who identify strongly with their companies are more likely to show a supportive attitude toward them (Ashforth and Mael, 1989) and to make decisions that are consistent with the company's objectives (Simon, 1997). Identification therefore produces strategic alignment, a unity of purpose between leaders and employees. Managers should therefore be keenly interested in discovering, understanding, and revealing the identity elements of their company in order to promote identification and alignment by employees with the constructed or desired identity of the company (Cheney, 1983; Pratt, 1998).

Identity management cannot and must not stop there, however. Being recognized externally as authentic can only happen when a company initiates a *process of external expression* designed to convey its core essence to all stakeholders in appealing ways. External expression involves crafting messages and launching initiatives that evoke emotional appeal – feelings of trust, respect, and liking among key stakeholder groups. When they work well, effective external expressions therefore generate not only internal alignment between company and employees, but also between the company and its *stakeholders*. The three processes linking identity and identification are captured in Figure 3.5.

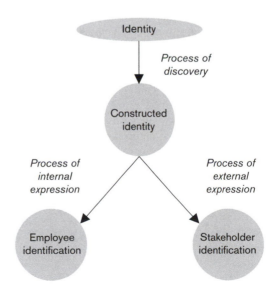

Figure 3.5 Linking identity and identification

Identification differs strongly across types of organization. Ideological or religious organizations have traditionally generated higher degrees of identification than commercial organizations. Individuals make sense of the world through the groups with which they identify. Through their sense-giving practices – their identity elements – organizations can capitalize on individuals' sense-seeking efforts (Gioia *et al.*, 2000). By projecting an attractive identity to employees, managers not only drive identification, but can steer the future direction of the company by effective socialization practices. For their part, employees that are inspired by the sense-giving initiatives of a company satisfy a psychological need for self-categorization ("I am a valuable person because I work for an important organization") and self-assessment ("I am valued for my work by the people within the organization").

In an influential study of New York's Port Authority, a quasi-private company that manages New York's airports and bus terminals, Dutton and Dukerich (1991) showed how employee identification was influenced by the interpretations people were making of the organization's actions, intentions, and identity. The situation involved the harsh treatment by the organization of the homeless people who used the public waiting rooms in the organization's terminals. Faced with customer complaints about the homeless, the Port Authority took aggressive action to expulse the homeless from its terminals. Harsh criticism in the media led to inconsistency between their understanding of the Port Authority as a "caring organization" and the seemingly uncaring policies imposed by management. Employee identification decreased significantly, and employees lobbied for a different, more progressive social policy. A change in policy ultimately re-aligned employees' self-concept with the identity elements of the organization, and improved identification.

More generally, managers can increase employee identification in two key ways: by tweaking the human resource management systems (reward and recognition practices, appraisal processes), and by guiding the communication system. The former are well-documented, so we will not dwell on them here. Use of the communication system as a tool for generating employee identification, however, is less well understood and we will therefore concentrate on it more heavily here.

Identification is influenced by both internal and external management communication. Internal communication enhances identification: (1) when employees perceive that they are receiving enough information with which to do their jobs, (2) when employees perceive that they are receiving enough information about what the organization as a whole is doing, and (3) when employees perceive that they are taken seriously by their managers. At the same time, external communication also enhances identification. It does so when the organization is able to secure a favorable reputation from its communications externally. The higher the organization's perceived reputation (Dutton and Dukerich refer to it as "perceived external prestige"), the more likely employees are to feel positively towards the organization (Mael and Ashforth, 1992). Employees are proud to identify with a well-regarded company. They bask in the company's reflected glory, as it were, and their personal sense of self-worth is increased.

Conclusion

This chapter focused on the concept of "organizational identity" and examined how identity elements create internal and external identification by employees and stakeholders. Although rooted in the study of visual aesthetics and design, the concept has evolved significantly from theoretical and empirical research conducted by a network of international academics.

The pragmatic implications of an identity approach to corporate communication is a five-step process to identity management described in Figure 3.6:

▌ *Step 1*: Objectively determine which characteristics the organization is currently projecting and test this according to three criteria of Albert and Whetten (continuity, centrality, and distinctiveness).
▌ *Step 2*: Simultaneously analyse: (a) what the top management sees as the most desired identity characteristic and (b) what the employees perceive as the projected characteristics.
▌ *Step 3*: Determine whether there are gaps between the four forms of identity.
▌ *Step 4*: Depending on the results of the gap analysis, it may be necessary to use one or more elements of the identity mix and possibly to use extra research to analyse the strong and weak points within the organization in these areas.
▌ *Step 5*: The previous steps should result in an action plan designed to close the gaps between the desired, projected, and realized identities of the organization.

Until recently, the general conception was that identity could be defined in terms of the beliefs held by members of an organization about what they saw as distinctive, continuous, and central elements of the organization. In recent years, other perspectives on identity have also found a receptive ear in the research literature. Perceived identity elements are an important component, certainly, of organizational identity. But they are complemented by three other identity components: the organization's desired identity, its projected identity, and its applied identity. Each component has a strong research tradition of its own, as well as specific measurement tools that we will examine more closely in Chapter 4.

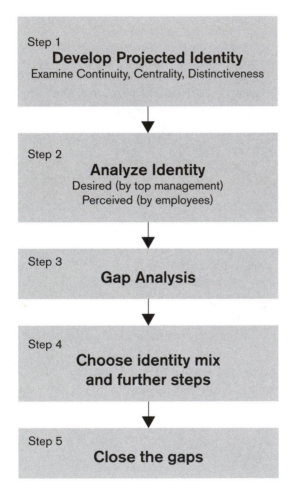

Figure 3.6 The process of identity management

Discussion Questions

1. Think about the identity of the organization in which you work. How would you describe the "actual identity" of that organization?
2. How many of those identity elements do you think are widely shared internally among employees? Which ones might not be shared?
3. Put yourself in the place of a customer. How do you think they would interpret the organization's identity? What would you call those identity elements?
4. How might you go about discovering and distinguishing the organization's actual, projected, and perceived identities? What would you do?

MEASURING CORPORATE IDENTITY

*Who am I? Wouldn't you like to know? I am
an oppressed King, the tree that was
forbidden to grow.*

*But you're not ready to open you eyes.
So just like me, you wear a disguise*
James Royster

Corporate identities are difficult to measure. Some researchers go so far as to suggest that organizations are so complex and unique that all attempts to develop general measurement instruments capable of defining their unique features are futile exercises.

We disagree. In our view, so long as we recognize that every measurement tool is colored by a particular point of view on the nature of "identity," it is possible to develop an appropriate measurement approach to the type of identity of interest. The purpose of this chapter is to examine the principal approaches to corporate identity, and to propose appropriate measurement tools capable of providing useful descriptions and analyses of those identity elements.

There are two principal measurement approaches to corporate identity. The first set of measurement methods are used to examine the four Identity Types described in Chapter 3. The second set of methods is useful in examining specific elements of the Identity Mix (behavior, communication, and symbolism). Table 4.1 summarizes these methods and they are discussed and assessed in detail in the rest of this chapter.

Table 4.1 Methods for measuring corporate identity

	Identity Types			Identity Mix		
	Perceived identity	Applied identity	Projected identity	Behaviors	Communications	Symbols
Desired identity		Laddering				
Consensus profile	Attribute scales		Design inventories	SOCIPO instrument	Organization communication	
Personality profile			Content analysis	ROIT instrument	Communication audits	Graphics audit

Measuring identity types

In Chapter 3, we described four identity types of interest to companies exploring their corporate identities, namely the desired identity, the perceived identity, the applied identity, and the projected identity. This section examines methods useful for deepening our understanding of these identity types.

Desired identity

There are two principal methods investigators can rely on to measure a company's preferred or desired identity elements: we describe them as the "Consensus Profile" and the "Personality Profile".

The Consensus Profile

In *Company Image & Reality*, the British author Bernstein (1986) describes a simple technique for building management consensus about a company's desired identity. He suggests bringing all senior leadership in the organization together in one room for a workshop. At the beginning of the session, participants are asked individually to write down those attributes which, in their opinion: (1) have played a decisive role in the development of the company, and (2) which are likely to be very important for its future development. The list should include all company values that seem relevant, even if some are currently out of favor.

Let us suppose that eight attributes are considered by all participants to be relevant attributes of the organization. Each participant is then given a form that lists all eight characteristics and is asked to score them on the degree to which the company: (1) is actually defined, and (2) should be defined by these attributes. The responses can be visually displayed as a cobweb diagram. Figure 4.1 summarizes the process and illustrates a prototypical identity cobweb for a particular company. Each axis on the chart forms a numerical scale, with the origin being 0. The diagram is used to energize a group discussion designed to determine the key elements and desired direction of the corporate identity.

Such a workshop is useful for putting managers' ideas into an explicit form. Areas of conflict within the management team can also be exposed. The most important function of the method is to bring out into the open the terms in which the managers are thinking, and to arrive at an unambiguous statement of the corporate identity desired by the management.

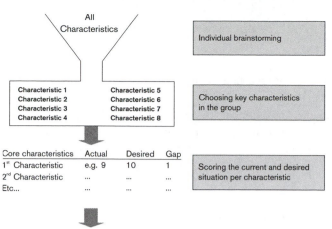

Characteristic 1	Characteristic 5	
Characteristic 2	Characteristic 6	
Characteristic 3	Characteristic 7	
Characteristic 4	Characteristic 8	

Core characteristics	Actual	Desired	Gap
1st Characteristic	e.g. 9	10	1
2nd Characteristic	...	...	...
Etc...	...	...	...

Plan a Cobweb diagram

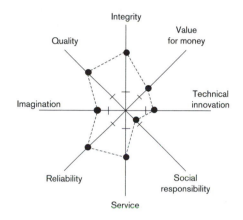

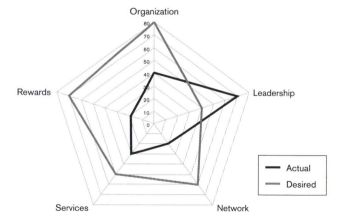

Figure 4.1 A consensus profile for describing a company's desired identity

This method measures in the first instance the picture that the managers have of their company, which is not necessarily the same as the view of the company held by other employees or members of target groups. This in fact constitutes the weakness of the method: it does not actually measure the existing identity of the company. It should perhaps mainly be considered as a method for initiating discussion of the goals of the organization.

The Personality Profile

The Personality Profile proposed by Lux (1986) takes as its point of departure the existence of seven core dimensions that can always be used to describe the "personality" of a company. He owes his views of "corporate personality" to studies of individual personality summarized by Guildford (1954) who suggested that there were seven character traits that could be used to describe all people. As Figure 4.2 diagrams, the seven core dimensions of a corporate personality profile are:

1. *Needs*: Needs are the central attributes of the personality profile. They are essential for the survival of the company, and provide the basic motivation for its actions. Examples are growth, security, and a healthy working atmosphere.
2. *Competencies*: The special skills and competitive advantages of the company.
3. *Attitude*: The philosophical and political background of a company. This is the key dimension on which the company views itself and its environment.
4. *Constitution*: The physical, structural, and legal space in which the company operates. The dimension encompasses its facilities, buildings, locations, structures, and description of its core business.
5. *Temperament*: The way in which the company operates (or fails to operate). This dimension is intended to describe the company's strength, intensity, speed, and emotional tone.
6. *Origin*: In this dimension we see the relationship between the present personality of the company and its past. It is primarily concerned with the attributes which have shaped the company in the past.
7. *Interests*: These are the concrete objectives of the company in the medium and long term. This dimension is concerned with what the company wants to do in the future.

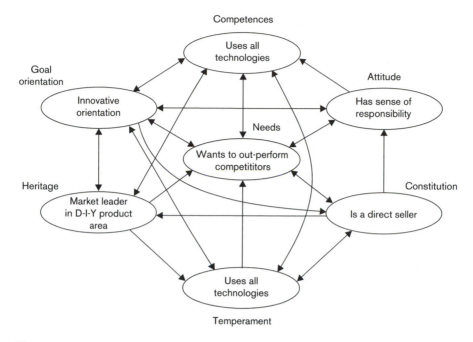

Figure 4.2   Core dimensions of the personality profile
Source: Lux (1986)

The value of the Personality Profile lies principally in stimulating management discussion about the direction in which the company's identity should develop. The dimensions of the Personality Profile can also be used as a tool for classifying the content of employee interviews, archival material about the company, or to summarize personal observations about a company. The main difference between the Consensus Profile and the Personality Profile lies in the selection of the identity elements used to define the company.

Perceived identity

Employees all have differing perceptions of the core elements of a company's identity. On one hand, context influences perceptions: employees therefore see the world from the perspectives of their location in the company – their level, function, and centrality, and so "see" different aspects of the company. On the other hand, employees also have different expectations and understandings of the way the company operates – and beliefs about the way it "should" operate. It is therefore predictable that different people in a company will have different interpretations about the identity elements that they believe to be core features of the company.

A common way to measure core identity features involves: (1) interviewing a representative set of employees and constituting a comprehensive list of those attributes most frequently mentioned, and (2) surveying a representative sample of employees to determine which characteristics are seen as most typical of the company. In their study of the Port Authority of New York, Dutton and Dukerich (1991) identified 84 identity elements which they grouped into five identity clusters deemed "most important" by employees:

1. Professional and unique technical expertise: 100 percent;
2. Ethical, free of scandals and altruistic: 44 percent;
3. First class, top quality organization, superior service: 36 percent;
4. High involvement in the well-being of the direct environment: 36 percent;
5. Loyalty of Port Authority employees (sense of belonging to a family): 25 percent.

In their study of a large rural cooperative, Foreman and Whetten (1994) began by conducting focus group interviews with members. From these interviews, they identified two "metaphors" that could be used to explain the existing tensions among internally: "family" and "business". The metaphors were used as inputs into a questionnaire created to measure the two identities. In the survey, members' identity perceptions and expectations of cooperatives in general were measured, as well as their attitudes about the legitimacy of cooperatives in general. The results showed how conflicting corporate identities are manifested in tensions among employees as well.

Gioia and Thomas (1996) investigated organizational identity at a university in order to develop a framework for managing change. They invited a sample of university administrators to rate their institutions on a series of identity elements derived from prior theorizing and research about universities. They also asked them to assess the degree to which their university was more or less "utilitarian" or "normative", and measured the "identity strength" of each institution (see Box 4.1).

Box 4.1 Identity scales used to describe a university

Identity type (U = Utilitarian, N = Normative)

To what extent . . .
1. do top administrators feel that the institution should not be "competing" for students as if they were clients or customers? (N)
2. are symbols and ceremonies important to the functioning of your institution? (N)
3. have budget cuts or increases usually been made across-the-board? (N)
4. are financial returns (e.g., from athletics, economic development, etc.) a measure of success for your institution? (U)
5. is your institution's mission focused on academic quality? (N)
6. is there a feeling that the university should be (or continue to be) actively engaged in marketing campaigns to attract students? (U)
7. are budget cuts or increases made selectively across departments or colleges at your institution? (U)
8. is cost-effectiveness the major criterion that guides programmatic or administrative change? (U)
9. is economic performance considered to be important to fulfilling your institution's mission or goals? (U)

Identity strength (attitudinal scale)

To what extent . . .
1. do the top management team members of your institution have a strong sense of the institution's history?
2. do your institution's administrators have a sense of pride in the institution's goal or mission?
3. do top administrators feel that your institution has carved out a significant place in the higher education community?
4. do the top management team members not have a well-defined set of goals or objectives for the institution?
5. does your institution have administrators who are knowledgeable about the institution's history and traditions?
6. does your institution have administrators, faculty, and students who identify strongly with the institution?

Source: Adapted from Gioia and Thomas (1996)

Measuring applied identity

A different approach to those described in the preceding sections was developed by van Rekom (1992, 1997; van Rekom *et al.*, 2006), and is frequently described as a "laddering" technique. According to Reynolds and Gutman (1984), laddering is "an individual depth interview technique, which is used to gain insight into the way in which consumers translate product attributes into meaningful associations relating to themselves."

In the standard laddering interview, attributes are generated by means of a Kelly Repertory Grid. This is a procedure in which three alternatives are presented to a group of respondents. They are asked to specify how each of the three is different from the other two, with scores given to each of the rated alternatives. The key question in the laddering technique is "Why is that important to you?" The question is repeated until a chain of meanings is built up which leads through levels of increasing abstraction from the concrete attribute, via its consequences, to the underlying values. All the chains relating to a particular product can be combined into a Hierarchical Value Map (HVM), which charts the associations across the different levels of abstraction expressed by the respondents.

The laddering technique was originally developed to determine the image of a product or brand, and to determine those aspects of the image which were most relevant to a respondent's purchase decision. Laddering exposes the meaning structure, which the respondent uses to decide about an action he or she is contemplating, namely the purchase or use of the product in question.

The laddering technique can also be used to determine the identity of a company. According to van Rekom, the measurement of identity is the detection of the structure of the collective meanings of the organization. The laddering method begins with a listing of attributes, but then examines the interpretations that respondents attach to their functions. The respondent is asked, for example, how quickly he or she assembles the parts of a mechanical device. Then comes the question: "Why is this aspect important?" The question is aimed, not at the results of using the product, as in product research, but at fulfilling the intended consequences of the action, i.e. the objective. The answer to the question (why a certain objective is important) sheds light on the underlying values of the company. In other words, the exploration starts with the concrete actions of the company, but quickly proceeds to uncover its personality. The Dutch company Overtoom, for example, guarantees delivery of office furniture anywhere in the Netherlands within 24 hours of receiving an order. Fulfilling that promise is critical to the image of "speed" and "reliability" that the company seeks to create.

Van Rekom recommends listing the identity elements revealed during the laddering interviews in a questionnaire, and using a survey to test how to represent the elements of the company's whole identity structure. The questionnaire is the instrument used to measure corporate identity. It contains all the attributes, characteristics, goals, and values, and the data are used to develop the final Hierarchical Value Map of the company.

Because they are rooted in the actual behavior of the company, the resulting map forms a legitimate basis for constructing communications aimed at the various target groups and for the use of company symbols. If the culture of the organization needs to be changed, the map clarifies which aspects of the culture are directly conveyed to outsiders.

Laddering enables constructing an overview of all the activities which a company directs towards its target groups, the values and objectives which lie behind these activities, and the relationships between them. Measurements can be carried out, not only for the company as a whole, but also for individual departments, and the results compared.

Although useful, laddering also has some disadvantages. For one, the method can only be applied by experienced interviewers, and requires well trained qualitative analysts. For another, the method takes considerable time and requires commitment, not only by the investigator, but also from the company itself. Nonetheless, it remains one of the more powerful methods for diagnosing and measuring the applied identity of an organization.

Measuring projected identity

Oddly enough, there are few documented methods for examining the projected identities of companies. Fombrun (1996) proposed a systematic framework for assessing a company's "messaging profile". As he suggested, projected identities develop from the communications that companies make through their print, visual, video, and web communications. Diagnosing the projected identity of a company therefore requires: (1) a compilation of all the formal communications and messaging used by an organization, including its online presentations, its financial statements, its social reports, newsletters, brochures, corporate advertisements, sponsorships, press releases, and executives speeches, and (2) a framework from which to induce the meanings expressed in those communications.

Design specialists often rely on visual inventories to make a description of all the visual expressions of the identity of organizations. This sometimes results in amusing discoveries of the varied ways in which organizations get represented internally both officially (logos, signing, etc.) and unofficially (bathroom graffiti, email slurs) – and becomes a "social fact" about the organization.

To get at a company's projected identity, however, it is important to focus on more than visual communications. After all, a company communicates its identity using a broad range of media, verbal communications, and symbols. Analyzing them together is therefore a vital aspect of developing a deep understanding of the company's projected identity.

A content analysis of all words used in a company's communications can provide a powerful complement to the visual analysis of symbolic elements that the company uses to position its products, brands, activities, initiatives, employees, history, and strategic direction. Through counts of word usage and verbal expressions, a deeper understanding of the projected identity is possible. To do this effectively, it is crucial to follow a systematic process from which to infer the core projected identity elements that lie dormant in the content analysis. Trained investigators are required to carry this out.

Figure 4.3 shows the results of a content analysis of the meanings expressed in the press releases and communications of a leading technology company. The connotative meanings evident in the identity attributes listed in the chart suggest that the "conversation" of the company's projected identity involves principally financial, strategic, and product performance attributes. In this example, minimal content is conveyed about the company's social performance, organizational attributes, corporate citizenship, or employee-related behaviors.

In *Fame and Fortune*, Fombrun and van Riel (2004) propose an inventory of messaging initiatives classified in terms of five key dimensions. Their examination of the messaging initiatives of leading companies in the US, Australia, Denmark, Italy, and the Netherlands suggests that stronger reputations are the result of corporate communication that produces favorable perceptions in the minds of the public and manifest "distinctiveness", "consistency", "visibility", "transparency", "authenticity", and "responsiveness". Figure 4.4 captures these dimensions in terms of a model for diagnosing a company's "expressiveness profile".

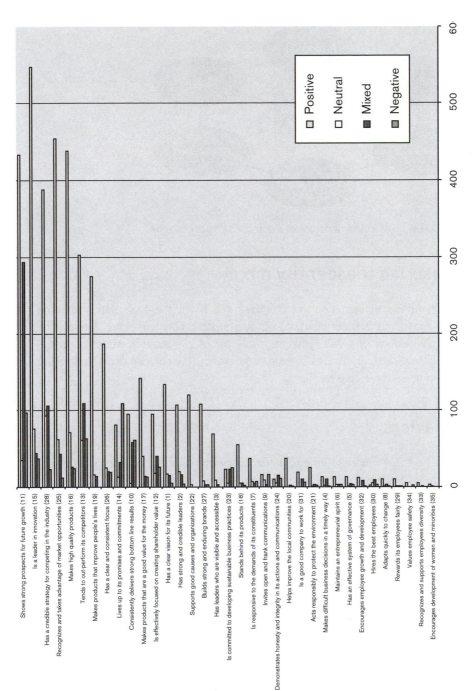

Figure 4.3 Sample results of a content analysis of a company's communications

Legend:
- Positive
- Neutral
- Mixed
- Negative

Y-axis categories:
- Shows strong prospects for future growth (11)
- Is a leader in innovation (15)
- Has a credible strategy for competing in the industry (28)
- Recognizes and takes advantage of market opportunities (25)
- Makes high quality products (16)
- Tends to out-perform its competitors (13)
- Makes products that improve people's lives (19)
- Has a clear and consistent focus (26)
- Lives up to its promises and commitments (14)
- Consistently delivers strong bottom line results (10)
- Makes products that are a good value for the money (17)
- Is effectively focused on creating shareholder value (12)
- Has a clear vision for its future (1)
- Has strong and credible leaders (2)
- Supports good causes and organizations (22)
- Builds strong and enduring brands (27)
- Has leaders who are visible and accessible (3)
- Is committed to developing sustainable business practices (23)
- Stands behind its products (18)
- Is responsive to the demands of its constituents (7)
- Invites open and frank communications (9)
- Demonstrates honesty and integrity in its actions and communications (24)
- Helps improve the local communities (20)
- Is a good company to work for (31)
- Acts responsibly to protect the environment (21)
- Makes difficult business decisions in a timely way (4)
- Maintains an entrepreneurial spirit (6)
- Has an effective system of governance (5)
- Encourages employee growth and development (32)
- Hires the best employees (30)
- Adapts quickly to change (8)
- Rewards its employees fairly (29)
- Values employee safety (34)
- Recognizes and supports employees diversity (33)
- Encourages development of women and minorities (35)

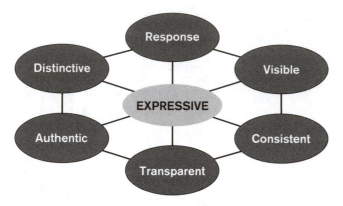

Figure 4.4   The key dimensions of a company's expressiveness

Measuring the identity mix

A number of instruments can be used to examine the three elements of the identity mix that contribute to building organizational identities: behaviours, communications, and symbols. In the rest of this chapter, we review some specialized tools used to develop insights about the company's profile on each of these three core elements.

Behaviors

There are countless empirical instruments that can be helpful in assessing the behaviors of employees in an organization. We have selected two of them here, largely because they have a communications orientation that can be useful for developing practical solutions. The first is the SOCIPO instrument developed by researchers at the University of Leuven in Belgium, and the second is the ROIT instrument developed by the Corporate Communication Centre at Erasmus University, Rotterdam.

The Climate Index (SOCIPO)

The Social Organizational Climate Index for Profit Organizations (SOCIPO) was developed by de Cock et al. (1984) and is based on the proposition that all companies are forced to choose between two central oppositions:

▌ Is the organization focused on personal development of people, or is the organization more focused on the realization of organizational goals?

▌ Is the organization flexible in its relationships with its environment, or does it try to control the current situation?

Answers to these two questions can be used to create a two dimensional map depicted in the diagram of Figure 4.5 and also in Table 4.2, producing a fourfold typology of organizational climates:

1. *Supportive*: The people/flexibility quadrant describes a company with a "supportive" environment.
2. *Rules based*: The people/control quadrant describes a company with a deep respect for rules.
3. *Goal oriented*: The organization/control quadrant describes companies heavily invested in developing effective flows of information.
4. *Innovative*: The organization/flexibility quadrant describes companies focused on stimulating innovation.

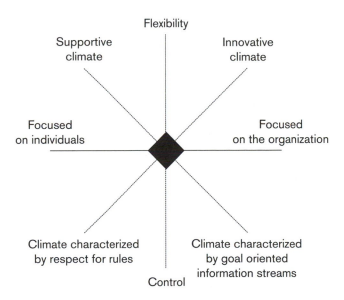

Figure 4.5 Dimensions for classifying types of organizational climate
Source: de Cock et al. (1984)

Table 4.2 Dimensions for classifying types of organizational climate

Name	Characteristics	Main focus of attention
1. *Supportive* climate	People oriented, value oriented	Cooperation, tolerance, support, maximization of human involvement
2. *Rules-based*: Climate characterized by respect for rules	Safety, continuity, uniformity, confirmation of the existing	Structure, formalization, centralization, and standardization
3. *Goal-oriented*: Climate characterized by effective information flow	Planning, clear policy, efficiency	Productivity, efficiency, workload, development of logical guidelines, organization
4. *Innovative* climate	Change, adaptation, individual iniative variety, competition	Growth and risk, stimulation of initiative, individual responsibility, optimal use of human resources, keeping track of academic findings

Source: de Cock *et al.* (1984)

A survey instrument is developed to measure the company's climate, and results are compared to a set of norms created by researchers at the University of Leuven. They applied the SOCIPO instrument to a representative sample of companies in Belgium and used it to identify "ideal types" in each quadrant. Figure 4.6 shows a comparison between a company's own scores on these attributes and the ideal type.

The value of the SOCIPO assessment lies in its ability to provide companies with data about the behavioral implications of initiating specific types of changes in a company. It provides a reasonable starting point for assessing the effectiveness of internal changes on the internal climate of the company. Repeated application of the instrument over time enables deducing the effectiveness of a company's behavioral change from identity-led initiatives.

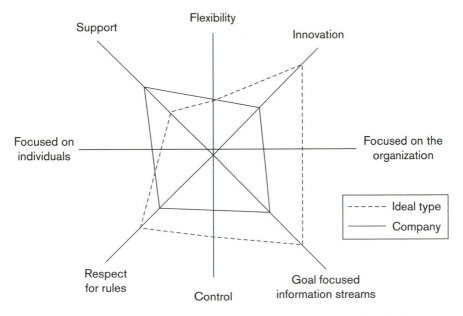

Figure 4.6 SOCIPO results for a medium-sized company compared to ideal type

From identity to identification

The Rotterdam Organizational Identification Test (ROIT)

When employees identify strongly with an organization, they are more likely to develop supportive attitudes to accept the organization's premises, and to make decisions that are consistent with the organization's stated objectives (Ashforth and Mael, 1989; Littlejohn, 1989). Identification with the organization is influenced by antecedents like "employee communication," "perceived organizational prestige", "job satisfaction", "goals and values," and "corporate culture". The ROIT instrument is designed to measure the impact of these antecedents on employee identification with the company (Rotterdam Organizational Identification Test) scale (van Riel *et al.*, 1994; Smidts *et al.*, 2001).

The complete ROIT instrument consists of 225 statements respondents are asked to respond to on seven-point Likert scales. The instrument has been tested extensively with a group of companies. ROIT is divided into four modules.

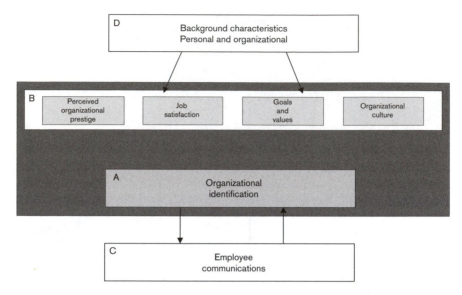

Figure 4.7   Measuring organizational identification using ROIT

The first module measures employee identification with the company using 15 attributes. The second module consists of 80 questions that measure the antecedents of organizational identification (perceived organizational prestige, job satisfaction, the perceived organizational goals and values, the means to attain these goals, and the perceived organizational culture). The third module assesses employee communications using 122 items, e.g. the quantity and usefulness of the information received on personal performance and on the performance of the organization, as well as the communication climate. In the final module, demographic data are obtained, including age, tenure, and organizational function. Figure 4.7 summarizes the structure of the ROIT model.

A ROIT survey enables organizations to develop indicators of the degree to which their employees identify with the company as a whole or only with the function or unit of the organization in which they work. ROIT also provides valuable information about how to improve employee identification by targeting the key antecedents of identification at the business unit or corporate levels.

From empirical research done using the ROIT instrument, it often turns out that employee identification with companies is strongly influenced by two key predictors: (1) employees perceptions of the company's *reputation*, and (2) by employees' own job satisfaction. These findings reinforce our understanding that employees are key stakeholders to whom managers must target both morale-enhancing and reputation-building initiatives.

Communications

Communications are a key component of the identity mix. Most practitioners interested in influencing corporate identity examine the effectiveness of their communications by performing an audit of the function. The term "audit" derives from the Latin verb "audire" (to hear), and is often used in the sense of "periodic review". The term "audit" is also closely related to the Latin word "auditor", which means "judge". Audits are generally evaluative and are typically used to change the way a company is managed. If auditing is done with care, there is usually little resistance to it, and the audit can stimulate improvements in both communication media, and the company's use of symbols.

There are different kinds of communication audits. The simplest ones involve a straightforward compilation and assessment of existing communication vehicles, and a subjective evaluation of their consistency and impact. More complex communication audits have drawn on the "organizational climate" literature. For instance, Redding (1972) distinguished five dimensions that were important for building an ideal communication climate: (1) supportiveness, (2) participative decision-making, (3) trust, confidence, and credibility, (4) openness and candor, and (5) high performance goals (Falcione et al., 1987). The "Organizational Communication" (OC) instrument developed by Roberts and O'Reilly (1973) relied heavily on Redding's early work. Also in the Redding tradition is the "Communication Satisfaction" (CS) that was proposed by Downs and Hazen (1977) to measure employee satisfaction with corporate communications.

The best-known communication audit is developed by the International Communication Association (ICA) in the US. It was initially referred to as the ICA Audit, but was subsequently adapted by Goldhaber and Rogers (1979) and renamed the "Communication Audit Survey" (CAS).

Finally, a valuable study initiated by the Finnish government led to an instrument for measuring the communication climate in working relationships (Wiio and Helsila, 1974). It was initially called the "LTT Communication Audit Questionnaire", but was later revised and renamed the "Organizational Communication Audit Questionnaire" (OCA). We examine these in turn.

Organizational Communication (OC)

The OC instrument enables comparisons between companies in how they communicate. It includes thirteen explicit communication variables. They are: (1) desire for interaction, (2) directionality upward, (3) directionality downward, (4) directionality lateral, (5) accuracy, (6) summarization frequency, (7) gatekeeping, (8) overload, (9) satisfaction, (10) written communication, (11) face-to-face communication, (12) telephone communication, and (13) other channels of communication. In addition, there are three other communication-related variables that are measured: trust in superior, influence of superior, and mobility aspirations.

Table 4.3 describes the most important elements of the OC scale (Greenbaum et al., 1988).

Table 4.3 The organizational communication scale

Dimension description and number of items in dimension	Illustrative items (7-point Likert scales)
1. Trust (3 items)	How free do you feel to discuss with your superior the problems and difficulties you have in your job without jeopardizing your position or having it "held against" you later? (Completely free to very cautious)
2. Influence (3 items)	In general, what do you feel your immediate superior can do to further your career in this organization? (Much to very little)
3. Mobility (2 items)	How important is it for you to progress upward in your present organization? (Not important to very important)
4. Desire for interaction (3 items)	How desirable do you feel it is in your organization to be in contact frequently with others at the same job level? (Very desirable to completely undesirable)
5. Directionality upward (3 items)	While working, what percentage of the time do you spend in contact with superiors? (Fill in percentage)
6. Directionality downward (3 items)	While working, what percentage of the time do you spend in contact with subordinates? (Fill in percentage)
7. Directionality lateral (3 items)	While working, what percentage of the time do you spend in contact with others at the same level? (Fill in percentage)

Table 4.3 continued

Dimension description and number of items in dimension	Illustrative items (7-point Likert scales)
8. Accuracy (3 items)	When receiving information from the sources listed below (superior, subordinate, peers), how accurate would you estimate it usually is? (Completely accurate to completely inaccurate)
9. Summarization (3 items)	When transmitting information to your immediate superiors, how often do you summarize by emphasizing aspects that are important and minimizing those that are unimportant? (Always to never)
10. Gatekeeping (3 items)	Of the total amount of information you receive at work, how much do you pass on to your immediate superior? (All to none)
11. Overload (1 item)	Do you ever feel that you receive more information than you can efficiently use? (Never to always)
12. Satisfaction (1 item)	Put a check under the face that expresses how you feel about communication in general, including the amount of information you receive, contacts with your superiors and others, the accuracy of information available, etc. (Respondent checks one of seven faces expressing range of happy feelings to unhappy feelings)
13- Modalities of 16. communications (4 items)	Of the total time you engage in communications while on the job, about what percentage of the time do you use the following methods? Written . . . %; face-to-face . . . %; telephone . . . %; other . . . % (Fill in percentage)

Communication Satisfaction (CS)

Employees are not always satisfied with the communications they receive from management, a factor that doubtless affects their morale, commitment, and identification with the organization. Downs and Hazen (1977) proposed an instrument to measure employee satisfaction with corporate communication. The instrument consists of eight communication satisfaction variables, six career satisfaction variables, and five demographic variables, scored on a ten-point scale. The eight communication satisfaction variables are: (1) *communication climate*: general satisfaction with the perceived effectiveness of the communication climate; (2) *supervisory communication*: satisfaction with upward and downward communication with the respondent's supervisor; (3) *Organization integration*: the extent to which employees receive information about their immediate work environment; (4) *media quality*: the extent to which meetings are well organized, written directives are short and clear, and volume of communication is adequate; (5) *co-worker communication*: satisfaction with horizontal communication relationships in the organization; (6) *corporate information*: information about the organization as a whole, such as information about company's financial standing; (7) *personal feedback*: what workers need to know about how they are judged and how their performance is appraised; and (8) *subordinate communication*: items that are only answered by super-visors, including "extent to which subordinates initiate upward communication" (Greenbaum, 1988).

Communication Audit Survey (CAS)

The CAS, better known as the ICA Audit, compares the perceived communi-cation environment with the desired situation of the company. The instrument examines the following core topics: judgment of the amount of information to be received; judgment of the amount of information to be sent to others; and judgment of the feedback received on the information sent. Items include: "In respect to information I send to my immediate supervisor, this is the amount of follow-up *I get now*"; and the same question, ending with "this is the amount of follow-up *that is needed*". Other items elicit judgments about the quantity of information ("the amount of information I receive"), the time-span within which the information is received ("to what extent can you say the information is usually timely?"), the communication climate ("to what extent can you say, I trust my co-workers?"), career satisfaction, and the channels used by the organization.

Organizational Communication Audit Questionnaire (OCA)

One of the few European communication audits, originally referred to as the LTT, and then reincarnated as the OCD and most recently the ICA, was originally developed in Finland by Wiio and Helsila (1974). The twelve variables at the heart of the ICA are:

1. overall communication satisfaction;
2. amount of information received from different sources – now;
3. amount of information received from different sources – ideal;
4. amount of information received about specific job items – now;
5. amount of information received about specific job items – ideal;
6. areas of communication that need improvement;
7. job satisfaction;
8. availability of computer information system;
9. allocation of time in a working day;
10. respondent's general communication behavior;
11. organization-specific questions; and
12. information-seeking patterns.

The information collected about the quality of communication in a particular organization gains extra value when it can be tested against outside standards. The most obvious comparison is against norms obtained from examining other companies in the same industry. Such comparisons are possible with the CAS Audit and with the OCA since extensive databases of audit results are available from the International Communication Association in the USA and the Institute for Human Communication in Finland.

Reliability and validity of communication audits

To be credible, organizations often call on outside experts to carry out communication audits. All of the audits described in this section have been tested for reliability and validity by various authors. Table 4.4 summarizes key features of these communication audits (Greenbaum *et al.*, 1988).

Symbols

Symbols such as logos, names, signage, music, styling, dress codes, design, and architecture, all play an important role in constructing corporate identities. Within the identity mix, symbols are actually the only elements that are fully under management control. Unfortunately, attention to symbols is uneven in most companies, and generally peaks during the adoption of a new branding strategy and house style, with a rapid drop thereafter. This is unfortunate since

Table 4.4 Comparing communication audits

	OC	CS	CAS	OCA
General structure				
Items: total	35	51	134	76
Communication items	27	40	109	54
Demographics	–	5	12	7
Outcome variable items	–	6	13	7
Comm.-related items	8	–	–	–
Org. specific items	–	–	–	8
Dimensions	16	10	13	12
Response format				
Type of scale	7-point	7-point	5-point	5-point
Open-ended	None	Limited	Extensive	Limited
Multiple choice	–	5 items	12 items	16 items
Inc. demographics				
Administration				
Ease of administering	High	High	High	Moderate
Ease of tabulating	High	High	Moderate	Moderate
Past use of instrument	Moderate	Moderate	High	High
Norms availability	None	Yes	Yes	Yes
Psychometric data				
Reliability				
Overall	0.70	0.94	0.838	n/a
Interim within scale	0.84 to 0.53	0.86 to 0.75	0.90 to 0.70	n/a
Item to total				0.39 to 0.22 (LTT items only)
Validity				
Face validity	High	High	High	High
Discrimination validity	High	High	High	n/a
Factor stability	Moderate	Moderate	Low	Moderate
Evaluated by other				
researchers	Yes	Yes	Yes	Yes

managers often neglect the valuable role that symbols can play in continued *sense-giving* to both internal and external stakeholders.

Symbols are "physical objects existing within an organizational context that connote meanings about the organization that are distinct from meaning connoted by these objects when viewed out of context" (Green and Loveluck, 1994). Symbols fulfil two functions. Internally, a symbol is a concrete visible object that is meant to increase someone's ability to identify with the organization. Externally, a symbol is supposed to increase the instinctive recognition of the organization. Research has shown that visual symbols tend to evoke greater recognition than verbal symbols (Edell and Staelin, 1983).

Graphics audits

A graphics audit consists of an inventory of the symbols used in an organization (Napoles, 1988), as well as the way they are conveyed through corporate communication. Virtually all objects which carry the company's logo are important in expressing the identity of the company. A graphics audit should therefore also include an inventory of all those objects that carry visual messages, e.g. the company's buildings, interiors, vehicles, and equipment. The logo on the average company truck, for instance, is capable of delivering millions of visual impressions to consumers every year. This gives an indication of the importance of the company fleet. Since visual impression is a means of communication, it is also an indirect sales tool.

An examination of symbols invariably leads to inquiring about all of the company's locations and the target groups they serve. It involves asking how space, color, lighting, and symbols are being used by the company in all locations to express the identity of the company. Armed with these diverse inputs, it is possible to create an overview of how each location is expressing the corporate identity, in pictures, videos, and messaging that either enhance or dilute stakeholder identification.

Henderson and Cote (1998) examined the relative effectiveness of various graphical elements in corporate logos. They suggested that logos demonstrated the following attributes in varying degrees:

- natural (figurative and organic);
- harmony (balance and symmetry);
- elaborate (complex, active, and depth);
- parallel;
- repetition;
- proportion;
- round.

They then tested the effectiveness of these logos questioning various experts. Certain characteristics of logos proved effective by stimulating repetition (natural, repeated elements, average level of harmony) while others were less important (complete harmony, round, parallel, etc.). They concluded that there were four types of logos, two of which are more effective and recommended (depending on the goal of the organization: whether to increase familiarity or improve image), whereas the other two should not be used.

- *recognizable*: very natural, harmonious, and relatively complex;
- *low budget*: below average natural, high degree of harmony, relatively detailed, parallel, and good proportion;
- *logos with a strong image*: reasonably detailed, natural, and great harmony;
- *badly designed logos*: not very natural, low harmony, and low detail.

Van Riel and van den Ban (2000) conducted an experiment surrounding the introduction of a new logo by Rabobank. The study demonstrated that people make different associations with each type of logo that is presented to them, and that they have differing levels of recall. As Figure 4.8 suggests, the set of associations they had with the logo increased when respondents were shown the name of the company behind the logo, leading to greater affect and lower false recognition. After the launch of the new logo, a nationwide advertising campaign in the Netherlands increased positive associations and reduced negative associations. The majority of interviewees were able to describe

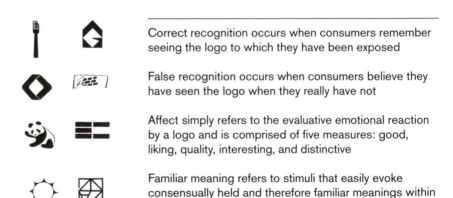

Correct recognition occurs when consumers remember seeing the logo to which they have been exposed

False recognition occurs when consumers believe they have seen the logo when they really have not

Affect simply refers to the evaluative emotional reaction by a logo and is comprised of five measures: good, liking, quality, interesting, and distinctive

Familiar meaning refers to stimuli that easily evoke consensually held and therefore familiar meanings within a culture or subculture

Figure 4.8   Testing effective and ineffective recall of logos
Source: Henderson and Cote (1998)

associations that matched the intended identity the bank had sought to express through its new corporate symbol.

Overall, despite the complexity of the identity construct, this chapter has reviewed a variety of practical tools that investigators can use to gauge the four principal identity types that exist in all organizations, as well as to measure the identity mix the company has put in place. In the next chapter, we explore how companies can draw on their corporate identities to strengthen their corporate brands and thereby build reputational capital.

Discussion Questions

1. Think about the identity of the company in which you work. What might the results of a Consensus Profiling session with the top management of the company look like?
2. What would you suggest would be the likely results of research about the identity of a company obtained from a questionnaire sent to a representative sample of employees. What conclusions could you draw from such a study?
3. Compare and contrast the results you might get from applying a laddering method to derive a set of identity elements compared to a personality profile.
4. Explain why symbols are important when formulating an identity policy.
5. Imagine that a company is pressed for time and is forced to start a corporate identity program (for example due to an IPO). Which method would you recommend they use to (1) determine the unique features of the company, and (2) to uncover whether a majority of the employees understand these features to be unique identity elements?
6. Under what conditions is it necessary to carry out the kinds of communication audits discussed in this chapter?

5

COMMUNICATING WITH THE CORPORATE BRAND

The magic of technology
Is it doesn't matter where
The sender and receiver are
Or in their underwear
But we've got lost in all of this
Checking for things here and there
What seemed like real time saving
Now makes us pull out our hair
We spend so much time receiving
And retrieving things on screen
When a simple conversation
Could have made clear what we mean.

David Keig

In this chapter, we examine the link between identity and corporate communication by posing the following question: how can managers ensure that their company's communication strategy leads stakeholders to make favorable associations between the company and its products? In the process, we explore whether it is feasible for a company to rely on its corporate brand to generate positive stakeholder associations with the company's core, central, and distinctive identity elements. Internally, companies struggle to ensure that there is alignment between what the company wants to do and how employees see the company and its strategic objectives. We will examine this question later in Chapter 7, and concentrate here on the intended logic of corporate branding.

By *corporate brand* we mean a visual representation of a company that unites a group of products or businesses, and makes it known to the world through the use of a single name, a shared visual identity, and a common set of symbols. The process of *corporate branding* consists of the set of activities undertaken by the company to build favorable associations and positive reputation with both internal and external and stakeholders.

Even cursory familiarity with the business world today demonstrates the growing visibility of corporate brands. Corporate brands are useful to companies seeking to create a coherent identity with consumers and investors. General Electric (GE), for instance, is among the most recognizable corporate brands. The GE name and logo bring together a very diverse set of over 200 different businesses operating in multiple industries. Similarly, Philip Morris changed its name to Altria Group in 2003 to recognize its involvement in both the tobacco business and the food business and to neutralize the negative effects of tobacco on its Kraft/General Foods division. Figure 5.1 shows an ad featuring Altria Group that highlights its role as the parent company to both food and tobacco companies.

In many industries, the only source of differentiation for a company consists of the way its products and services are experienced by customers. The growing interest in "experience marketing", for instance, recognizes the value of creating a coherent corporate experience for customers of companies, particularly those who operate in the services sector. The explosive growth of coffee retailer Starbucks, for instance, can be traced to a combination of factors that consumers link to its corporate brand, namely: the product (premium coffee beans, the roasting process, quality snack foods), the environment (lounge chairs, a social atmosphere), and the symbols (a specialized language for ordering coffee) (see Rindova, 1999). In similar ways, large casinos in Las Vegas such as Caesar's, Paris, Bellagio, Harrah's, have all become heavy investors in building a consistent and differentiating experience for their patrons in order to build customer loyalty and get repeat business, particularly from the high-stakes players they court assiduously. They cultivate their corporate brands systematically.

On the other side of the coin, the costs of maintaining multiple product brands are extremely high, so high that in many industries we see growing consolidation of brands and businesses as managers look for ways to exploit latent synergies between brands. Business consolidations therefore tend to stimulate corporate branding. As companies merge their operations, they are forced to contend with the need for a merged identity. Is the combination a "merger of equals" or "an acquisition"? The terms have major implications for

The value of seeing the whole forest.
by the parent company of Kraft Foods, Philip Morris International and Philip Morris USA

As a company that is the parent of both tobacco and food companies, we know what it is like to make the news – and not only in the financial reports. But what may not always make news is the long-term performance of a company like Altria Group, Inc.

We're not only one of the 30 companies that make up the Dow Jones Industrial Average, we're also one of the most profitable companies in the world. And we've had 39 dividend increases in the last 37 years. The family of brands made by our operating companies includes household names like Maxwell House, Marlboro, Velveeta, Virginia Slims, Philadelphia, Kraft, Nabisco. And many more.

We also know that in order for our companies to continue to be in business they need to strive to meet the expectations of Altria's shareholders, their consumers, regulators and society. It is simply the only path to the future.

For a company as newsworthy as ours, at times it can be hard to see the forest for the trees. But to look beyond immediate challenges and position our company for long-term success, we have to keep the whole forest squarely in sight.

And that's a vision we feel is worth sharing.

Our name is Altria Group.

 Altria

Kraft Foods
Philip Morris International
Philip Morris USA
NYSE: MO   altria.com

© Altria Group, Inc. 2006

Figure 5.1   Altria group highlighting its role as parent company

the characteristics of the corporate brand that the merged entity will adopt. The defining characteristics of the corporate brand depend in part on the type of "parenting advantage" that the company is trying to establish (Campbell *et al.*, 1995). The stronger the degree of synergy the parent company hopes to extract from its business units, the more important the corporate brand becomes in conveying to employees an understanding of the value created by the merger.

Managers can generate cost savings by building a single corporate name which they apply to all of their products. Nestlé and Philips are two companies that have relied on such a strategy for many years. More recent interest in corporate branding has been demonstrated by pharmaceutical firms such as Pfizer, Merck, Novartis, and GlaxoSmithKline as they seek to reduce the heavy branding burden imposed on them by their product focused strategy. The heavy dose of institutional advertising they have funded in recent years is a reflection of their growing interest in capitalizing on a more visible and distinctive corporate presence to endorse their activities. It also demonstrates the growing conviction of many companies that increased reliance on corporate branding can create added value for the organization. In Europe, the courier DHL is positioned as a member of Germany's Deutsche Post. In Poland, Bank Slaski holds itself up as a world-class company because of its endorsement as a member of the ING group.

Companies increasingly operate in the public spotlight. They are therefore forced to reveal more about themselves to the world and to justify their activities (Greenley and Foxall, 1997). Pressured by investors, consumer activists, journalists, companies are invited to disclose ever more information about their financial, social, and environmental activities. Legislation such as the Sarbanes–Oxley Act of 2002 in the US and the Revised Basel Capital Framework (Basel II) in Europe, define strict corporate governance guidelines and structures that companies must adopt to demonstrate their transparency. As companies are pushed to open up to outside scrutiny by regulators, they look for ways to present an attractive face to their other constituents as well. The societal call for transparency and openness is best addressed by personifying the company as a whole through a corporate brand.

In more general terms, academic research suggests that corporate branding is an appropriate strategy for companies to implement when:

- there is significant "information asymmetry" between a company and its clients (Nayyar, 1990); that is to say customers are much less informed about a company's products than the company itself is;
- customers perceive a high degree of risk in purchasing the products or services of the company (Aaker and Myers, 1991; Kapferer, 1992);
- features of the company behind the brand would be relevant to the product or service a customer is considering purchasing (Brown and Dacin, 1997; Keller, 1993).

Under these circumstances, a strong corporate brand can create bonds of trust between the company and its constituents, and thereby improve performance.

In the rest of the chapter, we examine how best to come to an internal decision about the features of the corporate brand and the specific nomenclature to adopt. In the process, we review various typologies of corporate brands, as well as empirical research in order to provide practical guidelines for developing corporate brands. The focus of the chapter is squarely placed on: (1) describing the process to follow, and (2) defining the specific circumstances under which managers should communicate about the institutional features of the company that stands behind the products and services it sells.

The drivers of corporate branding

Business unit managers vary in their degree of support for corporate branding. Interviews conducted with managers in four industries suggest a tug-of-war between those who support corporate branding and those who oppose it. Arguments used consistently express differing interpretations of the expected gains from having a shared identity and the expected losses in autonomy that are expected to result.

Those who favor corporate branding tend to argue that:

▌ a corporate brand will create a sense of internal coherence and will simplify internal cooperation;
▌ a corporate brand will help us demonstrate the strength and size of our organization to outsiders;
▌ maintaining a corporate brand will be cheaper than having to support a range of different product brands.

In contrast, opponents of corporate branding tend to argue that:

▌ investing in a corporate brand will imply that we have wasted huge sums in building our product brands;
▌ adopting a corporate brand means giving up a powerful local brand and losing market share;
▌ using a single corporate name will limit our distribution options;
▌ size may appeal to financial audiences in our home market, but will not help us with consumers in local markets;

■ increased importance of the corporate brand will reduce the influence of business unit management.

The tension between managerial advocates and detractors of corporate branding implies a need to build internal support among senior managers prior to the implementation of a corporate brand. A basic model can be developed to assess the willingness of business unit managers to use the corporate brand in their business unit communications (van Riel, 1994). The model (summarized in Figure 5.2) recognizes four key factors that drive managerial support for corporate branding: (1) *strategy*: the degree of relatedness among business units, (2) *organization*: the degree of centralization and control exercised by headquarters over the business units, (3) *employees*: the degree of identification by employees with corporate headquarters compared to business units, and (4) *value*: the expected performance and reputation gains to be obtained from adopting the corporate brand.

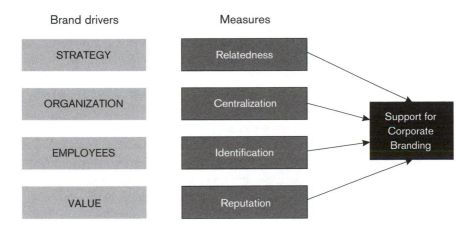

Figure 5.2   The drivers of corporate branding

Strategy drivers

Corporate strategy heavily influences the likelihood of support for a corporate brand. Strategy consists of "the pattern or plan that integrates an organization's major goals, policies, and action sequences into a cohesive whole" (Quinn *et al.*, 1988). Extensive studies of multi-business companies conducted since the 1980s demonstrate that companies whose portfolios demonstrated varying levels of relatedness among business units had different levels of effectiveness. The most significant predictor of the relative effectiveness of these companies was their ability to capitalize on the latent synergies in their portfolios by exploiting relatedness among its businesses (Rumelt, 1974).

Diversification creates tensions for portfolio and business unit managers. In what ways should they seek to create and exploit potential synergies among their business units? How "related" should the strategy of the company be? On what basis should relatedness be defined and crystallized? And who should be responsible for communicating about the company: should communications come from headquarters or from the business units? How homogeneous should they be? And how much information about the company's strategy should actually be communicated to outside audiences?

Studies about the risks of making information about a company's strategy publicly available indicate that open companies are more positively valued by the financial markets (Higgens and Diffenbach, 1989; Sobol and Farrelly, 1989). While true, however, managers also have to be cautious about revealing too much information to competitors, particularly sensitive information about the company's technology, corporate culture, or innovations. Auto industry ads by DaimlerChrysler, Ford Motor Company, and General Motors (illustrated in Figure 5.3) suggest how these companies have simultaneously sought to communicate their pursuit of a "relatedness" strategy by merging multiple car company brands into larger corporate portfolios. In the process, they have sought to infuse a corporate personality into the parent brand. The success of that corporate strategy depends significantly on the company's ability to convince audiences about the logic behind the integration of its product brands. The jury is still out on whether the companies have successfully created economic value from exploiting latent synergies at the corporate level.

Relatedness consists of "the degree to which the operational businesses augment or complement the parent's strategy and thus makes identifiable contributions to the financial and non-financial goals of the parent" (Jemison and Sitkin, 1986). Companies can build "relatedness" by pursuing businesses with common scope, shared technologies, common goals, and similar time horizons. Often relatedness develops from core competences that companies develop and that crystallize their distinctive histories, skills, and growth experiences (Prahalad and Hamel, 1990).

Figure 5.3 The search for synergy in the auto industry: repositioning
(opposite) DaimlerChysler, Ford Motor Company, and General Motors

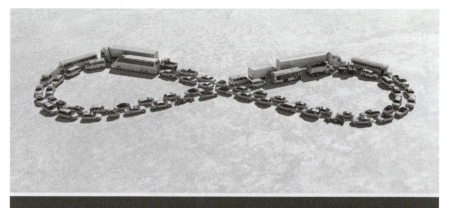

Infinite possibilities.

...to anywhere. As a leading car manufacturer, DaimlerChrysler offers countless solutions
for mobility. From small city coupés to heavy-duty buses. From 4-wheel drives to 18-wheel trucks.
Whatever your needs, we have vehicles that can take you from here...
Find out more at www.daimlerchrysler.com

DAIMLERCHRYSLER
Answers for questions to come.

"Scope" has to do with the nature and spread of a company's activities (Johnson and Scholes, 1989). It describes both the geographical and psychological borders of the company – the physical and social distance between its operations, technologies, and markets. The greater the similarity of the businesses in a corporate portfolio, the more desirable it will be for the company to communicate the strength of the company as a whole. Agricultural companies are a case in point. Often they control the entire supply chain from seeds, grain, and livestock through processing to final consumption of cereals, milk, dairy products, and meat by-products. Because of their vertical integration, such companies are often tempted to tell stakeholders that they can guarantee the "total quality" of their products. At the same time, however, describing their vertical integration too specifically can exacerbate latent fears among consumers and regulators that such a company has become too powerful.

Companies that can identify with a core competency tend to support corporate branding initiatives. Core competences signal the added value created by the company, both internally and externally. Take 3M, a company that has identified "innovation" as its core competence. 3M is widely known for its highly successful Post-It® notes. From its earliest roots in the mining industry, 3M has implemented a policy worldwide designed to stimulate innovation. Among the practices that have become institutionalized at 3M is one policy that allows its 7,000 R&D employees to take up to 15 percent of their time to think of new products that could benefit the company. The practice reinforces the company's core competence. At the same time it signals to external audiences the nature of the organizational glue that holds the company together.

Organizational drivers

Support for corporate branding depends in part on the degree of centralization already present in the organization itself. The more diversified and unrelated the corporate portfolio, the more likely it is that political coalitions exist in different parts of the company that vie for control of the company as a whole. In some companies, control is centralized: a central office fully directs and controls the business units. In others, decentralization prevails, and business units negotiate with headquarters and shoulder the responsibility for managing their units independently. The Dutch consumer goods giant Unilever has traditionally operated in a decentralized fashion, with the motto that everything that can get done at a business unit level should not get done at the head office.

A company with a more centralized communications function is also more likely to support the implementation of a corporate branding strategy. To accelerate support and facilitate implementation of a corporate branding policy, managers can also consider centralizing other administrative and support functions, including such functions as information technology (IT), finance, and marketing. For instance, having a single person responsible for all the European IT activities of the company (instead of allowing semi-autonomous country-level IT heads) significantly increases the likelihood of success in carrying out a coherent corporate branding initiative. A centralized organization structure facilitates the execution of corporate branding.

Employee drivers

Employees that strongly identify with the company as a whole are also more likely to support a corporate branding strategy (Ashforth and Mael, 1989). As Chapter 3 showed, employee identification appeals to individual needs for self-categorisation (Turner, 1987) and self-enhancement (Tajfel, 1981). By defining in-groups and out-groups, self-categorization enables employees to define the boundaries of their world at work. Identification also promotes self-enhancement and enables employees to feel valued in their work and to link their own success to that of the company (Dutton *et al.*, 1994).

The managerial challenge is to ensure that employees identify with the right parts of the company. People will generally identify more strongly with the grouping that is closest to them and through which their needs are met (Ashforth and Mael, 1989; Handy, 1992). Therefore employees will often identify less with the company as a whole, and more with their functional area or business unit. Various studies conducted at the Corporate Communication Centre at Erasmus University demonstrate that identification with the business unit is always higher than with the organization as a whole. Although this is not a problem in itself, local identification becomes problematic when the gap in identification between the corporate level and the business-unit level is so large that a "we–they" dynamic develops. Figure 5.4 and Box 5.1 illustrate four scenarios surrounding the disparity between employee identification with a sub-group or business unit and their identification with the company as a whole. Where gaps are significant (scenarios 2 and 3), only a weak endorsement branding strategy is feasible. Where the gap is small and identification is high, a strong endorsement strategy can be successfully implemented.

		Identification with the business unit	
		Low	High
Identification with	Low	Scenario 1	Scenario 3
the company	High	Scenario 2	Scenario 4

Figure 5.4   Employee identification with corporate and business levels

Box 5.1 Employee identification with corporate and business levels

Scenario	Description
1.	Low identification on both levels. Perform thorough research about the causes and start an intense motivation campaign before external steps are taken in the area of corporate branding.
2.	Strong desire to "seek shelter" with parent company, positive identification with the company behind the brand, usually caused by negative developments in one's own business unit. First, analyze why this feeling exists and especially what managers want to do with the business unit. If planned divestiture of Business Unit, do not develop a visible link with the corporate brand. If this is not the case, one could decide to apply a "weak endorsement" strategy.
3.	Strong identification with the business unit and weak identification with the corporate level. Often this occurs in a strong financially independent business unit that considers itself to be the cash cow of the company. A case is again made for a "weak endorsement" strategy.
4.	Strong identification with both the business unit and the company is an ideal starting point for developing a uniform corporate branding strategy.

Value drivers

Finally, support for the corporate brand also depends on local managers' perceptions that the corporate brand can create added value for them in their own markets, either directly by influencing product sales, or indirectly by casting a reputational halo over the company's product brands. Insofar as value and reputation are expected to result from a corporate branding program, managers are less likely to resist a corporate branding initiative.

Consistent with this line of thinking, empirical research conducted by the Reputation Institute indicates that companies that manage to hold a consistent line in their corporate branding strategies develop stronger and better reputations and are more likely to maintain these higher reputations over time (Fombrun and van Riel, 2004).

In the next section, we will examine in more detail how corporate brands can create economic value by improving product perceptions.

Generating value from the corporate brand

The purpose of a corporate branding initiative is to use the corporate brand to cast a positive halo over the products and businesses of the company and thereby generate more favorable impressions of those products and businesses than they would have on their own. Research suggests that it is only appropriate to build a corporate brand when two conditions are met:

▌ the corporate brand has a sufficiently *high level of awareness* with key stakeholders in the markets where the company's products are offered;
▌ the corporate brand transfers *incremental economic* value to individual product brands.

Marketing researchers refer to value creation as an "image spillover effect" (Sullivan, 1990). Most of the research in this area examines the value transfer from product A to product B that results from a line or brand extension (Aaker and Keller, 1998). A new brand can benefit from the image of an existing brand.

Corporate branding is a special form of brand stretching. In this case, new products are introduced under the corporate brand name (Keller and Aaker, 1998). Using a corporate name links an existing set of organizational associations with those of a product or business unit. It will be more successful if stakeholders perceive a degree of similarity between the corporate brand and the product brand extension (Bousch and Loken, 1991). If corporate and product associations are inconsistent, then the corporate endorsement might not only limit the new brand introduction, but damage the original product brand. Establishing a corporate brand is therefore not necessarily appropriate in all situations.

Organizational associations

Research on corporate brands suggests that, when prompted with a corporate brand name or symbol, people spontaneously make different types of mental associations. One study asked a group of individuals to describe what they associated with each of a long list of corporate brands (Maathuis *et al.*, 1998). The results were grouped into two clusters of associations: the first cluster consisted of *organizational associations* (e.g. company is listed on the stock exchange, has many employees, is profitable, is fun to work for, has good management, is good at conducting research). The second cluster consisted of *product associations* (e.g. makes expensive/cheap products, is well designed, has nice shops, makes product for kids, products do not wear out easily). The researchers then examined each corporate brand in more detail to identify whether product or organizational associations were more prevalent. The results showed that no corporate brand was 100 percent dominated by either organizational associations or product associations.

As part of the study, the researchers also examined whether some corporate brands could more easily stretch to endorse products. They concluded that corporate brands with more organizational associations could more easily endorse a broad array of products than those dominated by product associations. Endorsement by a corporate brand that has strong organizational associations has a more positive effect on assessments observers make about the quality and credibility of the company's products.

A corporate brand can help improve product perceptions by decreasing the perceived risk that observers feel from dealing with the company's products. A corporate brand is therefore a heuristic of sorts, a "script" that simplifies decision-making about the merits of a company's offerings. Organizational associations vary in their ability to help observers evaluate products (Brown, 1998). Therefore, it is important to understand: (1) what types of organizational associations are relevant, and (2) under what conditions these associations have a positive influence on product preferences.

"Corporate associations describe the cognitions, affects (i.e., moods and emotions), evaluations (attaching to specific cognitions or affects), summary evaluations, and/or patterns of associations (e.g. schemata, scripts) with respect to a particular company" (Brown,1998). Six dimensions of corporate associations are relevant:

1. *Corporate abilities*: What are the company's abilities?
2. *Interaction with exchange partners*: How fair is the company in its relationships with stakeholders?
3. *Interaction with employees*: Does one deal with the employees in a sensible way?
4. *Social responsibility*: Does the company fulfill stakeholder expectations of social responsibility?
5. *Marketing*: Do stakeholders have positive or negative associations with the way the company carries out its marketing communications?
6. *Product*: What associations do stakeholders have with the products of the organization?

Organizational associations have also been classified into two categories: Corporate ability associations and social responsibility associations (Brown and Dacin, 1997). Corporate competencies refer to the expertise that a company has in producing and delivering its products. Corporate social responsibilities speaks to the status of the company and the activities it is involved in which are perceived as social obligations. Keller and Aaker (1998) come to a similar conclusion. They make a further distinction between three types of organizational associations:

- *Corporate expertise*: the extent to which a company is able to competently make and sell its products and services.
- *Corporate trustworthiness*: the extent to which a company is thought to be honest, dependable, and sensitive to consumer needs.
- *Corporate likeability*: the extent to which a company is thought likeable, prestigious, and interesting.

Different authors have paid attention to the conditions under which organizational associations have a positive influence on product assessments. Brown (1998) provides a thorough overview of antecedents and consequences of organizational associations on product preferences. He also discusses the moderating role of individual attributes, the organization, and the products offered by the organization.

Another study researched the relationship between various types of organizational associations (corporate ability and corporate social responsibility) and product preferences (Berens *et al.*, 2005). They propose that a set of risk factors moderates the effects of a corporate brand on purchase intent (see Figure 5.5). Risk can be divided into financial, physical, psychological, social, and time related components. If the risk perceived by the observer is low, a high perceived fit (matching the demands and product attributes) will result in there being less need for information about the corporate organization. In the opposite case, if the risk is high, a high perceived fit will not offer enough information about the product quality and there will be heightened demand for information about corporate ability. After all, the target audience is often no expert concerning the product.

Finally, the study also indicates that the two main clusters of organizational associations (corporate ability and corporate social responsibility) differ in their influence on purchase intentions. Ability associations are the most important but cannot compensate for bad behavior in the area of social responsibility. Social responsibility associations, on the other hand, are important but only if corporate ability is relatively unimportant to the consumer.

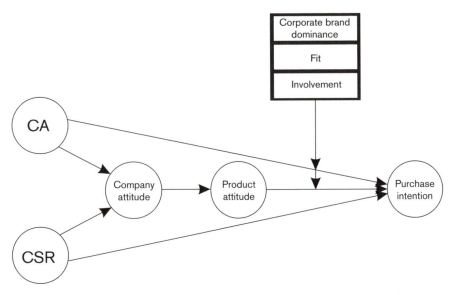

Figure 5.5   The moderating effect of corporate brand dominance, fit, and involvement on the degree to which capability and responsibility associations influence purchase intentions

Source: Berens *et al.* (2005)

Typologies of corporate brands

The preceding sections provided guidelines and a rationale for pursuing a corporate branding strategy. Once a decision to pursue corporate branding has been finalized, a choice has to be made from the types of available strategies. The academic literature proposes a variety of models that can help managers implement a corporate branding strategy (Aaker and Myers, 1991; Kapferer, 1992; de Chernatony and McDonald, 1992). We have found three models to be especially helpful.

Olins' branding strategies

The model proposed by Wally Olins (1990) is probably the best-known classification of corporate brand strategies. He proposes that there are three principal kinds of corporate branding strategies:

1. *Monolithic strategy* (Shell, Philips, BMW), in which the whole company uses one visual style. The company can be recognized instantly, and it uses the same symbols everywhere. Such companies have usually developed as a whole entity within a relatively narrow field.
2. *Endorsed strategy* (General Motors, L'Oréal), in which the subsidiary companies have their own style, but the parent company remains recognizable in the background. The different divisions can be recognized, but it is clear which is the parent company. These are diversified companies, the parts of which have retained parts of their own culture, traditions, and/or brands.
3. *Branded strategy* (Unilever), in which the subsidiaries have their own style, and the parent concern is not recognizable, "the uninitiated." The brands appear to have no relation to each other or to the parent concern. The separation of the brand from the identity of the parent concern limits the risk of product failure, but it also means that the brand cannot benefit from any favorable reputation, which the parent concern may enjoy.

Kammerer's action types

Kammerer (1988) shows different ways that corporate communication can be implemented internally. Specifically, he distinguishes four "action types" of corporate branding strategies:

1. *Financial orientation*: The subsidiaries are viewed as purely financial partici-pants. They retain their own full identity, and the management of the parent company does not interfere in the day-to-day running or in the strategy of the subsidiary.

2. *Organization-oriented corporate branding*: The parent company takes over one or more management functions of the divisions. In Kammerer's view, sharing organizational rules between the parent company and the sub-sidiaries is of central importance. In this situation, the parent company influences the culture of the subsidiaries to a far greater extent than in the case of the financial orientation. However, the functioning of corporate branding at the level of the whole organization is strictly internal, and not directly visible to the outside world.

3. *Communication-oriented corporate branding*: The fact that the subsidiaries belong to one parent company is clearly expressed in advertising and symbolism. One of the most important reasons for choosing this kind of corporate branding is to convey to the target groups the size of the concern. This can increase confidence in the subsidiaries, or respect for the whole concern. It also means that others can exploit goodwill achieved by one subsidiary. Communication-oriented corporate branding can proceed from organization-directed corporate branding, but this does not necessarily have to be so. It may be that nothing more than a common façade is created.

4. *Single company corporate branding*: The unity of action goes much further than with the other types. It is a really monolithic style of corporate branding: all actions, messages, and symbols come across as one consistent whole.

Van Riel's typology

Olins' classification evokes the suggestion that: (1) corporate branding is mainly dominated by visual choices, and (2) that multi-businesses have to choose either one of the three categories he has described. In reality, of course, as Olins readily acknowledges, companies mix and match these corporate branding strategies.

In fact, corporate branding does not only involve implementing a new name and selecting an appropriate logo, it also requires careful analysis about the *content* of the communications and attributes the company wants to express.

Van Riel's model takes point of departure from two factors that should be taken into account when developing a corporate branding strategy. The first is the degree to which the business units of the company are willing and prepared to communicate that they are part of a larger group of companies ("Agree on Parent Visibility"). Second is the degree to which the business units agree on the starting points of the corporate branding strategy ("Agree on Starting Points"). Figure 5.6 and Table 5.1 illustrates the four possibilities for the choice of corporate branding strategy.

As soon as an organization chooses to profile one or more of the business units with a high degree of corporate endorsement, it is necessary to determine what the parent behind the brand really stands for, what its values are, and how they can be used to communicate with the various target audiences. In exploring the company's core purpose and values, managers are well advised to carefully balance the selection of internal ideals against drivers of perceptions by external audiences.

Experience in applying this model suggests that it is wise not to force all units of the company to move to the selected model in one fell swoop. Global companies in particular should consider assessing each business unit's market fit on a case by case basis. A business unit should only move to a stronger degree of corporate endorsement in its commercial communications when:

▌ it can be shown through market research that the corporate brand is sufficiently well-known and valued in the local market;
▌ the local brand is losing strength in its local market due to the growing importance of the corporate brand.

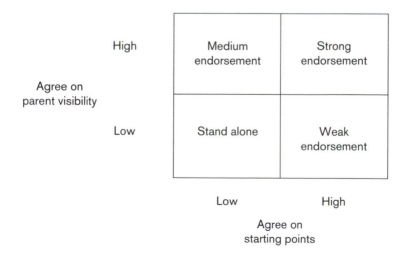

Figure 5.6   Typology of corporate branding strategies
Source: van Riel and van Bruggen (2002)

Table 5.1 Typology of corporate branding strategies

	A. No endorsement (stand alone)	B. Weak endorsement	C. Medium endorsement	D. Strong endorsement
Visualization	"Affiliate name"	"Affiliate name" member of "parent company name" (logo)	"Parent company name" (logo) "affiliate name"	"Parent company name" (logo) "specialization"
Example	Barings	Barings "Member of ING (lion)"	ING (lion) Barings	ING (lion) Investment Banking
Corporate branding strategy	Stand-alones, low degree of parent visibility, high degree of autonomy at business unit level, avoiding spill-over effects	Low degree of parent visibility, used by companies in a transition phase of complete autonomy towards integrated market approach	High degree of parent visibility, no consistent fits with the key elements of the corporate message, applied in Greenfields or in more mature markets where competitors already have achieved a strong position	High parent visibility, high degree of identification with the corporate level, high degree of transparency, strict coordination of communication strategy, showing the strength of the group

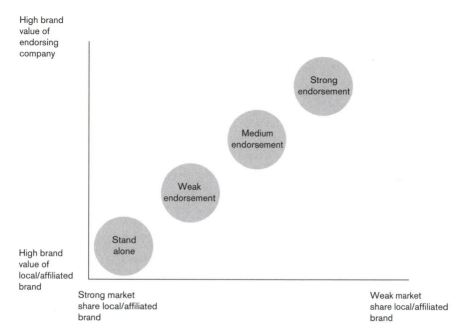

Figure 5.7   Levels of corporate endorsement
Source: van Riel (2002)

Figure 5.7 illustrates the progression we propose in moving towards a strong endorsement with the corporate brand.

Re-branding the company

Sometimes a corporate branding strategy requires a complete repositioning of the company. Often an entirely new name is developed in order to cast aside prior associations. For instance, re-branding is sometimes the path of least resistance for a post-merger company. Re-branding often enables by-passing the touchy political problems created from win–lose perceptions generated in merger siutations. In the accounting industry, for instance, early mergers between PriceWaterhouse and Coopers & Lybrand led to naming the merged firm as PriceWaterhouseCoopers – Lybrand was dropped entirely. When the accounting firm of Arthur Andersen developed significant revenues from its management consulting activities, it created a separate business unit that it named Andersen Consulting. When a rift subsequently developed between the accountants and the consultants in the 1990s, the firm broke out its Andersen Consulting group entirely. After much legal wrangling over use of the Andersen name, the consultants settled on a renaming of their division – and Accenture was born. The process took place very quickly – it took less than 90 days for the firm to select a new name, building eye-catching communications campaigns (see Figure 5.8), in order to build worldwide acceptance and recognition of its new identity with internal and external audiences. Ironically, the company that had sought so hard to keep the Andersen name – and lost it – turned out to have been the real winner: In 2002, its former parent Arthur Andersen was indicted and found to guilty of obstruction of justice charges relating to the collapse of the energy giant Enron. The firm was subsequently dissolved and the Andersen name has now completely disappeared from the corporate landscape.

Employee attitudes are a critical factor in a company name change. If the change is not communicated carefully to the employees, the whole campaign can founder on their scepticism (Muir, 1987). Employees need to have a feeling of belonging, and of being part of a shared culture. They need to be proud of the company they work for, and of everything connected with it. These matters cannot be left to chance. In order to arouse feelings of loyalty, the organization must create symbols, such as flags, rituals, and names. The company must make use of rituals and ceremonies to celebrate what it is, and the reason for its existence. Beliefs must be constantly confirmed (Olins, 1989). If this does not happen, the company can easily stagnate.

Consider British Airways, a company created in 1973 from a merger between BOAC and BEA. Observers indicate that there had been little preparation for the merger and no careful introduction of the new company. As a result, employees failed to identify with the new company, and some ten years after the merger, many still displayed flags of their old companies on their desks. The company was managed in a military fashion, and its service had a bad reputation. In the early 1980s, a start was made towards rectifying the situation. A new management team developed a strategy rooted in giving good customer service. A new logo was introduced to draw attention to the changes, and to the "reborn" British Airways. In this way, the company managed to lose its claim to being the "worst airline in the world" (Diefenbach, 1987). Indeed, in the early 1990s, dramatic growth enabled the company to claim title to the official tagline as "the world's favorite airline", based on its top rating as flying more passenger miles than any other airline.

Ultimately the symbols used by a company consist not only of its names, but of images that strengthen and support its actions and communications.

Figure 5.8 Corporate advertising for Accenture

Visual images such as photographs, illustrations, non-verbal graphics, brand marks, and logos are powerful symbols for implementing a corporate branding strategy. The power of these symbols lies in the increased attention which they attract to the communications of the company. A good symbol reduces the volume of redundant communication a company needs to broadcast.

A corporate brand generally consists of both a logo and a tagline. When effectively designed, the two work together as a script in eliciting organizational associations in people's minds with everything that the company is trying to communicate. Signs in shopping streets are an example. Even in strange cities, people quickly recognize internationally used symbols, especially when they are in familiar colors. The bright red and yellow colors used to feature Kodak products around the world readily comes to mind. It's a familiar guidepost signalling to tourists everywhere the presence of a retailer of film products.

The chemical industry is a good example of companies taking this approach. Having documented the negative reactions people have to the idea of "chemicals", firms have explicitly implemented a strategy of describing the industry using the more favorably received term "chemistry". For instance, the American Chemistry Council is the group that represents chemical manufacturers. Its tagline is "Good Chemistry Makes it Possible". Similarly, most pharmaceutical firms now self-consciously describe themselves as involved in the "Life Sciences" rather than the drug industry. Pfizer's tagline is "Life is our Life's Work".

Conclusion

Corporate branding has become more important in the past years. The veil of "corporate silence" that historically prevailed is no longer possible. Externally, legal rules regarding corporate disclosure are forcing a greater degree of transparency and openness than ever before. Internally, employees, customers, and investors seek greater clarity and understanding of a company's commercial and non-commercial activities. Everyone is therefore clamoring for knowledge of the company behind the brand, of its core competencies and socially responsibility.

Selecting a corporate branding strategy is no simple matter. Corporate managers are sensitive to the matter and often find themselves in conflict with managers of the company's diversified business units. Research shows, however, that the conflicts run along more or less predictable patterns. Problems that would normally take years to resolve can be prevented focusing corporate branding decisions on rational criteria.

Corporate branding strategies must of necessity be customized to the complexity of the market situations that organizations face. Endorsement by a corporate brand sets the context for the design of the total communication system that the company can carry out. It provides the bandwidth that local business units must fit into.

This chapter has set forth key considerations that managers should take into account in selecting a corporate branding strategy. To prevent lasting turmoil, we recommend initial internal and external research as input into the decision-making process. It should be followed by careful assessment of the rational factors involved in selecting a specific corporate branding strategy. Only when it can be convincingly shown that a significant parenting advantage can be achieved will corporate endorsements be accepted. Naturally this can partly be steered by intensely profiling the corporate brand in all relevant markets. An endorsement stemming from the company behind the brand is only useful if the corporate brand is strong. The corporate brand can only be used as an endorsement vehicle if it is known and appreciated by relevant stakeholders. Investing in corporate branding is therefore a matter of balancing potential benefits against costs.

In sum, our experience with re-branding programs suggests the following generalizations:

1. Corporate branding initiatives almost invariably develop from pressures by corporate audiences for increased clarity and transparency of communication from the company. These pressures are generally met with resistance from marketing-oriented managers.
2. No amount of negotiation will produce an optimal corporate brand. To develop and implement a corporate branding strategy requires strong and assertive leadership.
3. Symbolic support is important. Once a decision to implement corporate branding has been made, the launch must be signaled with appropriate internal and external messaging and hoopla.
4. Implementation of a corporate brand invariably generates resistance. Often the source of the resistance can be traced to lack of care in the setting of rules for business units to follow, and monitoring their execution. Managers of business units often ignore or bend the rules, and debate the way in which the organization is visually trying to communicate its identity. This is one of the crucial moments in the corporate branding process and requires

determined leadership to avoid slippage and a return to the *status quo ex ante.*

5. Branding is a Sysiphian process that has to be repeated over and over again: when a new CEO takes office, internal discussions about the merits of the corporate brand are likely to start all over again.

Discussion Questions

1. Identify corporate brands whose principal target audiences consist of either investors, employees, or consumers.
2. Explain how specific decision-making models can be applied in a company to identify points of resistance to a corporate branding strategy.
3. Describe the types of organizational associations that are essential in transferring positive brand value from the corporate level to the product level.

CHAPTER

6 DEVELOPING A REPUTATION PLATFORM

A reputation is not a play thing
A reputation is not a toy . . .
remember this one day
your reputation is what you make of it
not just what they say

Shana McMillen

The nomenclature that a company makes visible in the names, symbols, and house style it selects are a visual representation of the corporate brand. However, the corporate branding process involves, not only the selection and presentation of visual styles and other sensory input, but also the selection of specific *messaging content* that managers want to convey in their corporate communication. Careful examination of strong corporate brands demonstrates that most of them anchor their corporate communication around a core *reputation platform* that creates a "starting point" for more detailed descriptions of the company's strategic position and direction. Most reputation platforms and the communications derived from them are designed to create specific organizational associations in the minds of observers. In particular, reputation platforms are "starting points" for the development of what van Riel (2000) calls "sustainable corporate stories". Research confirms that strong and consistent application of symbolism and story-telling is associated with stronger corporate reputations and better valuations (Fombrun and van Riel, 2004).

This chapter examines how companies can build reputation platforms and select a nomenclature and corporate stories that follow from them. Logos, taglines, starting points, and stories are powerful expressions of underlying reputation platforms around which companies build strong corporate brands. The distinguishing characteristic of a reputation platform is that everyone recognizes the company on the basis of that platform. To use a musical analogy, a reputation platform is like the "hook" in a song or the major chords in a score – it consists of the melodic riff around which a score is built. Numerous improvisations of the melody are rendered throughout the company as business unit managers interpret and adapt the reputation platform to the needs of their local audiences (Hatch, 2003). The key to effective corporate communication lies in preventing day-to-day messaging from straying too far from the melodic line.

The nomenclature of corporate brands

"Nomenclature" is the summary term used by communicators to describe names and symbols. Whereas Chapter 3 discussed the general features involved in nomenclature, we focus here on the practical consequences of a corporate branding strategy for the nomenclature used by the company. Visual elements are vital in increasing short-term attachments to a company. As Olins (1990) suggests, it is critical to examine "how the visual style of a company influences its place in the market, and how the company's goals are made visible in its design and behavior." The identity of a company can be traced through the names, logos, sounds, colors, and rites of passage that the company uses in order to distinguish itself, its brands, and its associated companies. As Chapter 3 indicated, nomenclature serves the same function as religious icons, heraldry, national flags, and other symbols: they encapsulate collective feelings of belonging, and make them visible. They also proffer a virtual guarantee that the company is trustworthy, will deliver consistent quality standards, and deserves loyalty from its stakeholders (Olins, 1990).

Companies do not automatically have such symbols at their disposal. As Olins suggests: "Sometimes names and symbols need to be created, traditions and rites of passage have to be invented and reinvented for corporations, in the same way as they have always been invented for different regimes in different countries." Olins calls this "the invention of tradition", and gives several examples of political and military leaders who tried to create a sense of grandeur by using symbols taken from a historical period of which most people were proud. One can find examples of symbolism used in state-sponsored art, both in European capitals and in third world countries. The underlying strategy has penetrated the business world too. It is apparent in the tendency to locate

Company	Logo	Slogan/tagline	Starting points
Microsoft	*Microsoft*	Your potential. Our passion	Passion
3M	3M	Innovation	Innovation
Hewlett Packard	(hp) invent	Invent	Innovation
Kodak	Kodak	Take, share, enhance preserve, print, and enjoy pictures	Images
IBM	IBM	Leader in creation, development and manufacture of advanced information technologies	Technology
General Electric	GE	Imagination at Work	Performance
Nokia	NOKIA Connecting People	Connecting People	Networking
Pfizer	Pfizer	Life is our life's work	Life
Philips	PHILIPS	Sense and Simplicity	Technology
Nike	(swoosh)	Just do it	Action
Xerox	XEROX. Technology | Document Management | Consulting Services	The Document Company	Technology
McDonald's	M I'm lovin' it	A people company serving hamburgers	Speed and Service
ExxonMobil	ExxonMobil	Taking on the world's toughest energy challenges	Energy Challenges
BP	bp	Beyond Petroleum	Future Energy Sources

Figure 6.1 Nomenclature of some of the world's most visible corporate brands

corporate headquarters in impressive buildings. Attempts to regain prestige in the world and to stimulate loyalty from employees often involves extensive use of corporate symbolism: a new name, a flag, a company museum, an exhibition area, books about the history of the company, and selection of a house style, including its architecture, furnishings, and a dress code (Olins, 1978, 1989).

Figure 6.1 shows the names, logos, and taglines used by some of the world's most visible companies. Some of these companies rely on similar reputation platforms to build out their corporate communication. 3M and HP for instance use "innovation" as the bedrock of their strategic positioning. Pfizer's reputation platform, focused on "life," is emulated by most of its rivals in the pharmaceutical industry. Others like Nokia ("networking") appear quite distinct.

In choosing a company name and the way in which it should be supported, four areas should generally be considered as possible sources for building a naming system:

▌ corporate ability;
▌ corporate activity;
▌ corporate location;
▌ corporate responsibility.

These four choices in the way a company develops a new corporate brand name can be illustrated with the example of INVE, a global business-to-business firm that is active in the area of developing feed for animals in their first stages of life. The company's philosophy is to feed young animals with healthy ingredients so that people who subsequently consume these animals get healthier food. Consistent with that philosophy, the company selected as its tagline "Healthy Feed for Healthy Food". In choosing this tagline, the company sought to clarify what the company stood for. Naturally, it would also have been possible to choose among different kinds of capabilities (e.g. technology, value creation), or to emphasize the company's social responsibility (animal health, food safety) rather than its capabilities.

The key steps driving nomenclature choices are summarized in Figure 6.2. Choices depend on the relative benefits of ability, activity, location, and responsibility as the locus for differentiating the corporate brand.

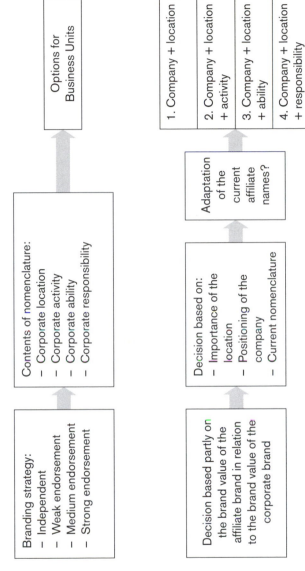

Figure 6.2 Developing a nomenclature for the corporate brand

What are reputation platforms?

Companies tell many stories about themselves; many stories are told about companies that do not align with the stories they choose to tell about themselves. As the well-known organizational psychologist Karl Weick puts it: "Stories allow the clarity achieved in one small area to be extended to and imposed on an adjacent area that is less orderly" (1995). Some stories paint a company in a favorable light, some become more popular than others, some tickle the fancy of the media, others are the stuff of folklore by NGOs. Companies therefore operate in an environment that is rich in narratives, stories, counter-stories, folklore, and strategic messaging – a world of social interpretations.

A *reputation platform* describes the root positioning that a company adopts when it presents itself to internal and external observers. It is a strategic choice. A strong reputation platform rests on a rendering of the company's history, strategy, identity, and reputation that rings true to internal and external observers. The quality of a reputation platform can therefore be tested on three key criteria:

■ Is the reputation platform *relevant*?
■ Is the reputation platform *realistic*?
■ Is the reputation platform *appealing*?

Many companies have interesting platforms and corporate stories to tell. Three themes seem to characterize the reputation platforms of some of the world's most visible companies:

■ *Activity theme*: Some companies try to build reputation around the key activities or businesses they are involved in. They convey the centrality of that activity to the company, be it online trading for e-Bay, transportation technology for DaimlerChrysler, or network computing for Sun Microsystems. Shell and ExxonMobil are in the energy business, Lucent is in the communications business.
■ *Benefits theme*: Others emphasize the attractive outcomes or benefits that stakeholders should expect from the company's activities as a way of inspiring allegiance. Sony entertains. Dell cuts your costs. Disney makes you happy. K-Mart and Sears give you "everyday low pricing". Bridgestone/Firestone makes "high performance" tires. Presumably auto-maker GM believes that bigger is simply better.

▌ *Emotional theme*: Finally, companies differ in their reliance on an emotional theme to inspire support. Volvo's focus on "safety", Pfizer's on "life", J&J on "motherhood", DuPont on "scientific miracles", Amazon on "personal service", and Southwest Airlines on "fun and friendliness" – all try to establish an emotional bond with stakeholders, to elicit a personal connection.

To illustrate the nature of reputation platforms and the corporate stories derived from them, we highlight three companies in this section: The UK's Virgin Group, Sweden's IKEA, and a small Belgian business-to-business company called INVE.

Many people are familiar with the Virgin Group – the British conglomerate created by Sir Richard Branson (see Figure 6.3). Some know the company for its products (e.g. Virgin Records, Virgin Cola, or Virgin Airlines). Others recall Sir Richard's cameo appearances on various US programs. Many more recall his many hot air balloon adventures and other publicity stunts.

Virgin's reputation platform is anchored around the dual notion of "creating value for money" and "having fun". The company exploits these by identifying businesses that appear to be at the end of their lifecycles, and re-invigorating them through a combination of organizational savvy and aggressive marketing.

The platform sets the seeds for the communication system. As Case Study 6.1 illustrates, Virgin's corporate website introduces the company to the world by telling "the Virgin Story". The story explains what Virgin strives for, what it has achieved, and why it has succeeded. It also describes the core competencies of the company: its focus on activities concerning products and services near the end of their life cycle. The real core competence of Virgin is its ability to combine an efficient internal organization with an innovative branding approach. Much of Virgin's success is attributed back to the personality of Sir Richard Branson, a public figure with considerable charisma and leadership who regularly offers his personal image in support of Virgin's corporate communication.

In similar ways to Virgin, the Swedish retailer IKEA builds its corporate story on a reputation platform that involves "value for money" and savvy marketing. Indeed, very few people in Europe or the US can claim not to own or to have purchased a single IKEA product. The company expresses its reputation platform using the distinctively bright blue and yellow color combination for all of its buildings. Around the world, it also offers to consumers the same value-oriented products, uses the same distribution system, and relies on the same promotional materials to reach consumers. Clearly IKEA has a strong reputation platform and, as Case Study 6.2 demonstrates, a concise corporate story to go with it.

Case Study 6.1   The Virgin corporate story: value for money

"Virgin – the third most recognised brand in Britain – is now becoming the first global brand name of the 21st century. We are involved in planes, trains, finance, soft drinks, music, mobile phones, holidays, cars, wines, publishing, bridal wear – the lot! What tie all these businesses together are the values of our brand and the attitude of our people. We have created over 200 companies worldwide, employing over 25,000 people. Our total revenues around the world in 1999 exceeded £3 billion (US$5 billion).

Figure 6.3
Virgin's Sir Richard Branson

We believe in making a difference. In our customers' eyes, Virgin stands for value for money, quality, innovation, fun and a sense of competitive challenge. We deliver a quality service by empowering our employees and we facilitate and monitor customer feedback to continually improve the customer's experience through innovation.

Virgin began in the 1970s with a student magazine and small mail order record company. Our growth since then has not only been impressively fast, it has also been based on developing good ideas through excellent management principles, rather than on acquisition.

We look for opportunities where we can offer something better, fresher and more valuable, and we seize them. We often move into areas where the customer has traditionally received a poor deal, and where the competition is complacent. And with our growing e-commerce activities, we also look to deliver "old" products and services in new ways. We are pro-active and quick to act, often leaving bigger and more cumbersome organizations in our wake.

When we start a new venture, we base it on hard research and analysis. Typically, we review the industry and put ourselves in the customer's shoes to see what could make it better. We ask fundamental questions: is this an opportunity for restructuring a market and creating competitive advantage?

What are the competitors doing? Is the customer confused or badly served? Is this an opportunity for building the Virgin brand? Can we add value? Will it interact with our other businesses? Is there an appropriate trade-off between risk and reward?

We are also able to draw on talented people from throughout the group. New ventures are often steered by people seconded from other parts of Virgin, who bring with them the trademark management style, skills and experience. We frequently create partnerships with others to combine skills, knowledge, market presence, and so on. Contrary to what some people may think, our constantly expanding and eclectic empire is neither random nor reckless. Each successive venture demonstrates our skill in picking the right market and the right opportunity.

Once a Virgin company is up and running, several factors contribute to making it a success. The power of the Virgin name; Richard Branson's personal reputation; our unrivalled network of friends, contacts, and partners; the Virgin management style; the way talent is empowered to flourish within the group. To some traditionalists, these may not seem hard headed enough. To them, the fact that Virgin has minimal management layers, no bureaucracy, a tiny board and no massive global HQ is an anathema.

Our companies are part of a family rather than a hierarchy. They are empowered to run their own affairs, yet other companies help one another, and solutions to problems come from all kinds of sources. In a sense we are a community, with shared ideas, values, interests and goals. The proof of our success is real and tangible."

Source: www.virgin.com

Virgin and IKEA are both large and prominent global companies. Reputation platforms, nomenclatures, and corporate stories are appropriate and relevant, not only for large well-known companies, but also for smaller, less visible companies. Consider INVE, a small business-to-business company involved in the aquaculture industry. The company is active in developing and supplying feed ingredients for animals in their first stages of life. The activities of the company are rooted in the belief that animals should receive high quality feed so that consumers will benefit from injesting healthier meat, poultry, and fish.

Case Study 6.2   The IKEA corporate story: improving everyday life

"The IKEA business idea is to offer a wide range of home furnishings with good design and function at prices so low that as many people as possible will be able to afford them. And still have money left!

Figure 6.4   An IKEA store

Most of the time, beautifully designed home furnishings are created for a small part of the population – the few who can afford them. From the beginning, IKEA has taken a different path. We have decided to side with the many.

That means responding to the home furnishing needs of people throughout the world. People with many different needs, tastes, dreams, aspirations . . . and wallets. People who want to improve their homes and create better everyday lives.

It's not difficult to manufacture expensive fine furniture. Just spend the money and let the customers pay. To manufacture beautiful, durable furniture at low prices is not so easy. It requires a different approach. Finding simple solutions, scrimping and saving in every direction. Except on ideas.

But we can't do it alone. Our business idea is based on a partnership with the customer. First we do our part. Our designers work with manufacturers to find smart ways to make furniture using existing production processes. Then our buyers look all over the world for good suppliers with the most suitable raw materials. Next, we buy in bulk – on a global scale – so that we can get the best deals, and you can get the lowest price.

Then you do your part. Using the IKEA catalogue and visiting the store, you choose the furniture yourself and pick it up at the self-serve warehouse. Because most items are packed flat, you can get them home easily, and assemble them yourself. This means we don't charge you for things you can easily do on your own. So together we save money . . . for a better everyday life.

How we're different

How is IKEA different from other furnishing stores? They offer a wide range, or good design and function, or low prices. While we offer all of these. That's our business idea.

Our heritage

It's no accident that the IKEA logo is blue and yellow. These are the colors of the Swedish flag.

In Sweden, nature and the home both play a big part in people's lives. In fact, one of the best ways to describe the Swedish home furnishing style is to describe nature – full of light and fresh air, yet restrained and unpretentious.

In the late 1800s, the artists Carl and Karin Larsson combined classical influences with warmer Swedish folk styles. They created a model of Swedish home furnishing design that today enjoys worldwide renown. In the 1950s the styles of modernism and functionalism developed at the same time as Sweden established a society founded on social equality. The IKEA product range – modern but not trendy, functional yet attractive, human-centered and child-friendly – carries on these various Swedish home furnishing traditions.

Many people associate Sweden with a fresh, healthy way of life. This Swedish lifestyle is reflected in the IKEA product range. The freshness of the open air is reflected in the colors and materials used and the sense of space they create: blond woods, natural textiles and untreated surfaces. In a climate that is cold and dark for much of the year, these light, bright living spaces create the sensation of summer sunshine indoors all year round.

The IKEA concept, like its founder, was born in Småland. This is a part of southern Sweden where the soil is thin and poor. The people are famous for working hard, living on small means and using their heads to make the best possible use of the limited resources they have. This way of doing things is at the heart of the IKEA approach to keeping prices low.

But quality is not compromised for the sake of cost. Sweden has an international reputation for safety and quality you can rely on, and IKEA retailers take pride in offering the right quality in all situations.

continued

IKEA was founded when Sweden was fast becoming an example of the caring society, where rich and poor alike were well looked after. This is also a theme that fits well with the IKEA vision. In order to give the many people a better everyday life, IKEA asks the customer to work as a partner. The product range is child-friendly and covers the needs of the whole family, young and old. *So together we can create a better everyday life for everyone."*

Source: www.ikea.com

INVE's reputation platform is captured in the slogan: *Healthy Feed for Healthy Food*. The environmentally friendly color "green" is all pervasive on the company's website and in its communications. Consistent with its core belief in "healthy feed," INVE's coherent corporate story is told in detail in Case Study 6.3.

Case Study 6.3   The INVE corporate story: healthy feed for healthy food

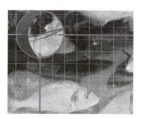

Figure 6.5   INVE's corporate story

"INVE is a family holding of more than 30 companies that provides nutritional and health solutions in animal rearing. INVE is active in more than 70 countries and has production units in Asia, Europe, and America.

The company started out of the integration of poultry farms and slaughterhouses in the early 1970s. A few years later the focus shifted to the basics in animal life: special ingredients and special application formulas. INVE's distinctive competence lays in its nutrition and health solutions for reared animals, especially young animals.

Today, the group focuses on solutions for aquaculture and agriculture based on experience and research. For aquaculture the most reputable products are Artemia (of different sources and for various applications), the Selco®-range of enrichment products, the Frippak® and Lansy®-range of dry diets. In agriculture INVE provides feed additives such as Toxy-Nil, Adimix® Butyrate, Salmo-Nil, Mold-Nil, feeding concepts like Lechonmix®, INVE Boar Vital, INVE NRJ Beef, plant extracts, and other advanced solutions such as specialties for conservation and treatment of raw materials and feeds.

INVE's high quality products focus on the critical phases in animal rearing and offer crucial benefits such as increased survival rate, improved growth rate, reduced risk of deformities and diseases, early and high feed intake. The development of these unique, innovative, even pioneering products that have given INVE an established reputation in the markets, is possible thanks to the continuous focus on research by highly skilled specialists. INVE's backbone is its strong global Research and Development Departments organized by INVE Technologies. INVE has its own test centers worldwide, participates in long-term projects with renowned universities and institutes, and conducts market verification of experimental research with selected customers. With the help of specialized software, INVE's nutritional engineers apply their profound knowledge of raw materials, premixes, specialties and additives to formulate an optimal diet, taking into account the animal's needs according to age and gender. INVE has the necessary knowledge and responsibility to produce safe and sound feed.

By means of an extensive network of First Line sales people, Solution Managers, INVE Shops and local Service Centers, INVE adheres to a strong personal market approach focusing on long-term, partnering relation-ships with customers. INVE simplifies feed management for farmers and hatcheries, resulting in more efficient working procedures and high quality results, offering economic benefits to customers. INVE's ultimate goal is to contribute to better nutrition and health for people around the globe. Therefore INVE commits to enhance the total food chain, providing safe feed for cultured animals that end up as an important part of our daily food. INVE not only strives for sustaining health in humans, but also works hard

continued

at promoting it. Through its premixes and additives, INVE balances the profile of fatty acids and vitamins in products from cattle, poultry and pigs. Drinking milk enhanced with conjugated linolenic acid, helps to protect against cancer; consuming eggs enriched with omega-3 fatty acids, stabilizes the heart beat; eating pork with high levels of some plant specific fats, is effective in reducing the potbelly. INVE also promotes the production of prime quality fish and shrimp through improving the nutritional value and safety of feeds and concentrates. For studies have revealed that this leads to less stress and disease. In animals as well as human beings.

INVE's philosophy is rooted in the strong belief of the company's founder, Mr. Flor Indigne, that people have to create positive things in harmony with nature. Happiness as a result, is what he wants to share with employees, customers, and all involved in the business activities of INVE. "Bringing solutions," the main core value of INVE, therefore stands for "Bringing Happiness." The more than 600 employees of INVE take pride in being part of a company that emphasizes social responsibility that goes beyond pursuing "standard" business goals. Respect for different cultures is also a strength of the company and is a substantial part of INVE's special reputation.

The INVE Group is a financially healthy firm with a current consolidated turnover of about €120m. The economic health of the company gives INVE employees, suppliers and customers' stability on a long-term base."

Source: www.inve.com

The building blocks of corporate stories

A corporate story is a structured textual description that communicates the essence of the company to all stakeholders, helps strengthen the bonds that bind employees to the company, and successfully positions the company against rivals. It is built up by identifying unique elements of the company, creating a plot that weaves them together, and presenting them in an appealing fashion.

Unique elements

It is not easy to identify unique aspects of a company. Most companies present have a great deal in common because they are institutionalized by professional managers, most of which have similar cultural and educational backgrounds, life experiences, and viewpoints. It should come as no surprise that researchers observe a striking similarity between the different value systems expressed by companies in credo-like statements reminiscent of the famous US Declaration of Independence that begins "We the people".

Unique plots

Unique corporate features have to be connected through a plot. Take a core element for a bank expressed as "customer focus". As a core element, it is hardly unique. Expressed through an active plot with actors and actions, it takes on distinct meaning. Consider how the Dutch Rabobank develops a unique plot for its customer-focused reputation platform:

> *The Rabobank does not have shareholders who are mainly interested in a high return on their investments. The only thing that counts is to have satisfied customers, now and in the future. The Rabobank chooses to build a long-term relationship with its customers. That means that the advice fits the wishes of the customers and that these are not the advice with which the bank earns the most. But it also means that, in bad times, the Rabobank will remain supportive to its customers.*
>
> Source: www.rabobank.com

A good story has to have a plot line. Folk tales, fairy tales, epic journeys, and romantic sagas are four typical plots. In the epic form, for instance, a heroic company finds itself confronting enemies or obstacles. As soon as everyone in the company pulls together, the company emerges victorious with growing market shares, profits, and job security. In the romantic form, for instance, the plot involves portraying a company as recovering from a bad fall or crisis, possibly stemming perhaps from excessive growth, scandal, or the death of the founder.

Unique presentation

It is also difficult to demonstrate unique presentation styles in telling a corporate story. Like other communications before them, after a period of ferment in which chaos reigned, most corporate websites now demonstrate remarkable standardization and homogeneity in what they communicate and how. Achieving distinctiveness through corporate story-telling is therefore something that will be difficult to achieve. Nonetheless, we believe it to be worthwhile, not least of which because of bandwagon processes from which even *small differences* in how companies present themselves can escalate into large effects on perceptions and reputation. In our experience, a good corporate story should be no longer than 400–600 words.

The more unique a company's reputation platform, the easier it will be to create a strong and distinctive corporate story for the company. Many of the companies listed in Figure 6.1 not only rely on distinctive logos and slogans, but tell a distinctive story about themselves that helps consumers and other stakeholders understand them better and distinguishes them in the reputation marketplace.

Consider LEGO, the company built on the foundation of LEGO bricks. The company uses primary colors to evoke a unique set of associations in stakeholders' minds that involve childhood memories, the ambitions of youth, and their manifestation in construction projects. The LEGO brick appears in all sorts of formats, including giant creations in front of toy stores at prominent locations (e.g. the high-end FAO Schwartz toy store in New York) and in the company's Legoland theme parks around the world that are built entirely out of LEGO bricks. Figure 6.6 and Case Study 6.4 illustrates how the company uses the LEGO brick as a corporate symbol to crystallize a reputation platform that is focused on the themes of imagination, play, and learning. The company tells its corporate story very appealingly:

Close inspection of LEGO's corporate story, like those of Virgin, IKEA, and INVE, shows that it has distinctive elements that are common to all good corporate stories:

- the story introduces *unique words* to describe the company;
- the story refers to the company's *unique history*;
- the story describes the company's *core strengths*;
- the story *personalizes and humanizes* the company;
- the story provides a *plot line*;
- the story addresses the concerns of *multiple stakeholders*.

Case Study 6.4   LEGO corporate story: imagination, learning and play

Figure 6.6   LEGO's reputation platform

"Ever since the LEGO® Company began in 1932, we have done things a little differently. Though we make toys, we are not a toy company. Though we make money, we are not driven by profit. Though we are famous for our product, we are defined by our philosophy.

Our name comes from the combination of the Danish 'leg godt,' which means to 'play well.' It is both our name and our nature. We believe that play is the essential ingredient in a child's growth and development. It grows the human spirit. It encourages imagination, conceptual thinking and creation. Play is at the very heart of our humanity.

Our intended brand position in the minds of children and adults is 'The Power to Create.' We provide the child with the capability to make their own fun, to develop their imagination and skills. 'Power' is the the power we help release in our children. 'Create' underlines our capacity to stimulate imagination and creativity. The Power to Create is our ability to release the best from within children of all ages, to provide the creative fuel for development and learning, to nurture the child in each of us.

The three B's: in Bed, in the Bath, and on a Bicycle. Those are the times when your best ideas usually pop up – when no one is pushing you to be creative and when your unconscious mind is free to work on its own. But what if you have to generate new ideas all the time? People who are curious, creative, and imaginative – who have not lost their natural urge

continued

to learn – are best equipped to thrive in a challenging world and to be the builders of our common future.

Over the past 60 years global sales of LEGO bricks have topped 320 billion – roughly the equivalent of 52 LEGO bricks for each of the world's 6 billion inhabitants. We have been making LEGO products since 1932, and today we are the only European toy manufacturer in the Top Ten of the World's Best-selling Toys. Our workforce comprises 8,000 LEGO enthusiasts – 4,000 of them work in Billund, the remainder are spread worldwide.

Right from the outset in the 1930s the company's motto has been 'Only the best is good enough.' So we have continuously reviewed our environmental and safety policies, making sure that our minimum standard was at least equal to the most stringent in the world.

It isn't possible to buy shares in the LEGO Company because it is a family-owned enterprise. But once a year we do publish an annual report, giving a statistical outline of the past 12 months.

By the way, we are also the world's biggest manufacturer of vehicle tyres: in 2000 the LEGO Company produced no fewer than 306 million of them.

In LEGO Company we have a long tradition of giving high priority both to protecting the surrounding environment and to the health and safety of our consumers and employees. Our environmental concerns are particularly linked to how we manufacture our products. LEGO elements have to be able to cope with being put in children's mouths, chewed, stamped on and used as hammers. We know that children play in this way. And that is why we have taken severe precautions."

Source: www.lego.com

Creating corporate stories

A corporate story is designed primarily to frame corporate communication. It is not necessarily appropriate for widespread distribution in its totality. It provides a useful briefing for advertisers, analysts, reporters, and other observers who want to capture the "essence" of the company. The success of a corporate story can be measured by the many ways in which different people inside the company tell that story. The story is even more successful if interpretations of that story are widely circulated *beyond* the boundaries of the firm.

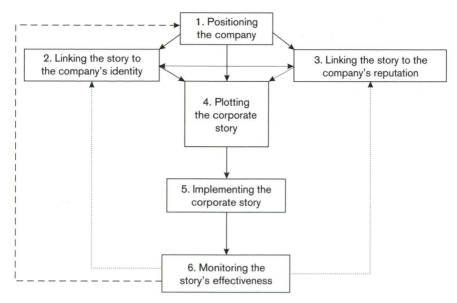

Figure 6.7 Creating a corporate story
Source: van Riel (2001)

The process of creating stories, and especially the integration of internal and external resources to create such a story has received limited attention in the academic literature, with notable exceptions (van Maanen, 1988; Roth and Kleiner, 1998; Senge, 1994; Collins and Porras, 1994). The common denominator in this research is the emphasis on involving organizational members with internal decision-making about strategic intentions in order to ensure successful implementation. Although they emphasize internal involvement, involving stakeholders is crucial in building a strong corporate story.

Corporate stories can be developed in many ways. In this section, we suggest six steps a company should take to arrive at a sustainable corporate story. A final draft of the corporate story should consist of a verbal text of 400–600 words (Figure 6.7).

Step 1: positioning the company

A good corporate story positions the company against rivals in the market and articulates its self-perceived competitive advantage (Porter, 1985). It also addresses the likely concerns of its key stakeholders. Building a corporate story must therefore begin by assessing the company's relative position vis-à-vis both rivals and stakeholders.

Competition

A first step in building a corporate story involves culling information from formal documents and archival research about the company's relative position against rivals. For a diversified company, it is useful to develop qualitative ratings of the relative "market attractiveness" and "ability to compete" of each of the business units. Figure 6.8 plots a typical positioning chart that suggests which "critical success factors" the corporate story should be built around.

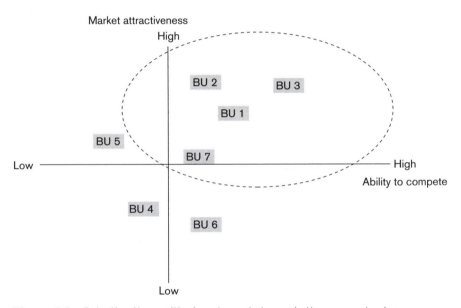

Figure 6.8 Selecting the positioning elements to use in the corporate story

Stakeholders

A second set of positioning elements for the corporate story should be developed from close inspection of the company's stakeholder environment. The most relevant stakeholders are those with the greatest degree of urgency, legitimacy, and perceived power over the company (Mitchell *et al.*, 1997; Grunig and Hunt, 1984). Representatives of each key stakeholder group should be interviewed to identify the key concerns they have about the company.

Step 2: linking the corporate story to the company's identity

A good corporate story must reflect the company's identity. As Chapter 3 discussed, a company's identity consists of internal beliefs about what employees know to be distinctive, continuous, and central "truths" about the company. These identity elements can be derived from internal surveys and focus groups held with employees and managers.

Managers who participate in these focus groups generally: (1) participate in open discussions about the company, (2) generate lists of key words they would use to describe the company, and (3) vote on the words which are perceived by most participants. Table 6.1 shows the possible results from such an analysis of identity elements.

A cobweb analysis of identity elements contributes another valuable "starting point" for developing a sustainable corporate story. The key words that are drawn out from this analysis reference the internal idioms of the company and will be credible to its internal stakeholders.

Step 3: linking the story to the company's reputation

A good corporate story should also speak to the underlying drivers of external perceptions of the company. Examination of external reputation surveys can also provide valuable input into constructing the corporate story.

Figure 6.9 illustrates a causal map that indicates the key drivers of a specific company's reputation. It suggests that another useful set of starting points for building the corporate story would be to emphasize those attributes that drive the company's reputation with its audiences. In this case, product attributes such as "reliability" and "value for money" are crucial contributors to the company's reputation, as are workplace attributes such as "skillful employees" and "good benefits", the financial attribute "strong record of profitability," and the leadership attribute "well-managed". These should be

Table 6.1 Results of a cobweb analysis of identity elements

Results from cobweb analysis	Actual			Desired			Difference
	Min.	Max.	Ave	Min.	Max.	Ave	
Worldwide company	5	8	7.2	8	9	8.6	−1.4
Business partner	6	8	6.9	8	10	8.8	−1.9
Quick delivery	8	9	8.6	8	10	8.9	−0.3
Consumer focus	4	7	6.2	8	10	8.5	−2.3
Good ability with large volumes	7	8	7.5	8	9	8.4	−0.9
Good employer	6	7	6.9	8	10	8.6	−1.7
Service delivery	4	7	6.0	7	10	8.7	−2.7
Trustworthy	8	8	8.0	8	10	8.7	−0.7
High tech	5	8	6.9	8	9	8.6	−1.7
Informal/open culture	6	7	6.8	8	9	8.1	−1.3

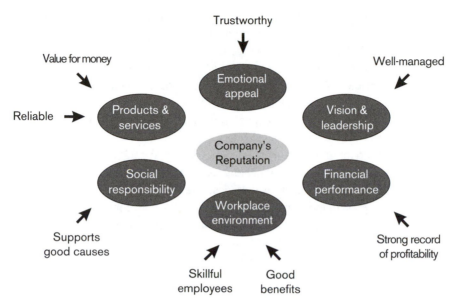

Figure 6.9 Using reputation drivers as starting points for story-telling

emphasized in creating the corporate story, and attributes that are less salient contributors to its reputation can be de-emphasized as starting points.

Step 4: plotting the story

Drawing on the research-based starting points developed in steps 1–3, a draft of the corporate story can be elaborated. The first step is to create a "positioning statement" – what the company proclaims to the world to be its distinctive strengths. Creation of the positioning statement should be done with a small group of no more than four to six corporate representatives. The resulting statement should be checked internally and externally. Checking will enable adaptations for relevance and realism. It will also increase consensus by involving as many people as possible in its creation.

A second step involves providing "proof points" for each of the starting points selected from steps 1–3. A proof for the starting point "worldwide company" could include "products are sold in more than 42 countries". A proof for the starting point "supports good causes" is "the company has donated more than XX hours of employee time to volunteer activities in local communities".

The third step involves selecting a "tone of voice" with which to tell the story. Key considerations include aggressiveness, humility, humor, modesty, and level of excitement. Does the tone come off as boastful or humble? In telling its story, does the company come across as exciting or dull? Conservative or avant-garde? Fun-loving or serious? Dry and caustic or humorous? Tone is an important contributor to the story's content and can significantly affect the company's emotional appeal to outside observers as well as generate cynicism or support from employees.

Although there are many possible plots that can be used in building a corporate story, a cause–effect logic is often the most persuasive. To cohere a story around such a plot, we propose the AAA model below. It begins with a description of the company's (1) *Abilities* – the core competences that have enabled it to be successful, (2) summarizes the core *Activities* the company is involved in, and (3) provides an overview of the company's *Accomplishments*. The AAA map is conceptually structured as shown in Figure 6.10 and can be built out in a focus group environment with senior managers.

Abilities

Abilities are identified by exploring:

■ how the organization is operating;
■ in which respect it is different from its competitors;
■ what makes the organization's identity enduring.

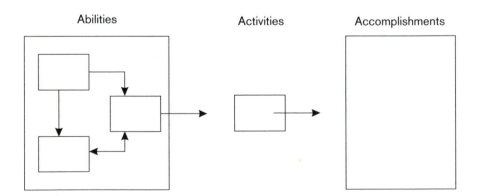

Figure 6.10 Building a cause-effect plot using the AAA model

Activities

Core *activities* are identified by raising the following questions:

■   in what business are we?
■   what are the main businesses of the organization?
■   in which countries do we operate?

Accomplishments

Accomplishments are identified by examining:

■   customer satisfaction scores, market share, employee morale;
■   return on investment;
■   reputation scores on external surveys.

Figure 6.11 illustrates a prototypical cause–effect plot for a specific corporate story.

Step 5: implementing the corporate story

To test external support for the draft version of the corporate story, we recommend conducting a survey of key stakeholders based on the IDU method of Rossiter and Percy (1997). The IDU method asks external audiences to evaluate the degree to which they perceive the starting points identified in building the story are "important" and "unique", and the extent to which they think the company will be able to "deliver" on these claims. The same technique should be used with multiple stakeholder groups in order to verify the draft story.

Once a version of the story has been tested and finalized, parts of the story should be incorporated into the multiple media through which the company communicates with its stakeholders. Figure 6.12 illustrates the messaging matrix that might be used to trace the use of the specific elements emphasized in the corporate story across the various media.

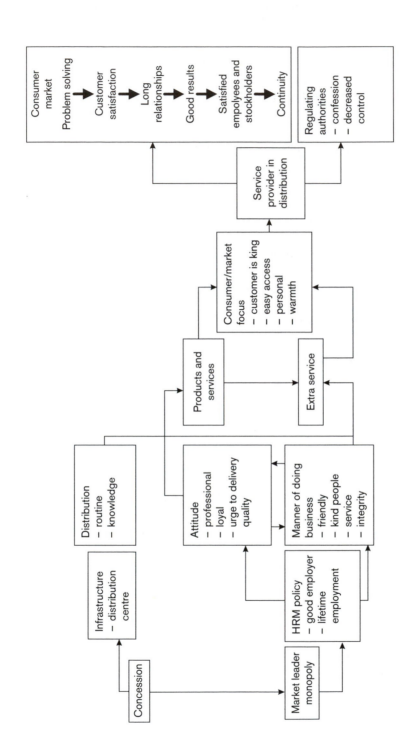

Figure 6.11 An example of the AAA model in practice

Source: van Riel (2001)

Starting points	Management speeches	Internal media	Website	Annual report	Corporate advertizing	Events and exhibits
Value for money						
Trustworthiness						
Skillful employees						
Supports good causes						

Figure 6.12 Embedding the corporate story in multiple media

Step 6: monitoring the story's effectiveness

A corporate story is dynamic, not static. It is dangerous to think that a story, once written, will remain unchanged. A good corporate story is as alive as the organization itself. As the organization changes to adapt to changing environmental circumstances, its story must change as well.

A good corporate story should stimulate both supporters and opponents to dialogue with the company. Online technologies enable culling broad-based input by numerous observers. Corporate websites themselves are becoming popular vehicles for facilitating dialogue with the company. Online feedback should be systematically analyzed for reactions to elements of the corporate story.

Traditional research tools are also valuable ways of monitoring a story's continuing effectiveness. A company can invite dialogue sessions with stakeholders in order to hear what stakeholders perceive to be attractive components of their corporate story, and what should be improved in the organization. Finally, the full spectrum of traditional market research tools can be used to track and trace public perceptions of the company and provide further input on the features of the corporate story that should be changed over time.

Conclusion

Companies build reputation platforms and select nomenclatures in order to achieve more effective corporate communication. They also create sustainable corporate stories by carefully identifying key starting points, proof points, and a plot that conveys the company's "essence" to stakeholders. A good corporate story is a tool that can increase mutual understanding between an organization and its key stakeholders.

A sustainable corporate story can be written down in a formal document such as a corporate brochure or a website page. But the true purpose of the corporate story is as a framework for guiding interpretations and conveying the essence of the company across multiple media.

Ultimately, the effectiveness of a corporate story can be judged on four criteria. The story has to be perceived by the company's key stakeholders as:

■ *Relevant*: It describes what activities appear to have added value.
■ *Realistic*: It describes what the company really is and does.

▌ *Sustainable*: It recognizes and balances the competing demands of multiple stakeholders.

▌ *Responsive*: It encourages an open dialogue with the company.

The effectiveness of a corporate story will also improve if the story is told and retold by top managers in the company in their own style and with their own interpretations, so long as they remain within the bandwidth created by the AAA model. Ultimately, however, no matter how appealing the story is, the story can only be effective when the gaps between the company's claims and the company's actions are minimal. The wider the gap, the greater the cynicism that will develop when observers hear the corporate story.

In the next chapter, we examine the pragmatic implementation of the company's reputation platform and corporate story. We then examine the specialized aspects of corporate communication with five key target audiences: employees, the financial community, governments, NGOs, and customers.

Discussion Questions

1. What factors should managers keep in mind when selecting a nomenclature for the company?
2. What is a reputation platform? Why should companies develop them?
3. What makes for a strong reputation platform?
4. What steps can be taken to create a sustainable corporate story?
5. Does everyone in a company have to agree with the corporate story before it can be implemented?

7

EXPRESSING THE COMPANY

Euphoric vitality
Exhilarates every molecule
Of this fluid life
As it surges and recedes,
Charting a course
Around and through me.

A universal concert
Surrounds me,
Permeating my atmosphere
With muted tones of energy,
Aspects of blue
Soothing my journey.
Pamela Waterbird Davison

Once a reputation platform is identified, managers should use that platform not only to build sustainable corporate stories, but to crystallize those stories into communication campaigns that are targeted to both internal and external audiences. This chapter examines the major factors that should be considered when building communication programs. It provides managers with a framework for identifying the broad targets of their communications and for building more expressive companies – companies that will be perceived by stakeholders as meeting key performance objectives of being consistent, distinctive, authentic, transparent, and responsive.

To implement a corporate story, managers take their cue either: (1) from a *market model* that calls attention to the benefits a potential customer or stakeholder will derive from the company's activities, or (2) from an *internal model* that focuses on the necessity for internal consensus among key implementers of communication activities.

The "IDU" model (Rossiter and Percy, 1987) takes a marketing approach to the design of corporate communication. It posits that in creating a communication program a manager should always define a "key benefit" that is:

▍ *I*mportant or motivating to the target group;
▍ *D*eliverable by the brand;
▍ *U*nique to the brand.

Other such marketing-based models describe the ideal configurations of communication activities (Cutlip *et al.,* 1994) and suggest that all planning for communication activities should depend on external market considerations (Reynolds and Gutman, 1994; Rossiter and Percy, 1997; Petty and Cacioppo, 1986).

A contrasting point of view is advanced by researchers who suggest that implementation decisions should be governed by internal cultural and political considerations (van Riel, 1992, 1994; Campbell and Tawdy, 1990; Grunig and Hunt, 1984). They call attention to the importance of creating internal consensus among key leaders and constituencies who play a central role in the implementation of the communication program.

The two approaches are complementary. Combining them leads to the following seven-step model for designing effective communications, taking the corporate story as a starting point (see Figure 7.1).

Step 1: test the corporate story

At the onset of a costly communications campaign, it will always be useful to assess the degree to which specific business units will or will not be involved in the communications program. Consensus-building exercises (one such exercise was described in Chapter 4) can be used to assess the degree to which key managers agree with the corporate story that was adopted. Experience suggests that not everyone will stand behind the corporate story that was created – some business units may even opt out.

Diversity in communications can be acceptable if there are good reasons for it. However, it will be paramount to know in advance who is and who is not

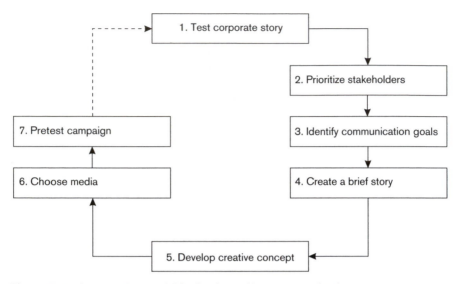

Figure 7.1   A seven-step model for implementing a corporate story

behind it, so that appropriate examples are selected to convey the corporate story elements. Consider ING Group. The Dutch financial services giant implemented its corporate story sequentially, by putting a clear emphasis initially on countries outside the Netherlands in which ING had a strong position. The first communication campaigns were launched in the United States, through the company's ING Direct subsidiary, and by sponsoring the New York marathon. Only later did communications cascade outward to Asia and back to the company's headquarters locations in Europe.

Step 2: prioritize your stakeholders

Companies have many stakeholders – too many to target them all. Effective communication therefore must begin by identifying a priority ordering of stakeholders, and targeting those that are most crucial to the company for implementing its goals. According to Freeman (1984) the term stakeholder can be defined as "any group or individual that can affect or is affected by the achievements of the organization." Two activities are necessary to priority-setting: (1) the selection of the most relevant target groups, and (2) segmentation of the selected target groups.

Selecting target groups

In selecting target groups, a distinction should be made between more important and less important target groups. A target group can simply be described as a key group through which a goal can be realized. In other words, there first has to be clarity about the goal before a definitive decision about the target audience or stakeholder can be made.

Target groups can be classified as primary or secondary based on how dependent the company is on those groups. Grunig and Hunt's (1984) "stakeholder linkage model" draws on Pfeffer and Salancik's (1978) resource dependency theory to classify groups on the basis of their "dependency relationship" (they call it linkage) – the ability of that group to control or influence resources that are crucial to the company's operations (see Figure 7.2).

Enabling groups are those with fundamental operating linkages to the company. They include shareholders and financial backers. Functional groups are those involving the company's inputs and outputs. They can be divided into input target groups (employees) and output target groups (customers). Normative groups are competitors or allies – groups that have the same interests as the company. Finally, diffuse groups are those whose linkages with the company cannot be identified by membership in a formal organization (Grunig and Hunt, 1984).

Stakeholder groups that are not directly commercially relevant are often the groups most likely to seek contact with the organization – and to seek contact that the company seldom welcomes but cannot be ignored. NGOs are generally not among a company's target groups and are often treated as irrelevant. But ask Nike about NGOs opposing child labor: they regularly complain about Nike's lack of responsible management of sub-contractors in

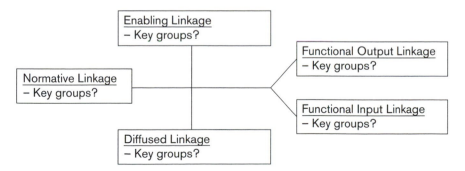

Figure 7.2 The stakeholder linkage model

developing nations, and make the company a target of its actions and communications. Clearly they have become an important group for Nike to target or consider in its communications.

Segmenting target groups

A better understanding of the target group can be gained by researching the socio-economic characteristics of its members, their motivations, their perceptions of the company (whether justified or not), their actual knowledge of the company, their lifestyles, and their media consumption patterns. Segmentation using these variables creates subsets of people that cut across standard definitions of target groups and can lead managers to customize communications that are appropriate to specific sub-segments.

From a marketing point of view, segments can be created around three categories:

1. Brand-specific characteristics of the group: These involve the way the target group feels about a corporate brand. An example would be a customer's loyalty to the beer brands of a particular beer beverage company such as Anheuser Busch or Heineken, and the frequency of consumption of its brands.
2. Product class characteristics of the target group. These involve the use of products in a limited product class, e.g. the consumption of alcohol-free beer.
3. The general characteristics of the target group, e.g. education, marital status, lifestyle.

Table 7.1 summarizes these definitions, and describes a typical approach to the segmentation of target groups.

Target groups can be defined on the basis of either their involvement with the company or on the basis of the specific "issue" about which the company wants to communicate Grunig and Hunt (1984). In designing a communications program, managers should pay attention to whether target groups are recognized internally as "problems" or as "constraints". If a simple two-way split is made on these two dimensions, the result is a configuration of eight target groups (Table 7.2).

Another approach to prioritizing stakeholders involves characterizing stakeholders by their relative power, legitimacy, and urgency (Mitchell *et al.,* 1997):

Table 7.1 Segmenting stakeholders

Segmentation strategy	Objective criteria	Subjective criteria
Brand-specific (use of a brand)	Brand loyal (behavior) Frequency of use Routines	Brand loyal (attitude) Preference Evaluation Buying intention
Domain-specific (use of a product class)	Frequency of use Substitution Complementarity Behavior	Interests, opinions Perception Attitude Domain-specific value
General (behavioral patterns or personal characteristics)	Income Age Education Place of residence Behavioral patterns	Lifestyle Personality General values

Source: van Raaij and Verhallen (1990)

- ▮ *Power*: The *power* of the stakeholder to influence the organization. A target group's power is high when "it has or can gain access to coercive, utilitarian, or normative means, to impose its will in the relationship".
- ▮ *Legitimacy*: The *legitimacy* of the relationship between the stakeholder and the organization. Legitimacy is high when "the actions of an entity are desirable, proper, or appropriate within some socially constructed system of norms, values, beliefs, and definitions".
- ▮ *Urgency*: The *urgency* of the stakeholder's claim on the organization: urgency is high when "stakeholder claims call for immediate attention". Two conditions apply to urgency: the relationship has to be time sensitive and critical.

The framework leads to a classification of stakeholders into seven key groups (see Figure 7.3):

1. *Dormant* stakeholders (groups with latent power);
2. *Discretionary* stakeholders (groups driven by legitimacy);
3. *Demanding* stakeholders (groups driven by urgency);
4. *Dominant* stakeholders (powerful groups with legitimate claims);
5. *Dangerous* stakeholders (powerful groups making urgent demands but lacking in perceived legitimacy);
6. *Dependent* stakeholders (groups with legitimate claims but no power);
7. *Definitive* stakeholders (groups with power, legitimacy, and urgency).

Table 7.2 Types of target groups

	High involvement (HI)		Low involvement (LI)	
	Behavior type	Type of public	Behavior type	Type of public
Problem-facing behavior (PF): High problem recognition, Low constraint recognition	HIPF	Active	LIPF	Aware/active
Constrained behavior (CE): High problem recognition, High constraint recognition	HICB	Aware/active	LICB	Latent/aware
Routine behavior (RB): Low problem recognition, Low constraint recognition	HIRB	Active	LIRB	None/latent
Fatalistic behavior (FB): Low problem recognition, High constraint recognition	HIFB	Latent	LIFB	None

Source: Adapted from Grunig and Hunt (1984)

Managers should recognize that they may have the upper hand in dealing with many of these stakeholder groups, though not always with all. Sometimes communication with specific non-targeted groups is unavoidable but necessary if the company is to maintain its license to operate. Identifying stakeholders solely from a marketing point of view can be dangerous – a marketing point of view often ignores many groups to which companies must also communicate their corporate story effectively.

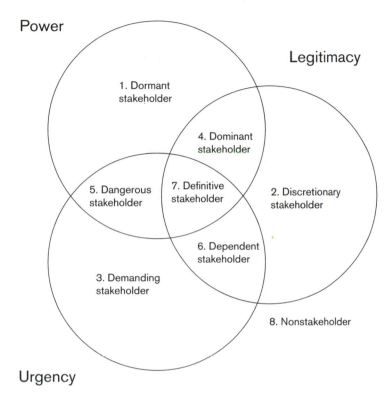

Power

Legitimacy

1. Dormant
stakeholder

4. Dominant
stakeholder

5. Dangerous
stakeholder

7. Definitive
stakeholder

2. Discretionary
stakeholder

6. Dependent
stakeholder

3. Demanding
stakeholder

8. Nonstakeholder

Urgency

Figure 7.3 Identifying key stakeholders
Source: Adapted from Mitchell *et al.* (1997)

Step 3: identify communication objectives

Companies can define their communication objectives in terms of whether
they are seeking to generate change in a particular stakeholder's "knowledge",
"attitude", or "behavior". Successful communication involves creating a
message, getting targeted stakeholders to pay attention to the informational
content of the message ("knowledge"), getting them to react favorably to the
content ("attitude"), and getting them to change a specific supportive behavior
such as purchasing or investing ("behavior"). This sequence is often referred
to as "the domino effect" and is illustrated in Figure 7.4.

Although the domino model provides a useful referent for outlining the
objectives for a corporate communication campaign, achieving those objectives

| Message domino | Knowledge domino | Attitude domino | Behavior domino |

Figure 7.4   The domino principle
Source: Grunig and Hunt (1984)

is often more subtle. In practice, the change sequence is often reversed, and attitude change can logically precede knowledge change as the target of a communication campaign (van Raaij, 1984). The assumed relationship between the cognitive, affective, and conative phases will strongly influence the way in which the communication campaign is constructed.

The co-orientation model shown in Figure 7.5 can be helpful in defining communication objectives (McLeod and Chaffee, 1973). The model takes the company's point of view to define existing "perceptual gaps" with its target groups. The model helps the company to prioritize the specific changes in knowledge, attitude, and behavior that are required.

The co-orientation model starts by defining Subject K as seen by the organization. Doing so can be difficult because of the widely varied internal perceptions of Subject K that are likely to prevail in the company. Consensus building often takes center seat here. Once a company-wide perception of Subject K has been established, the company must now assess the target group's likely perceptions of Subject K. To do so effectively requires carrying out research or dialogue that is designed to probe how members of the target group actually think about Subject K, and how they imagine the company perceives it. When juxtaposed, the perceptual gaps are very likely to emerge. McLeod and Chaffee distinguish four possible problems: (1) a lack of

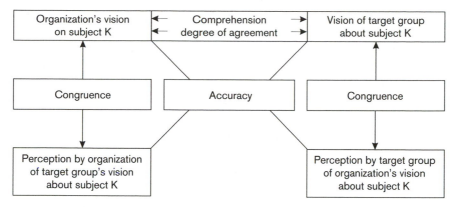

Figure 7.5 Defining perception gaps using the co-orientation model
Source: McLeod and Chaffee (1973)

congruence, (2) a lack of accuracy, (3) a lack of comprehension, and (4) a lack of agreement on how the situation should be defined.

Congruence is the level of agreement around the degree to which one person believes that he thinks the same about an object as another person. Accuracy is the degree of precision in the beliefs of both parties. Understanding is the level of agreement between the two sets of perceptions. Agreement is the degree of similarity in the evaluations of both parties.

Communication objectives can only be established if there is some understanding both of the situation as seen by the company and the situation as seen by the target group. If analysis indicates that the problem is principally one of accuracy, then forms of communication aimed at increasing comprehension should be the focus of effort. As Grunig and Hunt (1984) put it: "The recipients of the message do not necessarily agree with the message or plan to do anything about it. They simply remember what you said. Targets know the other's beliefs and evaluations. They do not necessarily hold the same beliefs and evaluations, however."

If the problem is one of understanding, then effort must be made to ensure that the message is received and accepted: the target should not only retain the message explaining the other's beliefs, but accept the message as its beliefs about reality.

Finally, if there are no perceptual gaps between evaluations of Subject K, there is agreement, and no change in attitude is required.

Take a situation in which accuracy is the problem. To overcome a gap in accuracy, the emphasis of the company's communication should be on increasing the target group's knowledge about the company before doing anything else. In other words, it's pointless to use communication to generate attitude change if the problem lies in factual mis-information. The Shell Group experienced this problem first-hand in its interactions with Greenpeace around the Brent Spar crisis in 1995. Greenpeace ultimately admitted that it was mis-informed about questions of fact – specifically, the organization had wrong estimates of the environmental impact of sinking the disaffected oil platform. Given the situation, Shell would have been wise to embark on a knowledge-based communication campaign before doing anything else. Lacking resistance, Greenpeace was able to convince the media and the public about erroneous data – and malign Shell in the process.

Step 4: create a brief

When preparing a corporate campaign, creative specialists from an external agency are generally invited to participate. They require a briefing – what is often referred to as a "copy platform". Such a "brief" should consist of three components:

1 Competitive context

A description of the market context which has brought about the need to create a communication campaign. This will normally include essential information about competitors, relating both to general strategy and to communication strategy.

2 Core mission

A description of the company's reason for being. Key questions to address include (Hamel and Prahalad, 1996; Campbell and Tawady, 1990):

- Why does the company exist?
- What are the core values of the company?
- What are the company's key sources of distinctive competence?
- What has the company done to make sure employees "live the values" of the company?

In the context of the brief, the fourth point may be the most revealing. For instance, many companies claim to have codes of conduct – most of which are unknown to most employees and unused – and so are unlikely to prove useful in creating a brief. In contrast, when the Shell Group revised its Business Principles in 1996, it was careful to make sure they didn't turn into just any other set of "corporate codes of conduct" – paper instruments that sit on shelves and gather dust. To bring the Business Principles to life, the company asked the top tier of the company to sign a declaration that stated that he/she was living up to the Business Principles. The consequences of not signing or not being truthful, would have drastic consequences for the manager. This is a powerful piece of information for the brief.[1]

3 Core message

The third component of the brief is usually a description of the core message the campaign should convey. In selecting a core message to communicate, two factors play a key role: What should be said and how it should be said. The PPT Model is a short-hand tool for organizing the creation of a messaging brief. It suggests that the three most important building blocks of a communication program are *proof*, *promise*, and *tone*, and these are principally conveyed through a core creative concept.

- *Proof*: The evidence that can be brought to bear, preferably linked to the main current of the creative strategy to be chosen.
- *Promise*: A short description of the central promises to be used in the campaign.
- *Tone*: Should the message be information intensive, or should it be conveyed with emotionally gripping content? Should the campaign adopt an aggressive tone, a humorous tone, or a provocative tone? What limits are there on formulating a firm message and making a credible impression on the targeted group?

Step 5: develop a robust creative concept

A reputation platform and corporate story can be implemented in innumerable ways. They are limited solely by the creativity of the design team that is interpreting the story for the targeted group. The appeal of a platform and story therefore depends heavily on the creative concept.

The creative concept brings the story to life – often through the use of visual stimuli that are combined with the story. The use of color, metaphor, sound, playfulness, and imagery all can impress themselves on the human sensory apparatus and can be applied to a story. Take the widely publicized

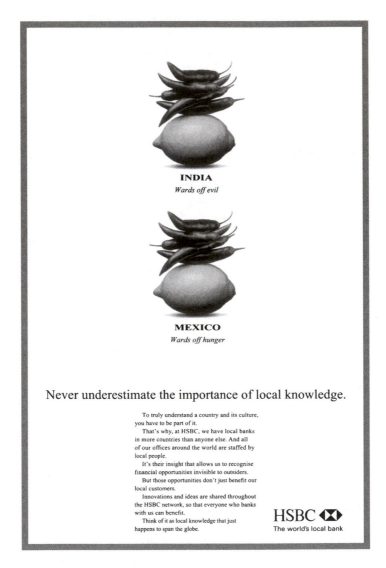

Figure 7.6   Positioning HSBC as "The World's Local Bank"

Source: Photography by Richard Pullar

HSBC campaign launched in 2003 that is illustrated in Figure 7.6. The campaign emphasizes HSBC's core message of "the world's local bank" through a variety of communications that demonstrate the bank's understanding of local practices. To do so, the campaign uses a distinctive combination of verbal content, local images, as well as fonts, colors, and symbols to crystallize its core message.

Practically speaking, a robust creative concept should provide a frame of reference for all of the company's communications – a distinct format and context through which all corporate messages can be filtered and that typifies the company behind the product brands. Few companies consistently maintain a creative concept over time. General Electric did so for many years through its core message "*We Bring Good things to Life*," but abandoned it in 2004 in favor of "*Imagination at Work*". The Dutch electronics giant Philips used the slogan "*Let's make things better*" for more than six years, but also dropped it in 2005 in favor of a new core message "*Sense and Sensibility*" designed to demonstrate Philips' commitment to technology for people. The US consumer goods, medical devices, and pharmaceutical company Johnson & Johnson has drawn on the mother–child bond to position the corporate brand of Johnson

Figure 7.7 Positioning Johnson & Johnson by emphasizing "nurturing" and "motherhood"

Figure 7.8   Johnson & Johnson's campaign: "Support Our Nurses"

& Johnson for more than 100 years. In advertisements Johnson & Johnson not only strictly limit the use of the Johnson & Johnson red color and logo, but they also limit their subsidiaries' ability to draw on the baby-based brand equity of the corporate parent in their own communications. The ads for "Johnson & Johnson" almost evokes the smell of a freshly powdered baby (see Figure 7.7).

In 2002 Johnson & Johnson launched a campaign intended to address the acute shortage of nurses in the US by encouraging people to consider nursing as a profession (see Figure 7.8). Called "Dare to Care" the campaign has raised money for nursing scholarships and education and has resulted in increased enrollment in nursing schools and more educational options.

The MECCAS model (means–end conceptualization of components for advertising strategy) of Reynolds and Gutman (1984) can be used to create more effective advertising content. It suggests that managers pay attention to five elements in building a creative concept:

▐ *Driving force*: The value-orientation of the communication strategy, the goal to focus on.
▐ *Leverage point*: The way the campaign will reach, realize the goals, or activate the communicated value. The leverage point addresses the link between the driving force (value) and the rational, moral, emotional components of the campaign.

■ *Executional framework*: The action plot and means through which the value is communicated to target groups. The framework provides the context within which the campaign will be developed, especially the tone and style elements to be used (layouts, visuals, and logos).
■ *Consumer benefit*: the important positive consequences for the targeted group that are explicitly communicated both verbally and visually in the communication. These benefits could be functional, psychological, or social.
■ *Message benefits*: The specific attributes, properties, or benefits that are linked to the product through the message and are communicated verbally or visually.

Ray (1982) suggests that once a creative concept has been developed, it should be tested by applying the following questions:

■ Is it consistent with the corporate strategy?
■ Does it suit the nature of the target group?
■ Does it fit into the total communication policy?
■ Does the idea have a "leverage effect" (= "multiplier effect")?
■ Is the concept too complicated?
■ Is the concept distinctive enough?
■ Could the concept be used in the different forms of mass communication?
■ Is there a danger of being ridiculed by competitors?
■ Will it last long enough?

Step 6: select the media

Marshall McLuhan is best remembered for his famous slogan "the medium is the message". Though abused, it remains the clearest statement of the crucial importance of the media mix to effective communication of the company's reputation platform and corporate story. The choice of which media to use to convey the communication message is at least as important as the other components of the communication program. An indication of the importance of a company's media strategy is the fact that about 90 percent of the total communication budget is spent on media buying – only 10 percent is all that goes into strategy-setting, production of the campaign, and evaluation of results.

The core of the media strategy is built around the notion that the selected media must be able to convey the creative content of the campaign in a way that meets the communication objectives and influences the targeted groups in expected ways (Rossiter and Percy, 1987). When an unknown company initiates a mass media campaign, its principal purpose should be to create awareness and familiarity. Subsequently, the campaign should be more narrowly targeted to specific groups through more direct and personalized communications, with different emphases for different adoption categories. The aim at that stage will be to *persuade* members of the target group, and thereby drive changes in the target group's attitudes or supportive behaviors.

In general, media are chosen according to four criteria: budget, range, frequency of exposure, and continuity. The "media balloon" describes a balancing of reach, frequency, and continuity. As Rossiter and Percy (1987) put it: "If the balloon is tied off (representing a fixed media budget), the manager cannot make one sphere larger without squeezing at least one of the other two." Figure 7.9 illustrates how, if the manager is allowed to inflate the balloon to any necessary size (representing an open media budget) then all three spheres will enlarge and a more comprehensive media plan will result (Rossiter and Percy, 1987). Increasing use can be made of computer models in the development of a media strategy. Examples include MEDICA (Little and Lodish, 1960) and ADMOD (Lancaster and Katz, 1989). The disadvantage of these models is that they were designed primarily for use in selecting advertising media, and are best suited to examining mass media options for advertising.

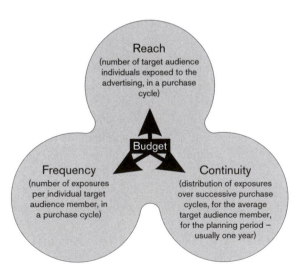

Figure 7.9
The media balloon
Source: Rossiter and Percy (1987)

Minekus (1990) identified a second order problem that routinely arises in the process of selecting communication media: "The most difficult task is to establish what combination of media will give the largest synergetic return in a particular case." As he asks pointedly, when does 1+1+1 equal 3, and when does it equal 5? When does the best solution to a situation involve a combination of advertising, PR, and direct marketing? And when is it better addressed through direct marketing, sponsorship, and product placement? At this point, specialists can provide little more than intuitive insights to such questions. There remains very little scientific knowledge about the effects of communication, about the effects of a single communication through a single medium, let alone of the synergetic effects of different media.

The *Handbook of Marketing Communication* (Rinnooy, 1988) suggests that the problem might be solved by assessing the available media on a number of features, and then deciding to what extent their weak and strong points can complement or compensate each other in the media mix. Naturally such an evaluation would have to be performed on a continuous basis, with reference to both the target group and the objectives of the campaign.

Step 7: pre-test the IMPACT of a campaign

Once a corporate campaign has been built around the company's reputation platform and corporate story, pre-testing the campaign is crucial. The IMPACT model [Internal Measurement for Predicting A Change on Targets] can be used to assess it (van Riel and van Bruggen, 2002). The model is designed to measure the probable impact and effectiveness of a corporate campaign *before* it is implemented.

The IMPACT model examines three areas: creativity, professionalism, and consistency. *Creativity* concerns the originality, uniqueness, and distinctiveness of the campaign. *Professionalism* addresses campaign characteristics such as clarity of message, link to company, attractiveness to employees, believability, modernity, and applicability to the targeted group. *Consistency* includes attributes such as stability, coherence, and how robust the concept of the campaign appears to be. The predicted success of the corporate campaign is explained through anticipated changes in knowledge, attitude, and behavior.

Pragmatically, implementing the IMPACT model typically involves asking people directly involved with the constructed campaign – both internal staff and outside agencies – to participate in replying to a structured questionnaire that asks them to anticipate the likely impact of the campaign on observers.

To do so, requires developing two or three alternative versions of the corporate campaign. These conceptual versions are presented to participants who rate them on the IMPACT questionnaire. A "best version" of the campaign is created based on the findings of the analysis. The revised campaign is tested once again to check that it delivers the highest positive test result. Once assessed, the campaign moves into implementation. Figure 7.10 summarizes the use of the IMPACT model in the pre-testing of a campaign.

Comparative research indicates that pre-testing a campaign solely with internal stakeholders generally delivers very similar results of pre-tests conducted with external stakeholders. Given the ease of reach, likelihood of response from internal groups, and lowered costs, it makes internal pre-testing by far the preferred and most affordable way to execute a pre-test. An added benefit of internally pre-testing is that the cooperation of the various managers in the company is likely to increase if they have participated in the pre-test and stand behind the final message and concepts introduced in the campaign.

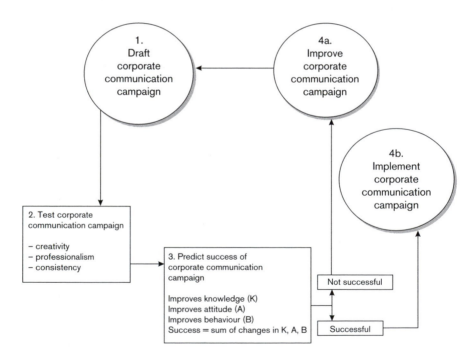

Figure 7.10   Pre-testing a corporate communication campaign using the IMPACT model

Source: van Riel and van Bruggen (2002)

Corporate expressiveness

Fombrun and van Riel (2004) extend the IMPACT model by suggesting that the anticipated benefits of a corporate communication campaign should be *reputation-building*. Reputation gains result when campaigns are expressive, that is, when they convey not only heightened visibility and distinctiveness for the company, but also transparency, authenticity, and responsiveness. It leads to the Reputational IMPACT model described in Figure 7.11. Pre-testing with either informed groups or test subjects can be carried out quantitatively using a survey instrument to ensure that the desired effects of the campaign are likely to be achieved.

Figure 7.11
The Reputational IMPACT model for assessing the expressiveness of a corporate communication campaign
Source: Adapted from Fombrun and van Riel (2004)

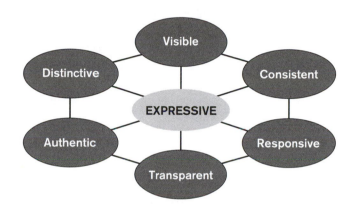

Conclusion

In implementing a reputation platform, communication managers can use models and checklists to prepare and execute their communications. The seven-step sequence that was discussed in this chapter is intended as a helping aid in formalizing the process of building a corporate communication campaign around a reputation platform and corporate story.

Our emphasis in this chapter was on the way that communication can be used to express the corporate story to targeted groups. However, one should not lose sight of the fact that the reputation platform and corporate story belong to the company as a whole – not just to the communication function. As such, the communication campaign should be seen as one necessary but not sufficient component of a broader process for institutionalizing how the company is seeking to position itself with key stakeholder groups.

When targeting the company's reputation platform and corporate story to more specialized internal and external audiences, a distinct but complementary set of factors must also be taken into account. These are addressed in Chapter 8.

Discussion Questions

1. Discuss how models for planning corporate communication can be used to build more effective campaigns.
2. How can a company prioritize stakeholders? Is it wise to put one group ahead of another?
3. What are the critical components of a communication brief?
4. What should be the relationship between the core message and the creative concept the company uses?
5. How should a company select which media to use to convey their core message?
6. What criteria should you use to judge whether or not a communication campaign is effective?

Note

1 Note that a comparable requirement was imposed on US companies by the Sarbanes–Oxley Act in 2001 when it insisted that CEOs personally would have to sign the financial statements released by their companies and would be held to it by law. It now prevents CEOs from claiming ignorance about the company's financial practices in the courts.

8 COMMUNICATING WITH KEY STAKEHOLDERS

Electric communication will never be a substitute for the face of someone who with their soul encourages another person to be brave and true.

Charles Dickens
Source: **ThinkExist.com Quotations.**
"Charles Dickens quotes".
ThinkExist.com Quotations Online
1 March 2006. 4 April 2006

Companies are dependent on five key stakeholder groups: employees, customers, investors, government, and the public. The public is often represented by self-appointed activist non-governmental organizations (NGOs) who identify themselves with a particular strategic issue. To address the concerns of these generic groups, most companies have created specialized departments responsible for communicating about and with these groups:

- *Internal Communications*: A group responsible for communicating with employees, that frequently interfaces with the human resources function in the company.
- *Marketing Communications*: A group responsible for communicating with the company's customer accounts and often interfaces with marketing and customer service functions in the company.
- *Investor Relations*: A group responsible for communicating with investors and analysts who monitor the company's financial performance and prospects.

■ *Government Relations*: Often called "public affairs", these specialists are generally responsible for improving the company's relationships with regulators, legislators, and other government representatives.
■ *Public Relations*: A group whose responsibilities would include interacting with the diffuse set of NGO and activist groups motivated by concern over a specific social problem to which the company may be contributing.

These five groups are diagrammed in Figure 8.1 and tied back to the stakeholder model discussed in Chapter 7 (Grunig and Hunt, 1984). Communication by specialists in these groups within companies has its own particular dynamic, and it is important to appreciate and address their concerns when giving shape to a corporate communication campaign. The subjects that these specialists communicate about differ, as does their relative interest in conveying information about the company that stands behind the brands. It is therefore important eliciting their support in developing as well as carrying out the campaign.

Despite the different dynamics of their specialties, experience suggests that all communications specialists benefit: (1) from having a solid appreciation and understanding of the company's reputation platform, and (2) from being provided with a clear version of the corporate story that is adapted to the interests of their target groups. Consistency in the articulation of the corporate story among specialists is more likely to increase awareness, understanding, and ultimately build trust and respect for the company with its key stakeholders. Reputation

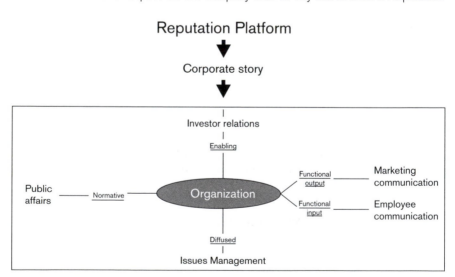

Figure 8.1 Orchestrating corporate communication

builds from repeating the core message, and from framing the content of the communications that the specialist will have with those stakeholders.

The rest of this chapter provides an overview of the concerns and approaches taken by specialists in each of these five domains, and discusses their role in implementing communications that can support the development and dissemination of the company's reputation platform and corporate story.

Investor relations: the role of financial communications

The investor relations (IR) function is only found in companies whose shares are publicly traded on a stock exchange. In such companies, the purpose of the IR specialist is to interface with current and potential financial stakeholders – namely retail investors, institutional investors, and financial analysts.

Despite the critical importance of the investment community to companies, however, scientific research about investor communications is limited and has only recently begun to develop a body of knowledge. In part, this is because financial management relies heavily on the dominant model of "market efficiency" developed and propagated by leading scholarship in finance. In an efficient market, all information about a company whose shares are publicly traded is supposed to be free, widely available, and easily understood. Under the efficient market hypothesis, therefore, there is no need for specialized financial communication since all investors have perfect access to all available information about the company.

The real world is different, of course, and market inefficiencies abound (Dreman, 2001). There are large gaps in the kind, quantity, and quality of information that can be accessed by large investors and small investors; investors do not have equal access to corporate information; there is information asymmetry between companies and investors and there are hidden incentives for companies and investors alike not to share private information about a company that is likely to affect its future performance.

Recognizing these facts, in 1952 General Electric was the first company in the world to start a specialized investor relations department. Doing so crystallized the need for a function that would not only manage the routine interactions between a company and its financial stakeholders, but could also strategically target these stakeholders in an effort to persuade them about the company's future prospects and thereby improve their chances of generating favorable appraisals of its shares and enhancing its access to financial capital.

Since then, a growing literature has become available that identifies not only the legally mandated requirements that investor relations specialists must fulfill, but also the more institutional role they play in conveying and positioning the company with financial audiences (Marcus and Wallace, 1997; Rieves and Lefebvre, 2002).

To take one example, the Dutch association for investor relations (NEVIR) defines investor relations as "the consistent building and maintaining of relationships with existent and potential suppliers of capital". Thönissen (2003) views investor relations as a function created to facilitate "meeting information disclosure obligations as opposed upon the company by capital market institutions and authorities, creating a favourable starting point with present and potential investors and their intermediaries." More generally, the London Stock Exchange (2001) describes investor relations "as an investor-targeted 'spearhead' in establishing a broader positive image for the company."

Overall, most observers agree that the role of investor relations is to fulfill three principal functions:

- comply with regulations;
- create a favorable relationship with key financial audiences;
- contribute to building and maintaining the company's image and reputation.

Ultimately, these roles come together because of a belief that good relationships with financial audiences will improve the company's reputation and thereby contribute to its financial performance. They do so, principally by improving access to credit, reducing perceived operating risk, and lowering the cost of capital (Fryxell and Wang, 1994; Fombrun and Shanley, 1990). Some empirical evidence exists of the link between perceived admiration of a company and its financial performance (see Fombrun and van Riel (2004) for a summary of that literature).

Investor relations specialists work closely with a number of key internal and external audiences. They are described in Figure 8.2. Figure 8.3 shows the broad playing field in which investor relations specialists operate both within and outside of the organization and their interrelationships (Larsen, 2003).

Internal audiences

Investor relations normally works closely with the departments of finance, corporate communication, and legal. The CFO and the CEO have to fulfill a crucial role in communicating investor relations messages to outside audiences,

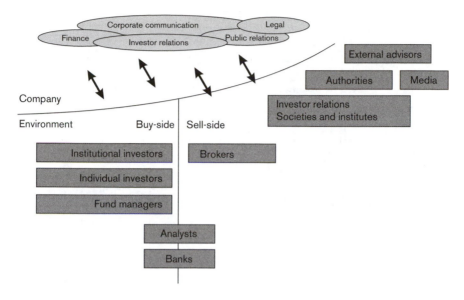

Figure 8.2   Target audiences for investor relations

and so these messages must be created, rehearsed, confirmed, and orches-trated. Most messaging emanating from investor relations should therefore embody the collective wisdom of the senior management team, and so are an important way the company's reputation platform and corporate story gets articulated and conveyed externally.

External audiences

Investor relations generally guides the company's senior team's messaging. This is normally carried out through investor presentations, analyst calls, company visits, webcasts, and other regular meetings designed to present the company to analysts and investors, and thereby to create positive regard for the company and its prospects. Key external audiences consist of two important target groups: the "buy-side" and the "sell-side". The sell-side includes investment banks and other intermediaries that regularly sell the company's shares. Sell-side analysts in these institutions are crucial stakeholders because they are tasked with objectively assessing all available information about the company in order to develop their personal recommendations ("buy", "hold", "sell"). Star analysts on the sell-side build personal reputations from their past

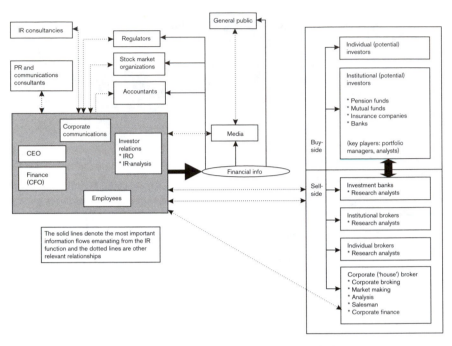

Figure 8.3   Investor relations: relationships between stakeholders
Source: Larsen (2003)

recommendations, and so often have enormous influence over the investment decisions of both individual and portfolio investors. They are therefore heavily courted by investor relations specialists who strive to convey information to them quickly, efficiently, and reliably. There is some evidence that companies whose IR departments offer more credible information to analysts tend to have better-performing shares (Brounen *et al.*, 2001).

In sum, the principal objectives of financial communications emanating from IR are to:

▌ create a pool of latent demand for the company's shares;
▌ reduce churn in the company's shares and keep price volatility low;
▌ give an accurate representation of the company's past performance;
▌ provide credible predictions of the company's future performance;
▌ monitor market reactions to the company's communications;
▌ align perceptions of the company's value by investors and by top managers;
▌ maximize the company's market value, minimize its financing costs, and reduce its cost of credit and cost of capital.

Achieving these goals, not only builds credibility and reputation, but proves especially valuable when a company seeks additional financing from the credit or capital markets for new projects or acquisitions (Brennan and Tamarowski, 2000).

In practice, IR activities vary greatly across companies and internationally. The active stock exchanges in the US and UK have created a longer tradition of financial communication in those countries. Historically, Europe and Asia have had less involvement with IR. However, the exponential growth in the market values of companies since the 1980s, combined with the proliferation of active listings of corporate shares on market exchanges around the world, has pushed the field forward.

Stock exchanges and national regulatory bodies prescribe much of the financial reporting that companies are obliged to divulge to all investors. In a bid to increase their "transparency", many companies also release more information than required. Although security regulations specify what should be contained in a company's annual report, many companies have taken to releasing information about their voluntary donations, pro-bono activities, and the many ways they address questions of ethics and social responsibility. Voluntary information disclosure of this sort varies greatly, and there is no consensus yet about the influence it has on financial valuations of the company. Consider the Dutch food giant Ahold. For many years the company was regarded as one of the organizations with the best IR departments in the Netherlands. After Ahold's financial difficulties with its FoodService division in the US that demonstrated extraordinary irregularities in its financial accounting practices, the company has limited its IR communications strictly to required disclosures. One can only conjecture whether this will have a long-term effect on Ahold's perceived transparency and reputation. A number of academic studies suggest that the mere act of listing on an exchange signal to investors a commitment to greater transparency and disclosure significantly enhances both analyst coverage and the accuracy of their forecasts of the company's likely future earnings; it also leads to higher market valuations (Doidge *et al.*, 2005; Lang *et al.*, 2002).

In recent years, the internet has dramatically increased the ability of IR specialists to convey information quickly and reliably to the financial markets, thereby increasing their perceived transparency and responsiveness, and the influence of IR departments over market valuations. So much so that a surrogate measure of the sophistication of an IR department is its ability to use information technology in its financial communications (Hedlin, 1999).

Employee relations: the role of internal communication

All companies communicate with their employees. As the volume of their communications grows, many companies create an employee relations (ER) function with dedicated staff to manage the numerous media through which senior managers can communicate among themselves and with the rest of the organization. Sometimes the ER function is embedded in the human resources (HR) department in order to capitalize on the routine interface HR has with employees in managing benefits, compensation, appraisal, and developmental activities. In most companies, however, ER will also report to the wider corporate communication function.

ER specialists are generally expected to fulfill one or more of the following four roles (Krone *et al.*, 2001):

1. *Efficiency*: Internal communication is used primarily to disseminate information about corporate activities.
2. *Shared meaning*: Internal communication is used to build a shared understanding among employees about corporate goals.
3. *Connectivity*: Internal communication is used mainly to clarify the connectedness of the company's people and activities.
4. *Satisfaction*: Internal communication is used to improve job satisfaction throughout the company.

Ultimately, the effectiveness and professionalism of the ER function depends on the particular role or combination of roles that a company adopts. In our view, however, none of them are sufficient onto themselves, and the true effectiveness of an ER function is better defined in terms of whether the ER specialists are helping or inhibiting the company's ability to implement its strategic goals.

To assess effectiveness, we therefore recommend distinguishing four types of activities that a professional ER function might be expected to address explicitly:

1. *Structure*: The formal and informal channels through which internal messages are conveyed.
2. *Flow*: The processes through which internal communications move vertically, horizontally, and laterally in the company.

3. *Content*: The specific content of the communication.
4. *Climate*: The emotional environment of the organization.

An effective ER function is one that manages internal communications within and between groups in the organization by systematically addressing structure, flow, content, and climate with a view to improving the implementation of the organization's strategic goals.

A by-product of more effective internal communication is organizational identification – the degree to which employees are proud to work in the company. People tend to identify more with a group when they have a sense of safety and security, and a sense of being recognized for the personal contributions they make. Internal communication plays a central role in increasing employee identification with the company: (1) by making the company's reputation platform more salient to individual employees, (2) by clarifying *ingroup* and *outgroup* membership rules – what it means to belong to the company, and (3) by communicating the benefits employees will have – implicitly or explicitly – when they participate in organizational life. Figure 8.4 describes the relationship we hypothesize to exist between employee relations, organizational identification by employees, and performance.

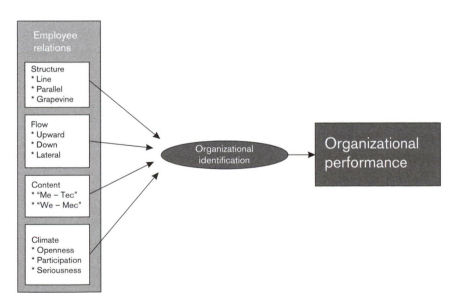

Figure 8.4   Employee relations: building organizational identification and performance

Source: van Riel and van Bruggen (2002)

Structure

Internal communication is heavily influenced by the official channels that are given life by the organization's formal structure of reporting relationships. The formal structure defines both the horizontal and vertical groupings of employees, as well as the coordination mechanisms that are used to integrate the differentiated groups (Fombrun and Shanley, 1990; Lawrence and Lorsch, 1966).

Information spreads in three ways in companies: formal communications occur through the organizational line and largely reflect the organizational chart. Top managers typically inform middle managers who inform the rest of the employees. The greater the number of levels in the hierarchy and the more distinct groups that were created for task purposes, the higher the probability of distortion and misinformation across the company, and the lower the likelihood of the company developing shared understandings among employees.

To supplement formal communications, most ER functions also rely on parallel media for communicating. Employee newsletters, internal magazines, video journals, notice boards, corporate television networks, and intranets are among the favorite media of modern ER functions. Parallel media are helpful to employees when they provide indirect feedback about the employee's effectiveness. If the information conveyed in these parallel media is perceived to be both credible and timely, and to reduce the costs to the employee of seeking out other information sources, then employees are more likely to seek them out (Ashforth and Cummings, 1985; Reinsch and Beswick, 1990; Jablin and Putnam, 2001).

Finally, information also gets conveyed through "the grapevine" – the informal side of the company. Rumours tend largely to form and get conveyed through the informal networks that take hold in all companies as people form friendships and develop other non-task related linkages (Tichy and Fombrun, 1979; Fombrun, 1982). The influence of informal channels can be considerable and savvy ER managers find it helpful to understand the workings of the grapevine – a channel that can be valuable for conveying some kinds of information (Johnson et al., 1994).

Flow

In most companies, internal communications are more likely to flow vertically rather than laterally, and downward rather than upward. Downward flows are typically decisions, assignments, and requests. Upward flows are more likely to involve reports and information. Research shows that negative information takes longer to flow upwards than downwards: employees are more likely to send information upwards if they feel that they have a trusting relationship with their manager. In such cases they are inclined to send more favorable and more important information upward. A comparable mechanism exists if employees are under the impression that the people with whom they are communicating can influence their career prospects: the greater the perceived influence of the recipient, the more effort the employee will make to share positive information (Trombetta and Rogers, 1988).

The proliferation of parallel media creates a crucial role for the ER function: maintaining consistency in the self-presentations of the company to all employees. Intranets quickly become outdated and must be updated. Newsletters written in one part of the company are not easily aligned across business units. Time lags separate the release of information online, in print, and on air. The sheer volume of information put out on parallel media have to be coordinated, orchestrated, and streamlined if they are to demonstrate not only coherence, but the singular imprint of the company's reputation platform and corporate story.

Besides consistency, another challenge for the ER function consists of developing credible spokespersons for communicating with employees through parallel media. Corporate news delivered by senior managers is preferable to information conveyed by ER specialists, particularly when the topic involves company-wide developments, strategic issues, or negative information. Third party endorsers are more credible than marketing staff when speaking about product features, positive market feedback, and success measures.

Content

The effectiveness of the ER function depends not only the structure and flow of internal communication, but also on the content that is distributed. Employees report greater satisfaction with communication content that is timely, readable, easily understood, and sufficient. Empirical studies report that employees generally feel they don't receive enough information. "More" is often perceived as "better" because it appears unfiltered, and therefore more "authentic" and "true" (Zimmerman *et al.*, 1996). This is particularly true when information is being conveyed by direct reports or by close colleagues.

Content that provides input to employees about their position in the company, clarity about their role, or their relative standing in the larger corporate scheme is generally well received. Research indicates that self-confidence grows when employees have a better understanding of their own role in the company and when they are conscious of the contribution they are making to the company's success (Varona, 1996).

Communications broadcast through parallel media help to institutionalize the "in-group" in the company, and so increases employee identification by those employees who see their interests as aligned with the established leadership in the company. Finally, the effectiveness of ER increases when employees have the feeling that top managers invite and welcome critical self-expression.

Climate

The communication climate is a subset of the broader "organizational climate" that develops within companies (Falcione *et al.*, 1987). The communication climate describes more focused employee perceptions about the nature of internal communications in the company – for instance its professionalism, innovativeness, breadth, or open-mindedness (Guzley, 1992).

All communication audits measure employee satisfaction with the "communication atmosphere" or "climate" (Downs, 1988). Research suggests that a positive climate increases employee involvement and trust in top management (McCauley and Kuhnert, 1992). Productivity results from a positive communication climate because it improves employee identification with the organization, enhances employee self-image and self-confidence, and creates a feeling of belonging by increasing the sense that employees are participating in the decision-making process (Rosenburg and Rosenstein, 1980).

Figure 8.5 summarizes the drivers of an effective ER function by pointing to the four components of internal communication and their effects on organizational identification. Ultimately, an ER function must create alignment between the formal and parallel channels of internal communication and the company's overall corporate communication. Increasingly, ER specialists must grasp the broader communication context of the company, its reputation

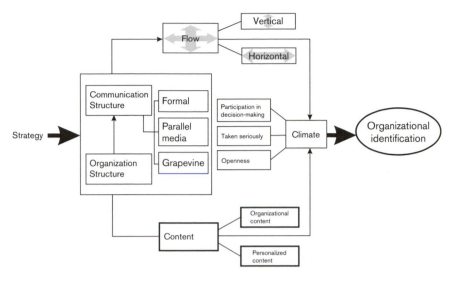

Figure 8.5 Effective employee relations: linking structure, flow, content, and climate

Source: van Riel and van Bruggen (2002)

platform, and look for ways to enhance the company's consistency and distinctiveness by infusing key elements of the reputation platform into the internal communication channels of the company. In this way, the task of internal communication consists not only of *expressing* the company's core values, but of *impressing* those core values on new employees through the corporate stories that are told formally and informally, in training videos and company programming, and through the corporate heroes that are praised both formally and informally through the grapevine.

Customer relations: the role of experience marketing

In most companies, a very large part of the communication budget gets allocated to marketing communications. These communications consist of (Kitchen, 1999):

▍ *Advertising*: Any paid form of non-personal presentation and promotion of ideas, goods, and services by an identified sponsor.

- *Sales promotions*: Short-term incentives to encourage purchase of a product or service.
- *Personal selling*: Verbal presentations in conversational form with one or more prospective purchasers for the purpose of making sales.
- *Marketing public relations*: Programs designed to improve, maintain, or protect the image of the company or its products.

Numerous research studies point to the deficiencies of marketing communications in building lasting gains for companies (Fombrun and van Riel, 2004). People are sceptical of corporate ads and other forms of paid corporate self-presentations and self-endorsements. Because it is self-referential, marketing communication therefore suffers from a lack of perceived authenticity and credibility (Scholten, 2002). The lack of credibility itself results, at least in part, because many of the programs that are created in marketing communications get developed with little or no connection to the organizational communications that emanate from the rest of the organization. A fundamental role of the reputation platform – and the corporate stories that are created from that platform – therefore consists in building commonality and consistency between marketing communication and organizational communication.

In recent years, we have witnessed growing interest in "experience marketing" – an approach to marketing that is based on getting potential customers to "experience" not only the product they could be buying, but the entire organization behind the product. Personalizing the experience increases the likelihood that the customer will confer a sense of "authenticity" on the company's communications – thereby creating a bond between customer and organization that will increase loyalty and repeat purchases. The goal of experience marketing is therefore to create an emotional involvement by potential customers. As marketing pioneers Pine and Gilmore (1999) put it:

> *While commodities are fungible, goods tangible, and services intangible, experiences are memorable. Buyers of experiences . . . value being engaged by what the company reveals over a duration of time.*

The Danish toy company LEGO builds its communications around a reputation platform of "creativity". LEGO's slogan "*The Power to Create*" is all pervasive in the way the company presents itself, not only in toy stores, but in its theme parks, DVD games, and on the internet. It demonstrates the kind of strong link that can be established between marketing communication and corporate communication, and how it can be leveraged to build up the reputation and value, not only of the company's products, but of the organization as a whole.

Facility tours have been a prominent vehicle used by major companies in recent years to link marketing communication to corporate communication. The German auto-maker Volkswagen uses its glass factory in Dresden to showcase to a large number of consumers daily what the company stands for and the way its products are produced. Tours are given regularly, and while sitting in the waiting area, visitors can create their own customized Phaeton cars, Volkswagen's new luxury brand. A simulator showcases how the new car will drive. Some customers even fly in to the factory by helicopter so that they can get to drive home in their new cars. When wrapped around the experience of joint dining in the factory restaurant, Volkswagen has clearly created an entirely new purchasing experience for the customer. The experience parallels that created by dealers of General Motors' Saturn brand in the US who, when they visit the company, are treated to a family experience that is designed to instil in new customers a sense of belonging and identification with their new Saturn cars, with the Saturn brand, with the Saturn corporate family.

Pine and Gilmore (1999) suggest that consumers have no resistance to paying a premium price for a unique brand experience. Starbucks, the rapidly growing Seattle-based coffee retailer, has built a comfortable business around selling its personalized version of "the coffee experience" (Rindova, 1997). Customers pay considerably more for a cup of Starbucks coffee than they do at other cafes, partly for the quality of the coffee itself, but also for the entire organizational context the retailer has put around it – the lounge environment, customized production process, specialized language used (try ordering a simple cup of coffee without knowing the specific terms to use!) and the sourcing strategy for the coffee bean itself. Judging by the company's financial results in the last decade, consumers around the world certainly seem willing to pay extra for the Starbucks experience.

Many years ago, the economist Abbott (1955) remarked that "what people really desire are not products, but satisfying experiences. People want products because they want the experience – bringing services which they hope the product will render." Experience marketing cannot be selectively applied – it must be conveyed holistically (Scholten and Kranendonk, 2003). To be convincing, the company must convey its reputation platform, not only by telling convincing stories, but by conveying those stories through "experiences" that breathe life into the reputation platform. When a company does it well, customers will recognize the company as genuine and authentic, and confer trust and reputation upon it. And that is effective marketing (Figure 8.6).

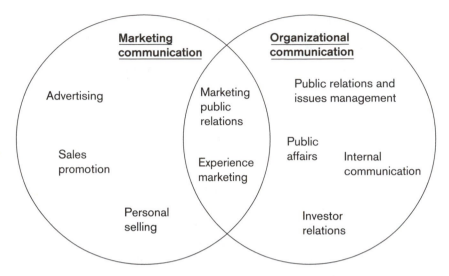

Figure 8.6   Overlap between marketing and organizational communication

Government relations: handling public affairs

One of the most powerful and delicate stakeholders companies have to interface with is government – the network of regulators, legislators, elected officials, and appointed representatives that constrain, control, tax, review, delay, authorize, punish, and otherwise maintain oversight of the activities of the private sector. Government relations (GR) describes the set of professionals who have specialized in this area in recent years, a field that is often referred to as "public affairs" because of its implicit focus on topics of widespread public interest.

Harris and Moss (2001) describe government relations as "the manage-ment of the often complex external relations between the organization and an array of governmental and non-governmental stakeholder groups." Leyer (1986) views the role of the GR or public affairs specialist as the management of strategic issues: "the strategic approach to situations which constitute either an opportunity for the company or a threat to it, and which are connected with social and political changes, formation of public opinion, and political decision-making."

To most people, government relations and public affairs are synonymous with "lobbying". A pejorative connotation is often attached to the term "lobbying" when it is interpreted as being a secretive, behind the scenes activity through which companies (and foreign governments) try to manipulate the political agenda to their advantage, using illicit means, such as the purchase of "favors". A different view of GR is advanced by those who advocate a view of lobbying, not as an illegitimate form of "strong-arming", but as a legitimate effort to provide balanced information to otherwise uninformed officials responsible for making policy decisions. In this interpretation, GR specialists are charged with ensuring that the opinions of the private sector are appropriately delivered to government decision-makers. Consistent with this view, van Schendelen (1993) defines lobbying as: "The informal exchange of information with public authorities, as a minimal description on the one hand, and as trying informally to influence public authorities on the other hand."

In practice, GR plays an important function for many companies, not only through lobbying (a process that principally revolves around the *legislative* process), but through the *regulatory* function. Energy companies, utilities, telecom operators, pharmaceutical companies, financial firms – all have significant interaction with regulators and have to deal with oversight from specialized government agencies. In the US, the FDA (Federal Drug Administration) regulates the testing and release of all prescription drugs. The SEC (Securities & Exchange Commission) regulates banks. To influence regulatory policies in their domains, industries themselves form associations whose principal purpose is to provide strength in numbers, and act to collectively influence regulators about actions being considered in the "public interest". The collective strategies of industries are evident in the actions taken by such groups as PhRMA – the Pharmaceutical Research and Manufacturers of America – in lobbying the FDA on behalf of the industry, or the American Petroleum Institute in its efforts to ease energy regulations. In the US, much of this activity occurs in the Washington DC area. In Europe, corporate lobbying is increasingly centred around Brussels – the capital of the European Union. Since the Maastricht treaty of 1992, the European Commission, the European Parliament, and the Board of Ministers are all in residence in Brussels.

Research on effective lobbying suggests a number of "best practices" GR specialists should apply.

▌ *Personal relationships*: A key requirement for effective functioning is the development of sustained, personal relationships between GR specialists and the regulators, politicians, and staffs who work on specific issues. Personal and frequent contact is the best means of communicating with these influential decision-makers – and trust is the foundation on which the relationship should be built.

■ *Appropriate timing*: The regulatory process involves a complex meshing of dates and decisions, with long "dead periods", and a rash of overlapping and interdependent cycles in which legislations are introduced and debated, and regulations are voted on and passed. The GR's role is to make sure that decision-makers have relevant information provided to them in a timely fashion at appropriate stages.

■ *Objectivity*: Decision-makers have to be convinced that they are receiving information that is objective, scientific, relevant, and relatively free of bias. Hence the growing importance for GR specialists to partner or affiliate with strong third-party endorsers whose credibility can help to guarantee the objectivity of the information being brought to bear.

Clearly the GR specialist has to be skilled in both the art of relationship management, and in the techniques and knowledge base of a specialized domain relevant to the issues the company is concerned about influencing. Box 8.1 suggests three sets of skills that the GR specialist should possess: scientific skills, specific skills required for the execution of the function, and specific skills needed to carry out fieldwork and be persuasive to targeted legislators (van Schendelen, 2002).

Box 8.1   Profiling the GR specialist

Scientific abilities

■ technical knowledge about industry topics;
■ descriptive and analytical capacities;
■ an ability to put things into perspective;
■ a critical way of thinking.

Specific preparatory skills

■ knowledge of political developments;
■ firm understanding of the organization and its strengths and weaknesses;
■ pragmatic efficiency.

Specific skills needed in the field

■ ability to make a connection between preparatory work and fieldwork;
■ diplomatic skills;
■ curiosity for developments in related areas;
■ strong involvement with the company's multiple stakeholders.

Adapted from van Schendelen 2002.

What constitutes effectiveness in government relations? In part, it can be measured through goal achievement – success in getting a law passed that is favorable to the company, in getting a threatening regulation eliminated, a subsidy cancelled, a burdensome law changed. However, a non-event (a measure not taken, a law not passed) can also be important in itself. Ultimately, success is often expressed in economic terms – the revenues gained for the company or cost burden removed. It can also be described in reputational terms – the effects of the GR's actions on the company's reputation with government representatives. Peddling influence can sometimes create short-term economic gains at the expense of longer-term costs to the company's image and credibility. Such a loss could significantly threaten the company's license to operate in the host country – with grave repercussions on its license to operate in other countries as well. The GR specialist's role is therefore crucial in arbitrating the company's fundamental competitiveness.

As GR specialists convey information and set out to influence key government agents, they get to introduce and personalize the company to a wide range of powerful stakeholders. Appropriate customization of the company's reputation platform and corporate story for targeted government representatives is crucial. Like all stakeholders, regulators and legislators need to understand and appreciate the company's position on an issue. A skilful GR specialist must create a sensible interpretation, one that rationalizes what the company does with what it stands for, and communicate the company's values in ways that convey credibility, authenticity, and responsiveness. Doing so is probably as important as the outcome of the influence tactic itself.

Public relations: issues management and the media

The general public is probably the most diffuse stakeholder group that companies address. For one, the public seldom speaks directly to companies. The public largely voices its concerns either through the mouthpiece of politicians claiming to represent the public interest, or through the activist initiatives of non-governmental organizations (NGOs) who claim to act on behalf of "the public".

In fact, the public consists of a large and diverse set of interests. After all, everyone is a member of "the public" – consumers, investors, employees, regulators, politicians – we are all part and parcel of the amorphous mass of people whose voice seldom rises above a whisper, and whose interests are only ever partially defended.

The role of the public relations (PR) specialist, in many ways, is to communicate with the general public in ways that serve the interests of the company. PR therefore consists of numerous specialty areas that convey information about the company to the public, including sponsorships, events, media relations, and issues management.

The effectiveness of PR has been widely questioned for years. Many have seen PR as a poor and distant cousin of advertising, without the resources. Others have made outsized claims about PR's ability to generate unpaid media coverage for a company, and thereby produce favorable impressions of the company with the public – a result that is obviously beneficial since third-party endorsements are not only cost-effective, but more lasting in their impact on consumers than are paid media.

In 2004, we conducted a content analysis of the press releases made by one US company over a two-year period. The analysis involved a detailed classification of the actual words used in over 373 press releases. A dictionary of key words was first built by defining synonyms and correspondences among words and naturally related expressions. Human coders then reviewed the text and identified natural groupings of words. Figure 8.7 provides a summary chart that documents the content of the press releases made by this company. The results suggest that the company's communication consisted principally of "product" and "performance" related communication, at the expense of communication that showcased its leadership, citizenship, workplace, or organization. In this case, the findings highlighted the fact that the corporate stories the company told were derived largely from a reputation platform

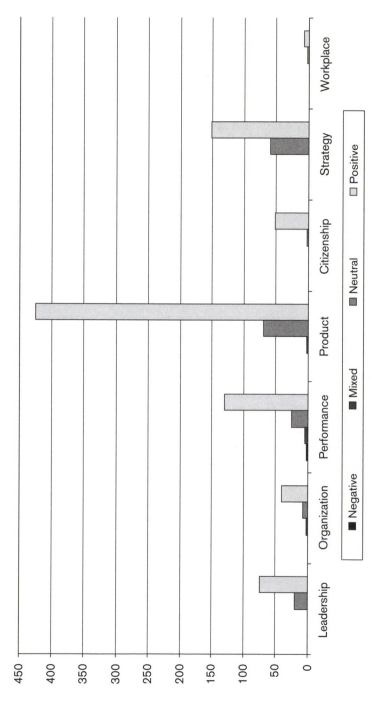

Figure 8.7 Content analysis of press releases by a major US firm (2003–2004)

that stressed product innovation. Far fewer stories were told of the company's other pillars of strength, and so could not and would not be received by the public.

Although a key role of the PR specialist is to make the company better known for traits and attributes that build the company's perceived distinctiveness and competitiveness with the public, it is not the only role. In recent years, PR specialists have become increasingly involved in helping companies manage strategic issues – public concerns about their activities that are frequently magnified by special interest groups and NGOs. Figure 8.8 shows a list of some of the most visible NGOs operating in the US and describes the results of a survey of public perceptions of these groups conducted by the Reputation Institute and Harris Interactive in 2003. Among the most respected groups by the public are clearly Doctors without Borders, Habitat for Humanity, and the Red Cross. Among the least respected were PETA (People for the

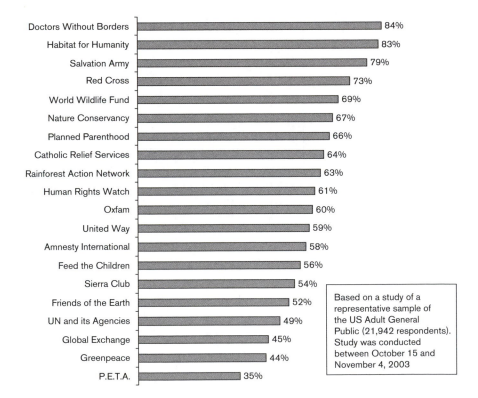

Figure 8.8 Which NGOs does the public trust?

Source: Harris Interactive and the Reputation Institute (2005)

Ethical Treatment of Animals) and Greenpeace – two of the most activist NGOs whose controversial tactics regularly infuriate many consumers and companies.

The role of the PR specialist therefore also consists of issues management, namely the "set of organizational procedures, routines, personnel, and processes devoted to perceiving, analyzing, and responding to strategic issues" (Dutton and Ottensmeyer, 1987). A strategic issue is one that compels a company to deal with it because there is "a conflict between two or more identifiable groups over procedural or substantive matters relating to the distribution of positions or resources" (Cobb and Elder, 1972).

The role of the PR specialist in carrying out issues management consists of three principal activities:

1. *early detection of issues* that can potentially become a threat to the organization;
2. *marshalling of internal resources and forces* to understand and prepare to address the issue;
3. *implementation of an issues management strategy* to react to the issue as soon as it proves necessary.

Most research in the area of issues management has focused on the development of methods for early detection. The sooner a company realizes that an issue can have a powerful effect on its ability to achieve its business goals, the more likely it is to limit potential harm. Companies have shown considerable interest in recent years in the development of "early warning systems" – tracking systems that can identify issues *before* they reach crisis proportions. "The idea behind such systems is that companies should try to identify strategic issues as early as possible, so that they have more time to respond to the issue, and can deal with the event while it is still relatively harmless" (Dutton and Ottensmeyer, 1987).

Strangely enough not much is known about what companies actually do when they detect a growing threat. Heugens *et al.* (2002) suggest that companies can address strategic issues in one of four ways: through dialogue, through advocacy, through silence, or through crisis communication. The selection of the appropriate issue response strategy depends on the degree of activism around the issue among the general public, and the allowable reaction time. Figure 8–9 diagrams these four strategies and suggests that PR specialists must build organizational capability in each of these four areas in order to be in a good position to address emerging issues as they arise.

The ability to dialogue with pressure groups is not given to all. For many years, Shell resisted dialogue with activist NGOs like Greenpeace, insisting that the group was too extreme. Lacking capacity for dialogue, in 1995 Shell found itself wholly unprepared to deal with the subversive tactics used by Greenpeace during the campaign the group mounted to prevent Shell from sinking the de-commissioned Brent Spar oil platform into the North Sea. To prepare for dialogue requires establishing two-way communication with the owners of the issue, and recognizing a loss of autonomy by the company in handling the issue on its own.

A capability for advocacy requires different skills from the organization. Advocacy-building owes much to the background of GR specialists – communicators skilled at presenting the company's point of view to groups like regulators and legislators. Persuasion is a key component of the skill-set, and the company learns to follow a clear and consistent line. The core message is often brought under the attention of a larger group through advertising in the hope and expectation that "opposing forces" will take a less negative stance. Philip Morris's campaign to create tolerance and understanding for the rights of smokers is a manifestation of the company's longstanding advocacy capability.

If an issue is unknown to many people and public resistance is barely perceptible, companies will often choose a silence strategy. Rigorous silence demands military-like discipline if it is to succeed, with explicit punishment doled out for those who break silence. Silence may be the preferred strategy for dealing with an issue that has developed little organized resistance from public groups, and for which there is little time pressure. Silence allows the company the luxury of careful preparation. The danger of adopting a silence strategy is that by condoning delay, it allows the issue to creep up slowly on the company, and sometimes to reach crisis proportions before being noticed.

Issues management is clearly not the same as crisis management. Crisis communication remains a critical capacity that organizations must master to effectively deal with issues that threaten their license to operate. In crisis situations, PR specialists get to work with small inter-functional teams for whom time is of the essence. Speed of action, strong networking skills, and decision-making abilities are crucial on these teams.

The critical balancing act for the PR specialist is between the short-term pressure of handling strategic issues, and the long-term concern with communicating consistently to the public and to NGOs who claim to represent the public about the company's position on issues of concern.

As one of the US's largest employers, Wal-Mart has been an attractive and vulnerable target for many NGOs. In recent years, the company has had to face class action lawsuits by minority groups claiming discriminatory behavior by Wal-Mart managers. A variety of private documentaries have been or are being released that feature Wal-Mart whistleblowers purporting to make revealing accusations about the company's abusive practices. At the same time, a rash of criticism has been leveled at the company by vociferous opponents who claim the company destroys the fabric of local communities when it moves into an area. On November 3, 2005, the *New York Times* featured a front page story describing Wal-Mart's new aggressive PR strategy, one designed to counter the mounting criticism. To enact it, the company recruited veterans of past US presidential and state political campaigns with extensive experience going as far back as the election of Ronald Reagan. The language of the group involves pre-emptive strikes, scorched earth practices, and the importance of counter-offensives against the company's critics.

One wonders at the wisdom of such a strategy when dealing with stakeholder situations. After all, Wal-Mart is not running for election – they are faced with stakeholders who will not be going away after the campaign. Viewing them as "the enemy" runs counter to the preferred strategy of engagement and dialogue that most observers recommend. The danger is that the aggressive play will work against Wal-Mart's best interests by institutionalizing an even more negative environment around the company and further defiling its image in the media and with the public. It is also inconsistent with a reputation platform that draws heavily on "being a desirable place to work".

In our view, companies should ensure that their reputation platform is consistently expressed to the company's diffuse stakeholders, and helps build reputation for the company as a whole. And that's what an effective PR specialist can do.

Conclusion

Five communication specialists help companies manage their critical stakeholder relationships internally with employees, and externally with investors, customers, regulators, and the public at large. Each of them contributes to the implementation of the company's goals.

Each communication specialty is built on two major pillars: knowledge of the subject matter and a set of communication skills. To be effective, corporate communication must first be corporate in nature – it must recognize its roots

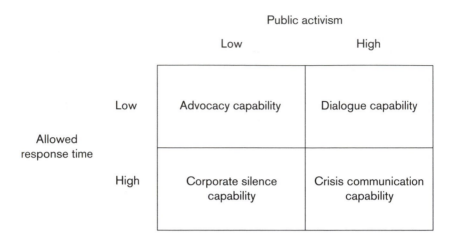

Figure 8.9 Four issues management strategies

Source: Heugens *et al.* (2004)

in an understanding of the functioning of the organization as a whole. The communication skills are secondary to the strategic orientation and training of the specialist.

No specialist, however qualified, manages alone. Cooperation between communication specialists is vital for a company to develop and convey a distinctive reputation platform and corporate story consistently to its stakeholders. When specialists identify too much with their narrow specialty areas, they are less likely to contribute to building the overall reputation of the organization. When that happens, corporate communication quickly deteriorates into a cacophony of misaligned messaging with little effectiveness in supporting corporate objectives.

Discussion Questions

1. What is the fundamental role of the IR function?
2. Are the interests of buy-side and sell-side analysts aligned?
3. How should a manager judge the effectiveness of the ER function?
4. What is experience marketing and how would you explain its growing popularity?
5. What is the role of the GR professional?
6. How can PR help a company conduct issues management more effectively?

9 ASSESSING THE EFFECTIVENESS OF CORPORATE COMMUNICATION

The act of Good-Will is a cover to kill
Butcher the rain forest and Mother Nature at will
Honorable ulterior motive is the motif
The hidden agenda of a covert thief

Josephine DixonBanks

Politicians are very sensitive to the fact that their re-election to an elected office depends heavily on the public's last-minute impressions of the candidates. Politicians therefore monitor closely the public's probable voting behavior by ordering tracking polls. Figure 9.1 shows the results of two tracking polls conducted by Gallup before the US presidential elections of 2000 and 2004. These polls provide simplified measures of each candidate's relative reputation with the voting public. They are therefore a measure of the effectiveness with which candidates have communicated with the public.

In recent years, companies have become almost as sensitive as politicians to the importance and benefits of conducting comparable opinion polls with the public and with targeted audiences. Reputational ratings make it possible for companies to explore what stakeholders are seeing – and how their feelings affect the judgments they make about a company and its products. Is the company thought to be selling life-threatening products, creating an unpleasant work environment for employees, paying extravagant self-serving bonuses to its managers? Or is it more favorably regarded – and thought to make high quality products and play a positive influence on the community?

Reputational ratings are empirical tools for making direct comparisons among firms and providing managers with a simplified interpretation of the

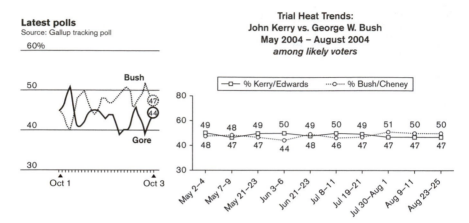

Figure 9.1   Results of a poll right before the 2000 and 2004 US presidential elections

effectiveness of their corporate communication systems. Although many companies already measure their reputations, experience shows that they often do so with poor measurement instruments, and without a roadmap for action based on findings. In our experience, few know how to use reputation research to guide resource allocation decisions across reputation management functions. And fewer still ever act on the research findings they commission unless a sense of urgency is created by a senior executive, a crisis, or a major strategic change. In our view, reputation research can help magnify those issues by creating benchmarks for organizations, and by stimulating the application of a correction mechanism for actions that deviate too far from stakeholder expectations.

Reputations are public, but reputation research need not be. A major advantage of conducting privately funded reputation research is the ability to use it internally as a diagnostic tool – a rudder for guiding change in organizational initiatives and in corporate communication and for addressing stakeholder concerns. As we indicated in Chapter 3 and throughout this book, a corporate reputation measures an organization's success at fulfilling the expectations of its stakeholders.

This chapter reviews the principal methods that can be used to measure the effectiveness of corporate communication. We emphasize two success criteria: (1) the effectiveness of corporate communication in creating strategic alignment internally, and (2) the effectiveness of corporate communication in building reputation.

Producing strategic alignment

One measure of the effectiveness of corporate communication is its ability to draw internal support from employees for the company's strategic objectives. By "strategic alignment" (SA) we mean a situation in which all employees "understand, "buy into", and are able to enact" their organizations' strategic objectives (Gagnon and Michael, 2003). Creating strategic alignment is vital because companies depend on their employees to successfully implement their strategic objectives. Research shows that when employees are supportive towards a company's strategic objectives, they are more likely to make decisions that are consistent with those objectives (Gagnon and Michael, 2003). Ultimately, the same research also suggests that strategic alignment leads to better organizational performance (e.g. Schneider, White, and Paul, 1998). Producing strategic alignment is therefore essential for the functioning of organizations – and corporate communication plays a crucial role in this regard.

Strategic alignment is influenced by the company's own internal control systems (Strahle *et al.*, 1996), the perceived fairness of the process of change (Caldwell *et al.*, 2004), and by employee communication (Farmer *et al.*, 1998).

A recent study found empirical support for the influence of various dimensions of employee communication on strategic alignment through its effects on employee behaviors at work (van Riel *et al.*, 2005). The findings confirm past research linking communication to employee attitudes such as job satisfaction and identification (Smidts *et al.*, 2001; Boswell and Boudreau, 2001; Noble, 1999), but elaborates the link to strategic alignment by emphasizing the influence of employee communication on employee behaviors at work. The real measure of what constitutes effectiveness for corporate communication is not whether employees feel more satisfied with the work they do, but whether employees behave in ways that support the company's strategic initiatives. This is measured with the EcQ® The Strategic Alignment Monitor as illustrated in Figure 9.2.

The chart describes internal communication in terms of six key attributes, three of which involve communication flows, two of which involve the content of communication, and one that addresses the wider "communication climate" in the company (see Chapters 2 and 3) (Greenbaum *et al.*, 1988). "Communication climate" has been defined elsewhere as "those molar factors, objective and/or perceived, which affect the message sending and receiving process of members within a given organizational group" (Falcione *et al.*, 1987).

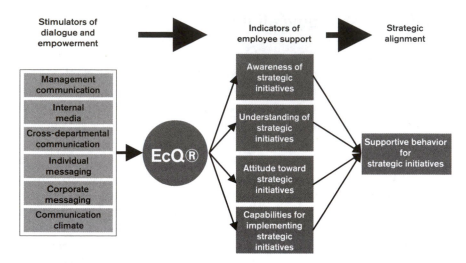

Figure 9.2   EcQ™ The Strategic Alignment Monitor: linking internal communication to strategic alignment

In other words, climate refers to aspects of the organization as a whole (molar factors) that influence how communication takes place.

Past studies have examined the impact of flow, content, and climate and showed that all three dimensions of communication have a strong impact on team performance (Choi and Kim, 1999), on trust in the manager, and on organizational citizenship behavior (Korsgaard et al., 2002). Companies that provided more information to employees following a merger announcement reduced uncertainty among employees and increased their job satisfaction and commitment (Schweiger and Denisi, 1991; Zimmermann et al., 1996).

A number of studies have also explicitly focused on the role of employee communication in fostering strategic alignment (Frank and Brownell, 1989, provides an overview of earlier studies). Farmer et al. (1998) showed that the degree to which a leader communicates about a strategic change influences the degree to which employees agree with the strategy. Similarly, Edmondson (2003) focused on the role of group leaders, and showed that the degree to which they informed group members about a change and created a supportive communication climate increased their success at implementing the change. Several studies have also investigated the role of employee communication in the context of managing a change in identity (which may accompany a change in strategic initiatives). They all stress the importance of management's use of rhetoric to generate employee support for the change (Chreim, 2002; Corley and Gioia, 2004; Fiol, 2002). Fiol (2002) found that in their speeches, managers studiously avoided the use of inclusive referents (such as "we" or "our") in order to establish de-identification with the company's old identity, and extensively used inclusive referents to establish identification with the new identity.

A comparative analysis of two large Dutch organizations demonstrated empirically that when employees perceive the flow, content, and climate of the company to be adequate, they are more likely to develop favorable attitudes toward the company's strategic initiatives (van Riel *et al.*, 2005). In turn, favorable attitudes tended to increase their willingness to behave in ways that were consistent with various organizational initiatives. The study also showed that direct communication from line managers was far more effective than communication from internal media in determining favorable attitudes regarding strategic initiatives. The flow of communication between departments influenced attitudes regarding strategic issues, but its influence proved less important than that of management communication. In addition, communication content related to the organization as a whole (corporate messaging) was more important for strategic alignment than communication content related to employees' personal roles. Finally, in both organizations communication climate also had a strong influence on attitudes toward strategic issues, and on strategically aligned behavior.

Overall, the results confirm that management communication, communication content related to strategic issues, and communication climate have a strong effect on employee attitudes regarding strategic initiatives, and on the degree to which employees behave in ways that are consistent with the strategy. A key way to judge the effectiveness of corporate communications internally is therefore to assess the degree of strategic alignment that the company is experiencing. Aligned companies are more likely to build reputational capital than companies lacking strategic alignment – employees are more likely to act as ambassadors for the company to outside audiences.

From alignment to reputation: measurement options

Although crucial, the effectiveness of corporate communication cannot be judged solely from examining internal perceptions. Good communication will also be reflected in the quality of the relationships that companies establish with their key stakeholders. As Chapter 7 indicated, companies build strong ties to stakeholders by *expressing* themselves fully. Expressiveness creates perceptions of transparency and trust in the company – and creates a stronger, more resilient reputation. Figure 9.3 diagrams the relationship between strategic alignment, expressiveness, and reputation.

Reputations are mental scripts that are more or less *elaborate* in the minds of these stakeholders. As we indicated in Chapter 3, the degree of elaboration depends on the perceived importance of the organization to the stakeholder. There are three ways to conceptualize corporate reputation, and they depend largely on whether stakeholders have a more or less *elaborated* understanding of the company (Poiesz, 1988; Verhallen, 1988; Pruyn, 1990). The greater the psychological and social distance between the organization and the stakeholder, the less elaborate the stakeholder's understanding of the organization.

The appropriate method to use in gathering reputation data depends heavily on knowing how much stakeholders know about the company – how elaborate are their cognitive structures? The best method will be one that enables respondents with an elaborated structure to demonstrate a sophisticated knowledge about the organization. The stakeholder with a less elaborate understanding of a company should rate companies using a method that does *not* require depth of knowledge, and should only invite them to answer questions about the organization's more general attributes. Table 9.1 contrasts the principal methods that can be used to generate reputational data.

Since organizations must communicate with multiple stakeholder groups in order to acquire and maintain adequate supplies of resources, corporate reputation research requires input from a variety of stakeholders. Each group will differ in how elaborate their understanding is of a company. Multiple

Figure 9.3 Strategic alignment, expressiveness, and reputation

Table 9.1 Approaches to reputation management

Degree of elaboration	Conceptualizing	Typology	Measurement implications	Measurement method
High	Reputation is saved as a network of meanings in the memory of the consumer	Reputation is structured in a complex manner	Qualitative research: deeper searching for associations	Free format method Structure method • Laddering • Kelly Grid
Medium	Reputation is the weighed sum of the perceptions of an object: perceptions of salient attributes multiplied by the importance of those attributes	Reputation is an attitude	Explicit methods: identify the salient attributes and put these forward in the form of statements	Attitude questionnaires • Thoughts • Valuations
Low	Reputation is a general, holistic impression of the place that the object is to take relative to its competitors	Reputation is a global impression	Implicit methods: relative positioning of the object through multi-dimensional scaling	Multi-dimensional scales of: • Likenesses • Preferences

methods may therefore be appropriate in creating an accurate reputation profile of the company.

Figure 9.4 and Box 9.1 list a variety of questions that should be addressed when launching reputation research. They involve questions about the "subjects" of the research – the stakeholder respondents whose opinions are of interest. A set of questions should also be addressed about the "objects" of the research – the organizational components which respondents are invited to assess.

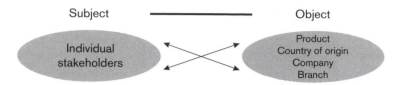

Figure 9.4   Questions to address in reputation research

Box 9.1   Questions to address in reputation research

Subjects

- Who should be questioned?
- Is it possible to segment the chosen target audiences?
- Are these groups reachable?
- Does the research evoke negative feeling, and if so, what is done with them?
- What will it cost?
- How long will it take to carry out the research?

Objects

- Which business units are of particular interest?
- Can the unit be subdivided into sub-units?
- Which sub-units contribute most heavily to the organization's performance?
- What specific information does the organization need?
- How will the research be used?

Reputation measurement techniques can be divided into open and closed techniques. Open methods invite respondents to describe an organization in their own words whereas closed methods invite respondents to judge a company on the basis of pre-selected characteristics.

Methods also differ in the specific tasks they ask the respondents to complete. For example, some methods invite respondents to examine a set of pictures and sort them. Others ask respondents to describe an organization using metaphors. Others ask for ratings of the organization on a pre-specified list of attributes.

Table 9.2 Types of measurement methods applied in reputation measurement

	Sorting	Metaphor	Rating
Open	Kelly repertory grid Natural grouping Card-sort	Photo-sort	
Closed	Q-sort		Attitude scales

To help researchers and managers select the optimal method, the rest of the chapter describes six tools commonly used by researchers to measure reputation: Kelly repertory grid, natural grouping, Q-sort, photo-sort, attitude scaling, card-sort, and laddering. Table 9.2 contrasts these methods.

Kelly Repertory Grid

The Kelly repertory grid (KRG) was developed by George Kelly in 1955 to gather public opinion. KRG presents respondents with the names of three companies or brands written on separate index cards and invites respondents to indicate which two are most similar, and which one does not relate to the other two. The explanations given by stakeholders constitute the dimensions that can be used to distinguish the companies. By presenting different combinations of companies, various dimensions of corporate reputations can be elicited. Stakeholders are then invited to evaluate or rank the companies on the derived dimensions, in order to provide a corporate reputation assessment.

Advantages and disadvantages

The KRG method is simple to conduct and requires relatively few respondents. It forces respondents to typify an organization, as far as their experiences allow them to do so, and to make them as elaborate as possible. The method is applicable to stakeholders with varying degrees of involvement with the companies. Stakeholders with a high degree of involvement tend to produce a wider range of dimensions when distinguishing the companies. KRG is generally attractive to stakeholders because it does not take much time and does not require a high degree of knowledge about the organization. Data analysis is moderately difficult, but costs are relatively low. KRG is especially useful in eliciting attributes of corporate reputation. In the classic Laddering interview reviewed below (Reynolds and Gutman, 1984), attributes on which companies are assessed are often generated by applying a KRG methodology (van der Veer, 1987).

Natural grouping

The natural grouping method is similar to the Kelly repertory grid (Verhallen, 1988). It involves presenting a large number of company or brand names (no more than 80) and asking a respondent to sort them into two subsets. Respondents are asked to specify the criteria they used to sort them, and to describe the resulting subsets in their own words. The process is repeated until the respondent can make no further subdivisions (Verhallen, 1988; Kuylen and Verhallen, 1988; Sikkel, 1991).

The criteria that respondents give when they split the dataset form the dimensions that are used to distinguish between competitors. For example, if respondents split a group of financial companies using criteria like "organizations for the wealthy" and "organizations for the middle class", it suggests that social status may be an important differentiator in the industry. The arguments that are given to make a first specification are clearly the important dimensions. Criteria that are named to split the next sub-groups provide insight into the mental map of the stakeholder.

Advantages and disadvantages

A moderate number of respondents are normally required for natural grouping research. The method offers less useful results when applied to respondents with a low degree of elaboration. Experts with deep knowledge of the firms and industry provide much richer insight and detail than uninformed respondents. The method provides little motivation, however, for respondents to be as open and elaborate as possible. Sorting objects is moderately attractive to stakeholders, and less monotonous than presenting them with attribute scales. Data are typically analyzed using multidimensional scaling techniques or correspondence analysis, making the method very complex to apply. Data collection time is relatively limited, however, and since only experts can do data analysis, it can be costly.

The natural grouping method can be useful when measuring a wide range of associations, features, and conceptions that stakeholders have about a company. The main purpose of this method is to generate attributes and to position a company on those attributes relative to competitors. Besides the perceptual dimensions resulting from the splits that are made, natural grouping also induces a tree structure (see Figure 9.5). This tree structure can be translated into relative distances between objects. By means of multi-dimensional scaling (MDS) or correspondence analysis, an *n*-dimensional perceptual map can be created from these data. In this "positioning-diagram", the dimensions on which the objects are plotted can be interpreted based on arguments articulated by stakeholders themselves.

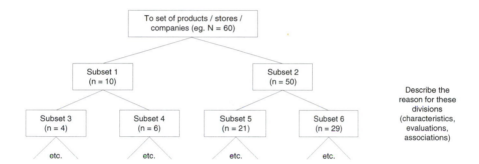

Figure 9.5   Reputation objects created from natural grouping
Source: Verhallen (1988)

Q-sort

Q-sort is a comparative rating method in which statements about a company are drawn from company and stakeholder communications. Multiple statements are put on cards and presented to the respondent who reads them and decides whether the statements apply or do not apply to the company (Boer *et al.*, 1984). Of the statements that apply, respondents are invited to rank order those that most apply to the company, and to do the same thing with the list of statements that do not apply. Respondents therefore start at the extremes and work their way to the less extreme statements. Respondents are asked to sort and rank a large number of statements, according to their degree of agreement (Brown, 1986; McKeown and Thomas, 1988). Typically, a normal distribution to the ranking is imposed, asking the respondent to rank few

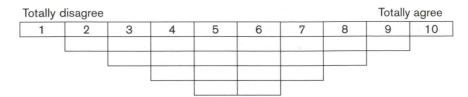

Figure 9.6   A typical distribution of attributes obtained from Q-sort

statements at the extremes of the scale and allowing the bulk of the statements in the middle (see Figure 9.6). The result of a Q-sort is a ranking of applicability of, or agreement with various statements or attributes, providing a detailed insight into the feelings of respondents (positive and negative) about the company. If Q-factors are computed, opinions of different sub-groups can also be obtained. The relative ranking of attributes within sub-groups can be used for benchmarking purposes.

Advantages and disadvantages

A major advantage of the Q-sort method is that it can be used with a small number of respondents (25–30) who have a moderate degree of elaboration about a company and can rank order the statements in a meaningful way. In Q-sorts, respondents are forced to make a decision; they cannot respond positively to every question. Another benefit of using Q-sorts is the ability to distinguish segments with significantly different opinions about the company. Unfortunately, Q-sorts are also complicated to conduct, take time, and are therefore less attractive to respondents because they require hard work. Q-sorts are also relatively expensive; data analysis requires advanced computer software and computation of Q-factors complicates the presentation of results.

Photo-sort

Various sorting methods can be used to carry out reputation research. The photo-sort method developed by FHV/BBDO is a projective research technique developed to increase creativity in advertising. It has also been applied to measuring corporate reputation.

Photo-sorts were developed as a result of dissatisfaction with having to ask respondents to verbalize their understandings of a company's reputation. Since reputations are perceptions, using photographs provides a way to by-pass the verbal realm and elicit reputational information using non-verbal techniques capable of surfacing subconscious feelings about the company. When non-verbal methods are used, respondents do not need to have a highly developed ability to put their feelings into words (Russell and Starman, 1990). In addition, whole reputations remain more or less intact, since they are not fragmented into attributes. The photo-sort method uses photographs of human faces. The respondents use these photographs to make judgments about an object. Russell and Starman (1990) find that respondents have little trouble making associations between the photographs and whatever objects they are asked to rate. When the subject has chosen a photograph to go with an object, he is asked to give the reasons for his choice. He is also asked to say what, in his opinion, should be taken as illustrative of the reputation the user has of the brand or company.

Applied to companies, the photo-sort method provides an indirect way of measuring reputations. Its advantage is that respondents are less inhibited in expressing their opinions, and emotions surface more easily. The use of a human face represents emotions in all their complexity. Each respondent gets to see the face as a complex whole, a "Gestalt" of emotions. People attach a wealth of significance to facial expressions and their interpretation.

The photographs used to rate companies or brands must meet certain requirements. The set of photographs must represent all major emotional categories likely to be relevant to people making judgments about a company or a brand. The meaning of the photographs should also be clear, so that the results can be interpreted unambiguously. The set of photographs must also be revised from time to time so that they do not become dated. As a result of its research, BBDO has compiled a set of 130 faces. The distinctive charac-teristics or attributes of the photographs are determined during preliminary research. During the reputation study, the respondent is typically shown a set of about 35 photographs relevant to the company or brand. Figure 9.7 shows an example of a photo-sort that was used to measure the reputation of British Airways.

Figure 9.7   Applying photo-sort to British Airways

Photonumber	Named F (%)	Affinity score (%)
309	41	34
310	33	47
329	27	57
216	27	72

Character E
Business-like, sophisticated, friendly, serious, decent. But also: old fashioned, distant, snobbish

Advantages and disadvantages

When photo-sort is applied in a qualitative study, it is important to know which photographs are associated with which objects. The respondents are watched through one-way mirrors or recorded during the selection of pictures that they believe to fit a certain object. In qualitative studies, the photographs function primarily as placeholders for discussions which are otherwise difficult to put into words.

If the photo-sort method is used for quantitative reputation research, a sample of at least 75 respondents per target group is necessary. This number must be increased in proportion to the number of target groups to be analyzed. The costs of photo-sort are otherwise relatively small, since administering the task does not take long. Respondents are observed through a one-way mirror, or recorded on video while they select and label the photographs that they believe typify the company being rated. An affinity score is calculated for each respondent that measures the affinity of that respondent with the person in the photograph. The final outcome of a photo-sort is the description of a brand or company in terms of a set of interrelated attributes, which together represent the "Gestalt" of that brand or company.

Card-sorting

Often too little attention is paid to the difference between associative reactions and judgments (van Westendorp and van der Herberg, 1984). It is appropriate to use the term "judgments" when the respondents in a study are reasonably well acquainted with a company and its many characteristics. However, in many cases, and especially in pure reputation research, it is not concrete judgments that are required, but a kind of associative knowledge that may be more or less remote from reality. These reputations resemble stereotypes of the kind discussed in social psychology, e.g. "Germans are industrious."

According to Spiegel (1961), a genuine reputation (or reputation feature) only exists if associative impressions of the kind described play a more important part in the significance of the object than knowledge based on reality. Van Westendorp argues that many of the usual methods of measurement that involve rating scales, include a mixture of associative and judgment tasks. The use of rating scales to measure judgments presents no problems; however, it is difficult for respondents to measure associations in terms of a marking system, since they tend to be of an "all or nothing" nature. The choice of measuring technique must depend, according to van Westendorp, on the kind of target group to be studied. If the respondents have solid detailed knowledge of the company as a whole, a judgment scale is appropriate.

NSS Market Research has further refined the card-sorting technique developed by the German Institut für Demoskopie. The card-sorting technique they favor is intended to apply to tracing associative reactions – what they term "genuine" reputation measurement.

Card-sorting is distinguished by its simplicity and speed of application. Respondents are presented with a series of attributes that are depicted on cards in personal interviews or that are read out in telephone interviews. They are asked to say which ones describe the company "well". The attributes are then presented a second time, and the respondent is asked to say which ones describe it "not at all". Presenting the attributes only once, and asking the respondent to place them into three categories can shorten the procedure: "fits well", "does not fit at all", and "no choice".

In most cases, two characteristics are derived from the card-sorting results, namely, profiling and relative reputation value. Profiling is based on the total number of choices made. It shows how far the attributes have meaning for the respondents in relation to the company. A high level of profiling indicates the importance of the attribute. Provided profiling occurs, relative reputation value indicates the quality of the reputation.

Advantages and disadvantages

The speed of this technique gives it a considerable advantage: it saves 25 percent or more of the time needed for the more usual methods based on rating scales. At the same time, van Westendorp and van der Herberg (1984) point out that it is better suited to the "all or nothing" character of genuine reputations than the usual rating techniques based on intervals or rankings. The procedure does not require developing word pairs, which can create difficulties when bipolar scales are used, and there are no difficulties with the interpretation of a "middle category".

With card-sorting, respondents do not have to make choices. "No choice" is a valid answer, and is used in the interpretation of results. The total number of choices made offers a direct indication of how meaningful the chosen attributes were for the respondents. It is easy to change the order in which attributes are presented to different respondents, thus avoiding sequential effects. Finally, multivariate analysis can be performed on the results obtained with card-sorting. Cluster analysis procedures are particularly appropriate. Cluster analysis makes it possible to trace the dimensions that underlie the pattern of associations that is observed (van Westendorp and van der Herberg, 1984).

Attitude scales

When respondents are likely to have a moderate degree of elaboration about a company or brand, the reputation may be regarded as an attitude. An attitude can be viewed as an aggregation of diverse perceptions about a company or brand. Attitudes can be used to explain and predict behavior (Fishbein and Ajzen, 1975). When an attitude is positive, the probability of positive behavior towards the company is increased.

An attitude can be measured explicitly. The researcher asks the respondent for an overall judgment about a company or about various statements describing specific organizational attributes. The respondent then indicates the degree to which they agree or disagree with each statement.

Attributes can be given different weights based on different methods. The Fishbein and Ajzen attitude model invites respondents to judge not only the attributes, but to attach a value from 0 to 1 for each of the attributes. This value is the weight, which is assigned to the attribute. Mathematically:

$$R = \sum r_i W_i$$

where R represents the overall reputation of the company, r_i the judgment the respondent makes about each reputation attribute i and W_i the importance of attribute i to the overall reputation of the company.

For example, consider a study that asks respondents to rate the reputations of a group of airlines by rating them on attributes of safety, reliability, on-time departures, and waiting times. All of these attributes are scored on five- or seven-point scales, ranging from "entirely agree" to "entirely disagree." Scales with odd-number points are generally used to allow neutral responses.

For each attribute, respondents also indicate whether they feel that the attribute is "very important" or "not at all important" (also on a five- or seven-point scale) to the overall reputation of the organization. The summed product of attributes by importance creates an overall reputation score (see Table 9.3).

Table 9.3 The results of an attitude scaling of airlines

Attributes	Evaluations	Beliefs				
	Totally agree	Totally disagree (importance)				
		N	G	E	A	F
Safety	93	93	85	81	74	71
Reliability	84	94	83	78	70	51
Punctual	79	87	81	77	68	62
Keep waiting times restricted	79	82	67	76	60	47
Service	77	85	73	76	70	27
Efficient timetable	73	78	60	71	63	56
Overall reputation-rank		1	3	2	4	5

Advantages and disadvantages

The results obtained from attitude scaling are easy to compare because they are measured along the same attributes. This makes it possible to obtain detailed insight into the strong and weak points of the various airlines. A disadvantage of attitude scaling is the need to know the attributes that are likely to affect reputation. Another disadvantage is that lengthy questionnaires are required which can demotivate respondents. Market researchers advise random rotation of questions as a way to overcome the problem.

Subsequent multivariate analysis, however, can provide valuable results. In particular, factor analysis can identify underlying groupings of reputation attributes for corporate communication to focus around. And regression analysis can be used to identify which groupings of drivers have the greatest effect on an overall measure of reputation.

Overall, the six methods reviewed in this chapter each have concrete advantages and disadvantages. Van Riel *et al.* (1998) compared the results of applying all six methods to the airline industry and across comparable groups of passengers with prior experience as customers of these airlines. Table 9.4 summarizes the advantages and disadvantages of these different methods of reputation measurement.

Conclusion

Assessing the effectiveness of corporate communication involves examining: (1) how successful the company has been in generating internal strategic alignment through its communication mix, and (2) how successful the company has been in converting alignment into reputational capital. That requires appropriate internal and external research that can diagnose internal alignment and external reputation.

Although reputation research is complex and expensive to undertake, it is an essential tool for assessing the effectiveness of corporate communication. It is therefore crucial for companies and communicators to understand the strengths and weakness of different research approaches, and to identify the optimal approach they want to take to the assessment process. Without assessment, communication lacks accountability. Without accountability, communication is without power.

We conclude this chapter with some advice for decision-making about reputation research.

▌ *Step 1*: Try to understand how managers in your organization are looking at the effectiveness of different functions and departments. What are their expectations about corporate communication? Are those expectations aligned with the strategic objectives of the business?
▌ *Step 2*: Design a reputation-management strategy that can benefit the whole organization. How is the communication department contributing to meeting organizational objectives?
▌ *Step 3*: Create a briefing for an external agency who can assist your organization in carrying out reputation research.

In such a briefing, the following must be taken into account:

- What "objects" is your organization interested in monitoring – a brand, a functional activity, an industry, or the company as a whole?
- Which "subjects" or stakeholder groups is your organization interested in monitoring?
- Which competitors do you want to compare your organization against?
- Is privacy of research important, or are you willing to participate in a syndicated study involving multiple companies?
- What is the rationale you plan to use to explain the research to outside groups?
- How do you plan to use the research results internally and externally?
- Are there methodological limitations to the research? Are there enough respondents in each stakeholder segment? Are respondents likely to participate? What will be the costs?

A great deal of effort is required to conduct reputation research. Managers of corporate communication should make sure they have a clear mandate for doing so, and a clear plan for how to use the results. In our experience, the most significant hurdle to overcome is the inherent difficulty managers have for viewing the organization as a whole. This chapter suggests that you cannot manage reputation if you do not measure it, and you cannot measure reputation without understanding methodological issues.

The next chapter examines the most prominent reputation measurement systems currently used by many companies around the world. We examine the relative strengths and weaknesses of these applied reputation research programs and discuss their applicability as tools for evaluating the effectiveness of the communication function.

Discussion Questions

1. What is strategic alignment and how is it influenced by corporate communication?
2. How does strategic alignment influence corporate reputation?
3. Explain each of the six major methods that can be used to develop measures of organizational reputation.
4. How would you develop an understanding of the reputation profiles of a group of banks in a specific country?
5. Describe key advantages and disadvantages of each of the six principal methods used to measure corporate reputations.

Table 9.4 Evaluating methods of reputation measurement

Reputation measurement method	Data collection	Usual number of respondents	Necessary involvement (degree of elaboration)	Attractiveness for respondent	Ease of analysis	Costs
Kelly repertory grid	Oral interview: choose 2 of the 3 objects that fit best or worst with each other and why. Open method.	Few: 10–40	Low/average	Medium/high	Average	Low
Natural grouping	Oral interview: split the objects on cards in more homogenous groups. Open method	Medium: 40–125	Average	Medium	Medium	Average
Q-sort	Oral interview: rank cards according to normal distribution, 10-points scale (agree – disagree). Open method	Medium/few: 30–50	Average/high	Low/medium	Low	Average

Photo-sorting	Oral interview: confront the respondents with powerful photo-set fitting a specific organization, evaluate using an affinity scale. Open method	Medium: 30–100	Few	High	High	Average/low
Attitude measurement	Questionnaire: measure ideas and evaluation of characteristics on a Likert scale. Closed method	Many/medium: 50 or more	Average	Low	High	Average
Card-sorting	Determining association through statements. Closed method	Many/medium: 50 or more	Average	High	Average	Average

10 APPLIED REPUTATION RESEARCH

*Common sense is the measure of the
possible;
it is composed of experience and prevision;
it is calculation applied to life.*
Henri Fredric Amiel[1]

Companies regularly fund customized research designed to examine the effectiveness of their corporate communications and related initiatives. Chapter 9 described six methods they can use in doing so. The strength of these custom programs is that they are tailor-made to the company's targeted stakeholder groups and initiatives. Their principal weakness, however, is that they lack a standardized comparison set, are only performed sporadically, and so make tracking difficult, producing an unfortunate lack of continuity and benchmarking capability for managers. J.D. Power & Associates is a research company that has made a business out of developing consumer ratings of products and brands. Companies in the auto, computer, electronics, airline, and other consumer goods sectors regularly uncover an attribute on which a J.D. Power survey rates them #1 – and use it for public relations. Continental Airlines boldly features its #1 rating in airline customer satisfaction on the outside of all of its planes, as well as in most of its ads. Nonetheless, J.D. Power surveys are normally purchased reports, and are not widely available. Figure 10.1 shows how General Motors uses a J.D. Power rating to trumpet its quality rating in a survey (note that the survey details are not specified, and it is anyone's guess if the survey only involved the mentioned plant in Oshawa or if it encompassed others).

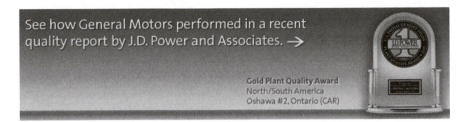

See how General Motors performed in a recent
quality report by J.D. Power and Associates. →

Gold Plant Quality Award
North/South America
Oshawa #2, Ontario (CAR)

Figure 10.1 How GM uses the J.D. Power & Associates #1 rating for publicity
Source: www.gm.com

A variety of applied research programs designed to measure corporate reputations have been developed by various research firms and media organizations. Because they are conducted on a regular basis, they create relatively large databases, some of which are exploited principally for commercial applications, others of which are used for academic research and analysis. Careful analysis of these research databases has led to a variety of practical insights about the effectiveness of communication programs and other initiatives that affect corporate reputation.

When people assess an organization, a question arises about the degree to which a single assessment should be used to represent the perceptions of all stakeholder groups. Does an organization have a single reputation or does it have multiple reputations? Some argue that organizations have multiple reputations because they embody the contradictory interests of self-interested constituents – investors want more profits, whereas employees want more income and customers want cheaper prices (Fryxell and Wang, 1994; Davidson, 1990; Dobson, 1989). Others insist that reputations are uni-dimensional because constituents incorporate into their reputational assessments implicit judgments about whether the organization is meeting the interests of all of the other key constituents (Wartick, 1992). In our view, the question is purely empirical: for some organizations, constituent images converge, and their strong reputations are an indication of that convergence. For other organizations, images diverge, and their reputations suffer from that divergence (Rindova and Fombrun, 1999). By measuring an organization's reputation using identical methods across constituents, it becomes possible to uncover whether stakeholder points of view differ and to study effects of those perceptions on an overall rating of the organization using sub-group breakdowns and multivariate analysis.

This chapter examines seven applied reputation research programs, summarizes some of their key features, and distills some of the major contributions they have made to the management of corporate communication.

Corporate reputation research: applied research programs

A variety of applied research programs are in place that measure corporate reputations. Most are US based programs, and many are principally focused on product brands. In 2000, the US based *Council of PR Firms* identified seven programs that were developed by either media organizations or market research firms, and that were being used by companies to assess or benchmark their corporate reputations. Of these, only two are conducted regularly and have broad visibility:

▌ "America's Most Admired Companies" by *Fortune* Magazine;
▌ the "Brand Asset Valuator" by *Young & Rubicam.*

Four other proprietary measurement systems are used by a number of companies to assess the effectiveness of their communications programs or initiatives: Harris Interactive's "EquiTrend" (developed by the former Total Research Corp. that Harris bought in 2001), WPP's "BrandZ", CoreBrand's "Brand Power", and the Reputation Institute's RepTrak® System. The latter is a successor to the original Harris–Fombrun Reputation Quotient (RQ) projects funded by the Reputation Institute and Harris Interactive. RepTrak® is a standardized scorecard that is now used by the Reputation Institute to measure corporate reputations on a continuous basis in over 20 countries. It has been adopted for benchmarking purposes by many leading companies.

Table 10.1 summarizes the key corporate attributes that are rated across these applied research programs. The methods differ significantly from each other in focus, rigor, and scope. Preference for one method over another partly depends on the kinds of information and analyses managers want to obtain. Common to all of these programs is the cumulation of both cross-sectional and longitudinal data that can enable benchmarking. However, because data are costly to gather, the sponsors of these research programs generally restrict access to the database. The BrandAsset® Valuator is only available to Y&R clients, although the company makes some of its data available for analysis to selected academics. Equitrend has also been similarly restricted by its sponsor, but made available to David Aaker who has used it extensively in his books and articles (e.g. Aaker, 1999). Topline results of annual RQ projects undertaken with the general public have been regularly published in major newspapers in a dozen countries, but detailed results have only been available to private customers. The same holds true of the databases created by WPP

Table 10.1 Reputation dimensions across major research programs

Applied corporate reputation research programs

Reputation attributes	Brand asset valuator	BrandZ	Equitrend	Brand power	USA's most admired	Reputation Quotient (RQ)	RepTrak
Leadership					X	X	X
Ethics and governance					X		X
Customer focus	X				X	X	X
Quality	X				X	X	X
Emotional bond	X	X		X		X	X
Social responsibility	X				X	X	X
Performance		X			X	X	X
Management quality					X	X	X
Employee skills					X	X	X
Relevance	X	X					
Reliability	X						X
Value	X					X	X
Presence/familiarity	X	X	X	X		X	X
Differentiation	X	X	X				X

with "Brand Z", by CoreBrand's "Brand Power". It helps to explain why so many academic researchers have had to rely on the publicly released scores produced by *Fortune* – they are the only ones widely available.[2]

Y&R's "brand asset valuator"

The large ad agency Young & Rubicam funded a start-up project in the summer of 1993 to collect data internationally about how consumers rated well-known brands. The initial research involved quantitative interviews with some 30,000 consumers a year in 24 countries, and rated some 7,000 brands. The project relied on the BrandAsset® Valuator (BAV) instrument, a proprietary tool that Y&R has since developed into a business unit and which it uses to assess a brand's achievements and stature, and to predict its future potential.

The BAV model defines a brand as "a set of differentiating promises that link a product to its customers." Since 1993, Y&R has conducted over 350,000 interviews with consumers internationally to rate popular brands. Each consumer is asked to provide more than 55 responses about the brand they rate, and consumers have collectively contributed to creating a database of consumer perceptions about over 20,000 brands. The core of the questionnaire consists of 32 attributes that are used to determine which aspects play a role in the perception and evaluation of brands. Respondents are asked to evaluate brands in relation to all of the brands they know.

The strength of the BAV is its international scope and the ability to assess a brand against rival brands in the same industry or product category. The difficulty with the BAV is the opacity of the model, its proprietary nature, and the difficulty therefore for non-Y&R clients and academics to access the data.

The four key dimensions "pillars" measured in the BAV are:

- *differentiation*: how unique the brand is;
- *relevance*: the degree to which a brand meets personal needs;
- *esteem*: the degree to which consumers admire the brand;
- *familiarity*: the degree to which the brand is part of the consumer's daily life.

From proprietary analyses, Y&R reports that these four attributes of the BAV are consistently linked to a brand's ability to deliver revenues and profits across industries and countries.

In Y&R terminology, the pillars determine the current power and future potential of the brand, and derive from two core brand drivers: the *authority* of the brand, and its *vitality* (or strength). Vitality results from multiplying differentiation by relevance. Vitality provides insight into the future potential of the brand: a differentiated brand that is also relevant to many consumers has more growth potential than one that is undifferentiated.

Similarly, a brand has more *authority* when it is both familiar and well regarded by consumers. Authority measures the brand's current power in the marketplace, how firmly implanted the brand is in the minds of consumers. Together, the two dimensions determine what the brand has achieved. Figure 10.2 shows the relationship between the four pillars schematically.

Y&R has developed an elaborate conceptual framework to analyze brands on these dimensions. The most important is the *power grid* that plots in two dimensions the vitality of the brand against the authority of the brand, and is central to all BAV analyses. Figure 10.3 shows a typical power grid. According to Y&R analysts, brands tend to begin their lives in the bottom left quadrant and move to the upper left where they have great potential for growth. Here, a brand has to increase its vitality, and the challenge for an emerging brand is to convert vitality into authority. New brands in this quadrant are therefore potential challengers of more established brands that reside in the top right quadrant. Over time, BAV analysts suggest that brands eventually lose vitality, move to the bottom right quadrant, and have to be re-energized or "reborn".

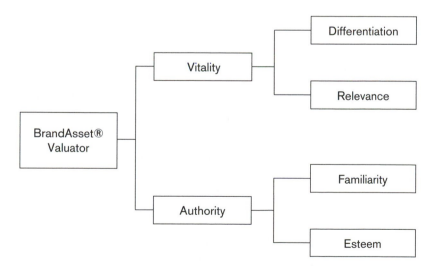

Figure 10.2   The brand pillars measured in Y&R's BrandAsset®Valuator
Source: Alhers (1996)

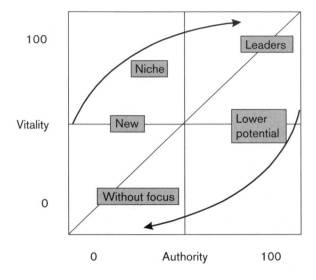

Figure 10.3
The power grid
Source: Alhers (1996)

Once a brand is placed on the grid, researchers conduct two diagnostic tests to explore why they are there, and what can be done. "Reputation Factor Analysis" involves identifying the factors in the product category that are important and see how it compares on those factors against its competitors. "Brand Cluster Analysis" enables a comparison of brands from different product categories in an effort to learn from them by analogy.

A researcher from Y&R explained the results of Figure 10.4 in this way:

> *Budweiser launched onto the Dutch market in 1993 and over four years it grew into a niche brand. Häagen Dazs made the transition from niche brand to marketleader (in the premium ice cream market). Albert Heijn continues to be a strong brand. It is located exactly where a market leader should be. Prodent's position is suffering serious erosion, so the brand has to resort to price offers. Sisi pulled out of its negative slide and is on its way back. Zanussi's proposition is too unclear and consumers are starting to see it as a brand without focus. Timex is a watch brand making a comeback, climbing back from being a lost brand to becoming a brand with cult status.*

A joint venture labelled BrandEconomics and launched in 2004 has created an interesting juxtaposition of research data by combining the BAV database with the database of EVA ratings developed by financial consultants Stern Stewart & Company. The BrandEconomics approach is based on multivariate

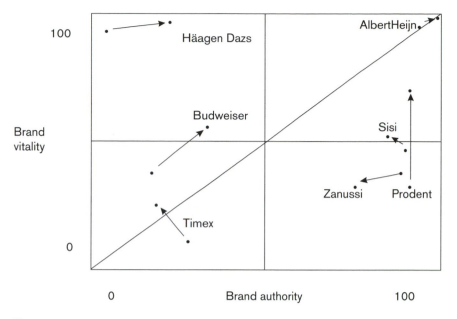

Figure 10.4 Movement of a number of brands in the power grid

analysis of the relationship between brand health and financial performance. In aggregate research across all industries and years, the results suggest that financial factors explain around 55 percent of the differences in the market values of companies, whereas brand factors explain around 25 percent, with other factors (such as "industry context" and the "business cycle") explaining the remaining 20 percent.

The analysts use these data and models to express the market value of a company as a function of its business model and its brand. The effectiveness of a company's business model shows up in its profitability (measured using the EVA spread). The strength and durability of the company's consumer brand shows up in the brand pillars. The model produces estimates of the relative contributions to value creation from improving operating performance versus brand health, and so suggests optimal value-creating strategies for a business.

In 2005, Y&R subsidiary Landor Associates and BrandEconomics released a study of more than 2,500 brands drawn from the BAV database in 2001 to 2004 that identified those brands that exhibited the greatest increases in *brand vitality*, the combination of differentiation and relevance (Figure 10.5). These brands were found to command greater premiums and to have a broader sales footprint as a result of their brand improvements, directly affecting the

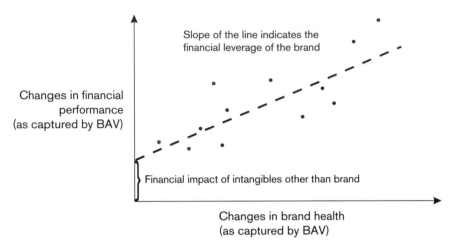

Figure 10.5 Linking financial value to brand health
Source: BrandEconomics

value of their operations and allowing them to expand more easily across categories and geographies, enabling significant future value growth. For each of these, Landor and *Fortune* magazine evaluated key actions the brand owners took to improve the brand's performance, leading to major gains in their financial value. The list included a range of consumer and business-to-business brands, and was topped by the following brands:

❚ Google: internet;
❚ LeapFrog: educational toys;
❚ Sony Cyber-shot: digital cameras;
❚ Sierra Mist: soft drinks;
❚ Subway: quick serve restaurants;
❚ BP: oil and petroleum;
❚ DeWalt: power tools;
❚ iPod: consumer electronics;
❚ Eggo: packaged foods;
❚ Gerber: baby foods.

WPP's "BrandZ"

Many of the member companies of the WPP group draw on a large research database called BrandZ to develop insights about brand positioning and brand strategy. The raw data from BrandZ are collected annually by interviewing consumers and professionals. Each respondent is asked to evaluate brands in a competitive context from a category they actually shop in. The data have considerable face validity since they represent the opinions of people who know the category and who judge a brand solely based on the attributes that are important to them.

In total, BrandZ has asked over 650,000 consumers and professionals across 31 countries to compare over 21,000 brands. For each brand, each person interviewed is assigned to a specific "level" of the brand pyramid shown in Figure 10.6 depending on their responses to a set of questions. The BrandDynamics Pyramid shows the number of consumers of a specific brand who have reached a specific level. The five levels (from high to low) that they can be assigned to are:

- *Bonding*: Rational and emotional attachments to the brand to the exclusion of most other brands.
- *Advantage*: Felt to have an emotional or rational advantage over other brands in the category.
- *Performance*: Felt to deliver acceptable product performance and is on the consumer's short-list.
- *Relevance*: Relevant to consumer's needs, in the right price range or in consideration set.
- *Presence*: Active familiarity based on past trial, saliency, or knowledge of brand promise.

Proprietary research conducted on the database by member companies of WPP using BrandZ data suggests that purchasing loyalty increases at higher levels of the Brand Pyramid – bonding-level consumers are likely to be strong advocates of the brand and to own a higher "share of wallet": the proportion of consumer expenditures within the category that is spent on that brand increases at higher levels of the pyramid.

In BrandZ analyses, the rate at which a brand converts people from one level to the next is first calculated, and compared with what one would expect given the brand's size. This defines the strengths and weaknesses of a brand relative to other brands in its category, regardless of size.

Figure 10.6 The brand dynamics pyramid of BrandZ

Source: BrandEconomics

Every brand has a "signature" that highlights how strongly a brand converts consumers into higher-level loyalists. A cult brand is not widely known or relevant to everyone, but the people for which the brand is relevant are committed and often fanatical fans.

BrandZ researchers have developed a typology of eight brand signatures:

1. *Clean slate*: A brand that is unknown to most consumers. The brand's relevance and advantages are not established. A corporate brand that is not well known to consumers or has not previously marketed to consumers.
2. *Little Tiger*: Relatively unknown but with a strong following amongst a core group. Can become an Olympic brand if it can increase familiarity and relevance to a wider group without alienating its core. It could also continue to develop amongst a loyal group and become a strong group brand.
3. *Weak*: A brand perceived as having little to offer – but still well known enough for many to decide they don't like it.
4. *Specialist*: Relatively well known but not a brand with a mass audience. Likely to be too expensive for most. Has small groups of passionate users, and would have difficulty widening its franchise without alienating core users. Must beware of pricing at too high a premium and becoming irrelevant to users.
5. *Classic*: A well known and well loved brand with a large core following. Good but not great. Must retain its status by constant reinvestment in its product and image.
6. *Olympic*: Well known, well loved with a large core following. Talked about in everyday life as a part of the cultural fabric of the country.
7. *Defenders*: A good balance between product performance and price – but no real product-based or emotionally rooted advantages.
8. *Fading Stars*: Previously known and liked by all. Still relevant to a mass audience, but has lost appeal and now has little product or image-based advantage.

Most companies know how people feel about their brands. And all companies know how their brands are performing in the marketplace. BrandZ links the two and provides managers with a diagnostic tool that evaluates the strength of brands and can relate it to future changes in market share through the company's Brand Voltage™ indicator, a measure of the brand's growth potential given its current size in the market that helps diagnose key drivers of effective marketing programs.

BrandZ analysts typically plot a brand's ubiquity (presence within its category) against its brand voltage to depict the brand's position, that is, the brand's growth potential given its current size in the market. Figure 10.7 shows brand maps for the brand typology, and provides examples of brands in each type.

Most corporate brands have relatively complex brand signatures – a different one for each line of business. British retailer Marks & Spencer (M&S) is a case in point. The company operates in three core businesses: as a department store, an apparel maker, and a grocery retailer. Figure 10.8 shows that consumers are more likely to bond with M&S as a department store than they are as a grocery retailer. The brand has stronger presence as an apparel maker than as either a department store or as a supermarket. M&S is a classic brand as a department store, but lacks style as an apparel manufacturer. As a grocery retailer it is an aspirational brand, costing more than consumers are willing to pay.

Harris Interactive's "EquiTrend"

Originally developed by Total Research Corp. before it was bought by market research firm Harris Interactive, EquiTrend is a study that has relied on a simple measure of "brand equity" to track a total of over 1,000 brands since 1989.

In its annual surveys, EquiTrend asks some 20,000 consumers to provide a "snapshot" evaluation of a brand they are familiar with on five key attributes:

▌ familiarity;
▌ quality;
▌ purchase intent;
▌ brand expectations;
▌ distinctiveness.

Different typologies typically fall in different map positions

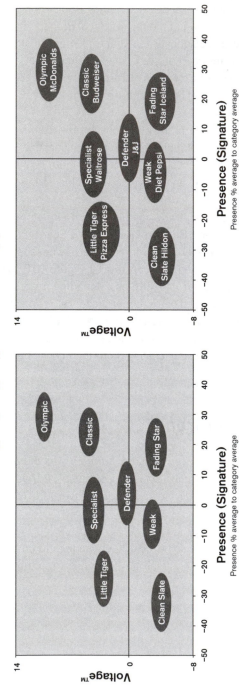

Figure 10.7 Conceptual and empirical BrandZ maps

Source: BrandEconomics

Marks & Spencer as a multi-faced brand
(% of consumers in the UK who bond with the M&S brand as …)

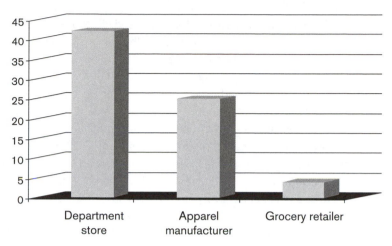

Brand signature™ for Marks & Spencer

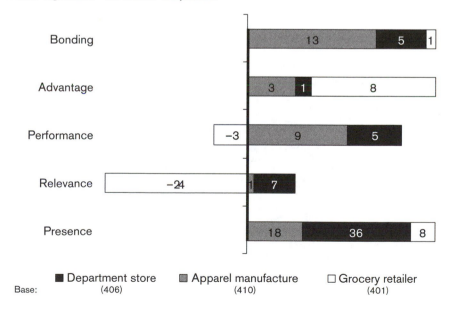

Figure 10.8 Different brand signatures for Marks & Spencer

Figure 10.9 describes the model used in the study. "Perceived quality" is the measure used to describe "brand equity," and the study reports results for about 133 US brands in 39 categories.

Research conducted on the EquiTrend database indicates that the average quality rating among those with opinions on brands is strongly associated with brand liking, trust, pride, and willingness to recommend. For instance, an analysis by Aaker and Jacobson (1994) reported in *Advertising Age* indicated that brand building for 34 major US companies paid off for shareholders. The researchers examined the extent to which brand equity provided information about firm performance that influenced stock prices above and beyond current-period return on investment (ROI). The results showed that stock returns, as expected, were positively related to changes in ROI. They also showed that changes in brand equity mattered. While not quite as large an effect as the market's response to favorable ROI, the results indicated a strong positive association between brand equity and stock market returns. In their book, *Brand Leadership* (2002), Aaker and Joachimsthaler reaffirmed the causal link between brand equity and stock market return that was uncovered using the EquiTrend database. As they put it:

> *Firms experiencing the largest gains in brand equity saw their stock return average 30 percent; conversely, those firms with the largest losses in brand equity saw stock return average a negative 10 percent. And brand equity impact was distinct from that of ROI – the correlation between the two was small. In contrast, there was no impact of advertising on stock return, except that it was captured by brand equity.*

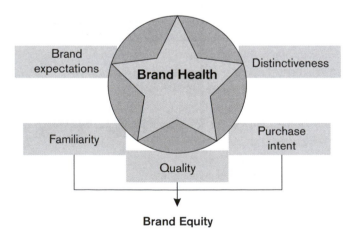

Figure 10.9
EquiTrend's measure of brand equity

The authors suggest that the brand equity/stock return relationship might stem from brand equity's tendency to support a price premium, which contributes to profitability. "This relationship is undoubtedly based upon a two-way causal flow – a strong brand commands a price premium, and a price premium is an important quality cue," they write. "When a high level of perceived quality has been (or can be) created, raising the price not only provides margin dollars but also aids perceptions."

CoreBrand's "Brand power"

CoreBrand is a US based brand development and management firm that tracks the corporate brands of 1,200 companies in 47 industries. The measures collected include familiarity with the company, and favorability on three key attributes: management effectiveness, investment potential, and overall repu-tation. In addition, CoreBrand acquires data on financial performance and communications spending for each company. Familiarity and favorability are combined into a single score termed "brand power", and serves as the dependent variable in CoreBrand's models and is the key measure against which they recommend creating brand-building programs.

"Brand power" is a score based on familiarity and favorability toward a company. Familiarity is the degree to which an audience feels they know a company. The more one feels he knows about a company the more he is favorably disposed. Among those familiar with a company, favorability is the percentage that are favorably disposed toward the company. They like the company's management, reputation, and investment potential. The favorability measure tells companies whether their story is selling or not. Paid media advertising is one of the ways companies build brands. But, it is not necessarily the only or most effective way. Some would say that paid media advertising is less effective today because people's media consumption habits continue to change at a rapid rate. Table 10.2 shows partial results from the Brand Power survey conducted in 2004. Top rated brands include Coca-Cola, Johnson & Johnson, UPS, and FedEx. Oddly enough, however, the study rated Google a lowly 686 in the third quarter of 2004, and dropped it further to 1,007 in the fourth quarter. Given Google's broad consumer appeal and extraordinarily successful IPO the following year, this ranking seems a bit odd.

CoreBrand contends that its proprietary analyses across industries show that advertising spending is one of the chief drivers of brand power. Companies that advertise more tend to have higher brand power. This is

Table 10.2 Brand power of selected brands

Company	Q3 2004	Q4 2004
Coca-Cola Company	1	1
Johnson & Johnson	2	2
UPS (United Parcel Services, Inc.)	3	3
FedEx Corp.	4	4
PepsiCo, Inc.	6	5
Land O'Lakes, Inc.	14	6
Campbell Soup	8	7
Hallmark Cards, Inc.	7	8
Harley-Davidson, Inc.	9	9
Hershey Foods Corp.	13	10
Lowe's Companies, Inc.	5	11
Microsoft Corp.	10	12
General Electric Co.	11	13
IBM	15	14
Walt Disney Company, The	12	15
Sony Corp.	16	16
Toyota Motor Corp.	19	17
Colgate-Palmolive Company	17	18
American Express Company	18	19
Levi Strauss and Co.	23	20
Home Depot, Inc., The	25	21
Wal-Mart Stores, Inc.	21	22
Starbucks Corp.	24	23
Quaker Oats	20	24
General Mills, Inc.	22	25

Source: CoreBrand (2004)

because advertising has a measurable impact on sales when it gets through the media clutter, and companies who spend a great deal on advertising usually also make coordinated efforts to orchestrate it with their other branding and communications initiatives as well.

From analysis of more than 800 *Fortune 1000* companies, CoreBrand also claims to have demonstrated that corporate branding efforts have a significant, measurable impact on financial performance. Specifically, they report that a stronger corporate brand image positively impacts stock price by an average of 5–7 percent, and that the results vary by industry. When managed properly, CoreBrand founder Jim Gregory contends that brand ROI effects can be even greater. Unfortunately, no empirical evidence has been provided for academic scrutiny, so these results remain somewhat questionable.

Stock price and Brand Power influence

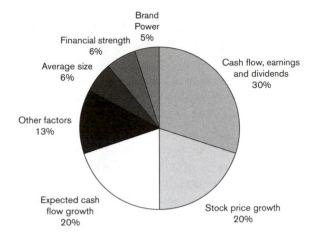

Factors impacting corporate Brand Power

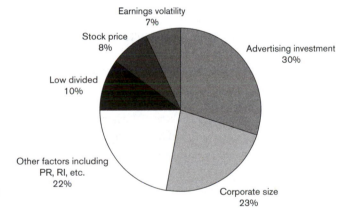

Figure 10.10
Brand power:
drivers and
effects

Source: McNaughton
(2004)

Figure 10.10 reports how CoreBrand describes the drivers of "brand power" and its effect on market value.

Fortune's Most Admired Companies

Fortune's annual study of the "Most Admired Companies in America" (AMAC) is the most prominent monitoring system used by academics and practitioners to measure corporate reputations. The project was launched in 1982 and provides the longest-running, relatively consistent source of empirical data on corporate reputations that can be drawn on for research and analysis. Practitioners also find it useful because the database provides them access to benchmarks.

Methodologically, reputation ratings are derived by inviting participation from a large group of managers, analysts, and corporate directors. Questionnaires are circulated among potential respondents in the companies to be rated, and "official responses" are obtained. In each questionnaire, raters are asked to respond to eight questions that constitute the "key reputation attributes" on scales from 0 to 10:

1. quality of management;
2. quality of products or services;
3. financial soundness;
4. ability to attract, develop, and keep talented people;
5. use of corporate assets;
6. value as long-term investment;
7. innovativeness;
8. community and environmental responsibility.

Fortune reports that there are more than 10,000 respondents to their survey each year, and provide ratings of the largest companies in their own industries. Respondents are grouped by industry, and the top-ten rated companies are then determined from those ratings. In the last few years, *Fortune* has also added an overall question that muddles the water somewhat – it consists of a single question posed to respondents and that asks them to name the ten companies they most admire.

Most of the academic research on corporate reputations conducted since the 1980s has relied on the *Fortune* ratings. A number of critics have also pointed to the limitations of the database: (1) its financial bias – managers are more likely to assess on the basis of a more elaborated understanding of corporate financials, (2) its stakeholder bias – the data represent, not a broad measure of reputation, but the viewpoint of a financially oriented subset of stakeholders relatively unconcerned with questions of social responsibility or workplace environment and, (3) the lack of theory behind attribute selection, and the failure to apply rigorous methodology in conducting scale development (such as the use of multi-item scales, reliability analysis, or factor analysis).

Early studies that used the *Fortune* ratings as measures of reputation tended to treat the eight attributes as if they were independent of each other (Chakravarthy, 1986; McGuire *et al.*, 1988). In their seminal analysis, however, Fombrun and Shanley (1990) showed that the ratings were highly correlated and loaded on a single factor. They concluded that when respondents rated firms on these seemingly distinct attributes, they were assessing a single underlying construct that could be called "reputation". Following the work of Fombrun and Shanley (1990) and Fryxell and Wang (1994), most researchers now recognize the "financial halo" in the *Fortune* ratings and either remove it statistically, or work with it directly (Sobol and Farrely, 1989; Dowling and Roberts, 2003). *Fortune* itself now recognizes the uni-dimensionality of the construct and no longer even provides the single attribute ratings.

Many researchers have sought to establish the relationship between the *Fortune* ratings and other variables. For instance, Fombrun and Shanley (1990) found that, although the ratings were best predicted by financial performance variables, they were also influenced by measures of the overall visibility of the company in the media, their advertising expenditures, and their charitable contributions, thereby suggesting that respondents may unconsciously factor other constituents' concerns into their judgments.

Table 10.3 shows a chart of the most admired companies in the USA from *Fortune*'s data in 2004 and 2005, and juxtaposes it against operating results (profitability). Although many of the most admired companies nominated are doing well, there is clearly no simple relationship between returns and reputation. This is confirmed by Fombrun and Shanley's (1990) original study, as well as by other studies reported since the Reputation Institute's first conference held in 1997 at New York University's Stern School of Business (Srivastava *et al.*, 1997; Black *et al.*, 2000).

In sum, despite their availability, there are serious limitations to relying on *Fortune*'s ratings as a comprehensive measure of corporate reputation. The ratings reflect the biases of a largely managerial stakeholder group, and the attributes represented in the instrument are not comprehensive. Finally, *Fortune* has made little effort to test the validity and reliability of the attributes internationally.

Many of the weaknesses inherent in using *Fortune*'s measure of corporate reputation are addressed in research conducted by the Reputation Institute since 1999, and mirrored in the early development of the Harris–Fombrun

Table 10.3 The USA's most admired companies

Top ten		Total return	
Rank	Company	2004 (%)	1999–2004 (%)
1.	Dell	24.0	-3.7
2.	General Electric	20.7	-4.8
3.	Starbucks	88.1	38.8
4.	Wal-Mart Stores	0.4	-4.7
5.	Southwest Airlines	1.0	8.8
6.	FedEx	46.4	19.4
7.	Berkshire Hathaway	4.3	9.4
8.	Microsoft	9.1	-12.4
9.	Johnson & Johnson	25.1	8.0
10.	Procter and Gamble	11.9	2.1
	Top ten average	23.1	6.1
	S&P 500	10.88	-2.3

Source: *Fortune*, March 7, 2005

Note: Survey asked businesspeople to vote for 10 companies that they admired most, from any industry

Reputation Quotient®, and the more recent RepTrak® system introduced in 2005.

Harris-Fombrun "Reputation Quotient" (RQ)

The Reputation Quotient (RQ) is an instrument developed by Charles Fombrun with the market research firm Harris Interactive. Between 1999 and 2005, the Reputation Institute sponsored annual RQ surveys of consumers whose topline results have been featured in the *Wall Street Journal* and other prominent newspapers around the world. Since 1999, the RQ has been used to measure corporate reputations in over 26 countries.

The RQ measures corporate reputations by asking respondents to rate companies on 20 items grouped around six dimensions: (1) emotional appeal, (2) products and services, (3) vision and leadership, (4) workplace environment, (5) social responsibility, and (6) financial performance. Figure 10.11 summarizes the standardized structure of the RQ model. These six dimensions and their 20 underlying attributes were determined through a mix of qualitative and quantitative research conducted in the USA, in Australia, and

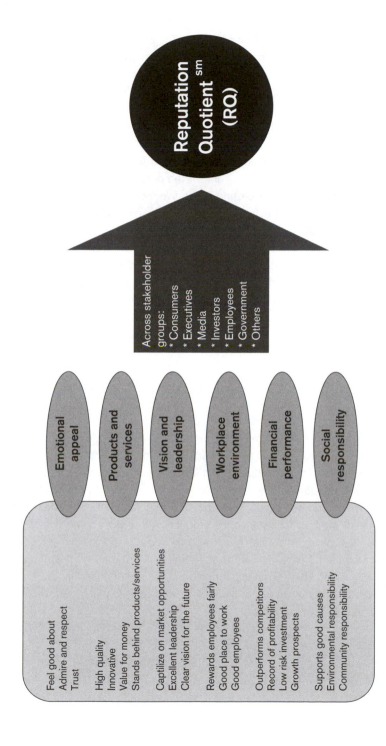

Figure 10.11 The six dimensions and 20 attributes of the Harris–Fombrun Reputation Quotien (RQ)

in Europe between 1998 and 2000. To get at these attributes, existing measures of reputation were compiled from examining the criteria used by *Fortune*'s AMAC, and by rival ratings in *Asia Business*, in *Far Eastern Economic Review*, in Germany's *Managers Magazine*, and in the UK's *Management Today*.

Literature research and an analysis of the strong and weak points of existing methods were used to create a prototype of the instrument. The prototype was then tested in a pilot project that examined consumer perceptions of the airline industry and of the personal computer industry. Items were subsequently adjusted, and qualitative focus groups were run with three stakeholder groups (technical, professional, and general) in three different continents (USA, Netherlands, and Malaysia). The Reputation Institute used these discussions to determine how people in different parts of the world thought about companies: which attributes were dominant, were there differences between countries, should these attributes be standardized as part of the RQ? Although there were differences across countries and among stakeholder groups, the researchers concentrated on the commonalities and built a final version of the RQ that has been applied since to both generic country studies and in specific company analyses (Fombrun *et al.*, 2000).

The RQ projects were important in addressing weaknesses of the *Fortune* survey. By surveying consumers, they provided a different stakeholder viewpoint on the reputations of companies. By using 20 attributes rather than eight, they overcame some of the limitations of the single item scale used by *Fortune* to measure complex dimensions. What made the RQ a particularly powerful contributor to reputation measurement was its ability to untangle the possible reputation drivers by close examination of the interrelationships between attributes, dimensions, and an overall rating of corporate reputation. In most countries, for instance, the products and services dimension has proven the most powerful predictor, followed by social responsibility and workplace environment. This reinforces the stakeholder interpretation of reputation – the public cares little for financial performance and leadership, in contrast to financial and managerial stakeholders who tend to place performance and leadership above all others.

International applications of the RQ in Australia, Denmark, Netherlands, France, Germany, the UK, and South Africa made possible interesting comparisons of the drivers of reputation in those countries. Much work can still be done with the RQ databases to develop and test hypotheses about reputations across countries and across stakeholder groups.

Another strong point of the RQ approach is its ability to guide corporate communication. Analyses of responses on attributes can provide useful information to managers eager to identify the highest leverage points for improving reputation with targeted groups. A segmentation analysis of RQ results demonstrates that some sub-groups tend to esteem a company more than other sub-groups. Such an analysis provides potentially valuable information to communicators interested in developing strategic targets. Table 10.4 indicates the prescriptive implications that might derive from understanding: (1) how well a company is rated by stakeholders on specific dimensions, and (2) what it can do to influence those ratings through strategic communication. Figure 10.12 indicates how the dimensions of a reputation scorecard such as the RQ can be used as key performance indicators against which to set objectives for improvement by the corporate communication department.

Table 10.4 How managers can impact reputation with corporate communication

	Marketing Communication	Investor relations	Employee Communication	Public relations
Emotional appeal	XXX	X	X	X
Vision and leadership		X	X	X
Social responsibility		X	X	XX
Workplace environment			XXX	X
Products and services	XXXX			
Financial performance		XXXX	X	X

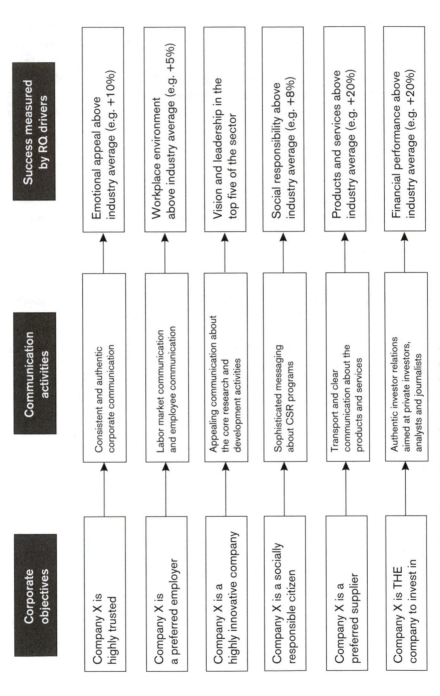

Figure 10.12 Using RQ dimensions as key performance indicators

The Reputation Institute's "RepTrak® System"

The Reputation Institute (RI) has been studying the dynamics of reputation since 1997. In 2005, RI introduced the RepTrak® system, a cutting-edge toolkit designed to track and analyze corporate reputations. The system relies on the RepTrak® Scorecard – an instrument developed by the RI in 2005 that tracks 23 key performance indicators grouped around seven core drivers that were created from qualitative and quantitative research conducted in six countries.

The starting point for creating RepTrak® was the cumulative research on the RQ conducted around the world since 1999. The first step was to address some fundamental weaknesses of the Harris–Fombrun RQ instrument that crystallized over the years (Fombrun *et al.*, 2000; Gardberg, 2005). In particular:

1. the six reputation dimensions identified in the RQ, although conceptually distinct, did not factor together empirically;
2. RQ studies demonstrated consistently high levels multi-colinearity among the 20 attributes used to measure corporate reputation;
3. the dimension of "emotional appeal" has proven to be very highly correlated with a measure of overall reputation, suggesting the possibility that they are merely components of a single dimension;
4. the dependent variable "reputation" used to partition variance in reputation was a single item variable, and subject to higher sampling error;
5. all attributes in the RQ carry equal weights, despite their demonstrably different impacts on overall reputation.

Additionally, researchers had raised questions about the validity of the scale internationally, and the need for further examination of reputation attributes since the wave of corporate scandals that had washed over the business community since 2001, and might have changed how stakeholders viewed corporate reputations.

The Reputation Institute therefore embarked on a journey to remedy the weaknesses of the RQ instrument. Focus groups were held in six countries in spring 2005. Prompted and unprompted questions confirmed many of the existing attributes used by the RQ, but suggested some additional attributes involving "ethics" and "governance" that were not measured by RQ, and new wordings for some existing attributes.

A new prototype for measuring corporate reputations was therefore created from the qualitative research. Preliminary quantitative tests were then held with consumers in six countries using a continuous online polling process. After the first two months of data collection, data sets were combined across the six countries and factor analyses were conducted. Seven factors emerged from the analysis, involving 23 attributes. Figure 10.13 shows the structure of the RepTrak® Scorecard that was created based on these factor analyses.

Multivariate regressions were then run to examine the relative contributions of attributes to dimensions and dimensions to an overall measure of reputation constructed from four items – an overall reputation measure, and the three "emotional appeal" attributes (like, trust, and admire) that were used in the RQ. The predictive strength of each attribute on its dimension score was used to represent the net contribution the attribute made to the overall reputation measure.

The RepTrak® is the world's first standardized and integrated tool for tracking corporate reputations internationally across stakeholder groups. Companies choose the data they want to see in their RepTrak® and can juxtapose both perceptual surveys with analysis of media content. For instance, tracking polls conducted daily around the world provide companies with direct access to the perceptions of consumers, investors, and employees.

Real-time monitoring of selected groups makes it possible for companies to see if branding activities are inducing the kinds of supportive behaviors they were intended for, if PR strategies are influencing public opinion, and if media coverage is hurting or helping the company's reputation. All this, benchmarked against your key rivals.

The strength of the RI's RepTrak® instrument is that, unlike the RQ, the dimensions of RepTrak® are statistically independent of each other. This reduces problems associated with multi-colinearity in data analysis and strengthens conclusions about the relative impact that specific attributes and dimensions have on the company's overall reputation.

More importantly, however, the RepTrak® Scorecard is used by the Reputation Institute as part of an integrated analysis of corporate communication. Reputations are viewed as outcomes produced as stakeholders interpret what they hear and see based on the company's communications and on media coverage. Figure 10.14 describes the integrated approach applied with the RepTrak® System.

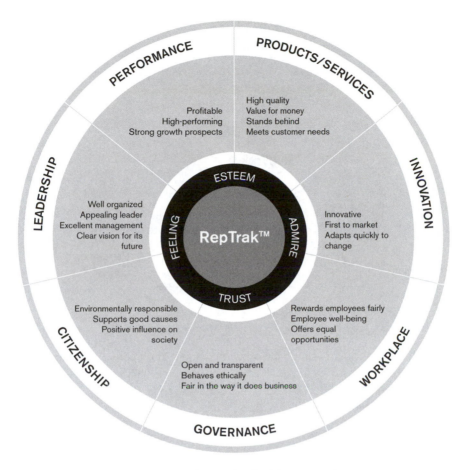

Figure 10.13   The Reputation Institute's RepTrak® scorecard

Figure 10.15 describes the results of an application of the RepTrak® system in one company. It shows that:

▌ perceptions of the company's products were the most important driver of the company's overall reputation, followed by perceptions of its "vision" and "financial performance";

▌ a comparison of the company's media coverage against its press releases demonstrated that four attributes were particularly well received by the media;

▌ the company's press releases were well leveraged for these four attributes, but not so for the other reputation attributes.

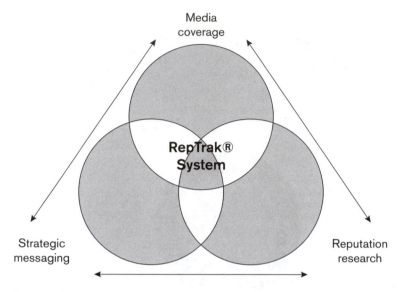

Figure 10.14   The RepTrak® system

A RepTrak® analysis clearly offers managers of corporate communication systematic insight into the effectiveness of their initiatives. It also presents a powerful platform for addressing areas that the company is not leveraging and that could therefore improve reputation.

Conclusions

Reputational ratings offer a powerful way to draw attention to public perceptions of firms' relative success at meeting stakeholder expectations. Although most reputation ratings in use have limited validity, their growing popularity offers the tantalizing possibility that better-constructed polls of the public's beliefs about firms can capture and stimulate both the economic and the social dimensions of corporate performance.

Design a strategy together that is beneficial to the entire organization in the area of reputation management. Each department should be able to contribute to the success of the organization. The communication department should ensure that everyone's interest is taken into consideration in creating a management plan for reputation management. A powerful way to galvanize integration is to create a briefing for external agencies providing assistance with reputation research, corporate branding, and corporate communication. The briefing should address:

- Which business level should be the focus of the company's reputation building efforts – the company as a whole or particular business units?
- Which stakeholder groups' opinions matter most to the future success of the company?
- Which competitors does the company want to benchmark itself against?
- What objectives will the reputation research fulfill for the company?
- Will research be used to inform decisions only once, or is tracking important to the company?

Answering these questions raises implicit questions about the organization of the communication function itself – a subject to which we now turn in the final chapter of this book.

Discussion Questions

1. Describe the advantages and disadvantages of using attitude measurement scales.
2. What are the principal weaknesses of relying on *Fortune*'s AMAC data and method to measure corporate reputations?
3. How would you compare the BrandAsset® Valuator approach to the Reputation Institute's RepTrak® method?
4. Explain how RepTrak® results can be used in the daily practice of a communication department in an organization of your choice.

Note

1. Source: ThinkExist.com Quotations. "Henri Fredric Amiel quotes". *ThinkExist.com Quotations Online* 1 March 2006. 4 April 2006.
2. Researchers interested in measuring corporate social responsibility have relied heavily on the ratings produced by KLD, a private ratings group that grades companies on various features of the social performance of over 3,000 US companies. Their ratings provide a window to the "reality" of corporate behavior in selected areas likely to affect reputation, and more closely resemble expert ratings than reputational measures.

A driver analysis was carried out for this US company based on examining the perceptions of consumers, employees, and influentials. The results indicated that the most significant driver of reputation was perceptions of the company's products.

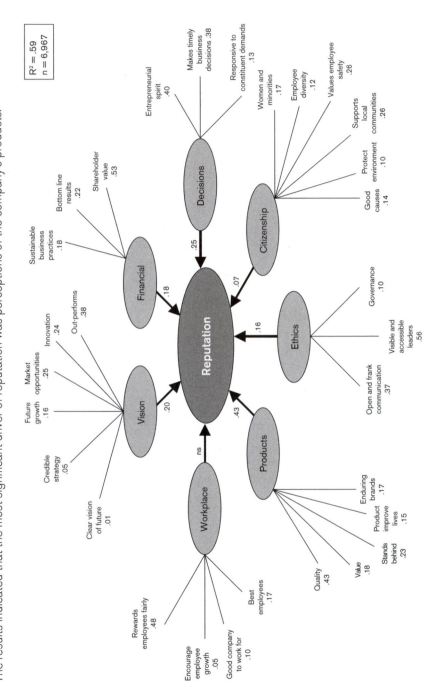

R² = .59
n = 6,967

Further data analysis led researchers to single out four key reputation attributes: comparisons of press releases against media coverage for these four reputation attributes showed that there was a high rate of return from press releases involving them. The most heavily mentioned attribute was "shows strong prospects for future growth," followed by "has a credible strategy for competing." Both had positive ratios of favorable to unfavorable coverage.

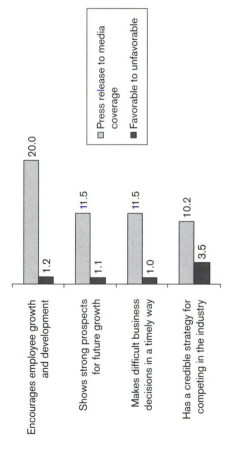

Figure 10.15 A RepTrak® driver analysis

11 ORGANIZING CORPORATE COMMUNICATION

Working together, handling the job well,
Each of us should be like a human cell.
Who knows the part what to do,
To make the next person's job easier, is a must, we always knew.
We are really working for each other,
Like a link in a chain or a drop of water.
Fair, good leadership can guide,
Every business into success and harmony, worldwide.

LaSoaphia QuXazs

The final chapter of this book examines the organizational aspects of corporate communication. How should a company structure its communication function in order to implement reputation management? Although organization theory tells us that "one size doesn't fit all", it does suggest various considerations managers should take into account when making decisions about the most effective way to implement a reputation-sensitive, corporate communication system. We address them here.

The first prescription is that *structure should always follow strategy* (Chandler, 1962) – and not vice versa. A company should therefore design its communication function in a way that reflects its business strategy. A company whose corporate strategy is built around unrelated diversification should have a very different communication structure than a company whose strategy is built around a set of highly related businesses. Similarly, a company whose business strategy is anchored around a business strategy of "differentiation" should organize its communication structure to reflect that strategy – and will do so differently than a company pursuing a "low-cost" strategy in the market-place. We will examine various implications of strategy for the management of corporate communication.

A second prescription is that the leadership of the communication function must be *included in the process of strategy formulation* of the company. That means involvement in the dominant coalition if the communication function is to play a strategic role in major decisions that are likely to require communication support and to affect the company's reputation. All too often companies consider communications only as a tactical tool of strategy implementation rather than of strategy formulation.

A third organizational prescription is that the communication function be treated as a *creator of value* – and get measured and rewarded accordingly. In many companies, communication is viewed as purely a "staff" function, and so is not regarded as a contributor to the "bottom-line". In order to make a "business case" for corporate communication, the function must commit itself to measuring its activities, tracking the effects of its initiatives on a set of key performance indicators, and receive rewards and punishments when its actions do not meet the strategic objectives set for it.

Finally, as we have expressed throughout this book, the focus of the communication function must be *holistic* – internal and external communications must be organized to build, maintain, and defend the reputation capital of the company. To provide anything less is to abdicate a fundamental responsibility of the function for corporate communication.

Structuring communications for strategy implementation

The communication system must serve the organization's strategic choices. Decision-making about the organization of corporate communication should therefore be taken in light of larger decisions made about the company's broader corporate and competitive strategies (Rumelt, 1974; Chandler, 1962). As the well-known organization theorists March and Simon (1958) put it: "The purpose of organizational structure is to achieve more calculable and predictable control over organizational members in order to enhance organizational performance."

Helping to create synergy at the corporate-level

A large literature on corporate strategy proposes that companies can be distinguished in terms of the "relatedness" of their corporate umbrellas (Rumelt, 1974). Corporate strategy involves the strategic selection of: (1) how diversified a portfolio of businesses to hold, and (2) how related to make the businesses in that portfolio. Much of the early research on corporate strategy set out to demonstrate the performance implications of diversification, and concluded that there were significant financial benefits to increasing the degree of "relatedness" in the portfolio. Higher operating profits were found to accrue to companies pursuing related diversification because of their implicit ability to capitalize on synergies of different types across businesses – synergies in: (1) marketing and distribution, or (2) production and technology.

A weakness of that literature was its limited focus on differences in implementation – after all, differences in performance would also result if some companies were simply better at *implementing* diversification than others. In fact, the ability to capitalize on any synergies across businesses depends heavily on managers' ability to implement appropriate communication systems.

"*Marketing synergies*" consists of the ability to exploit cross-selling opportunities across business units by virtue of identifying common customers and setting out to meet their needs with the products of different businesses in the corporate portfolio. Banks that diversified into the broader "financial services" sector were often motivated by the desire to exploit marketing synergies. Communication conglomerates such as WPP, Omnicom, or Interpublic were also similarly motivated to capitalize on offering integrated advertising, public relations, and lobbying services to a pool of shared clients. Cross-selling to common clients requires centralization of the communications function – an ability to gather information about these clients, share them across business-unit departments, and present a "common face" to clients. Many of these mergers also sought to exploit distribution synergies – the ability to reach out to and service the needs of those clients in more customized fashion, with all its implications for presenting a common "face" to the client.

A corporate strategy of related diversification that is motivated by a search for "*production synergies*" requires enhanced coordination of internal communications. Diversification by the global auto industry into parts manufacturing and the adoption of shared technology platforms, for instance, was motivated by a desire to consolidate operations and decrease costs incurred across business units involved in related businesses. In the 1990s, the mergers of Daimler-Benz and Chrysler, the numerous acquisitions made by Ford and

General Motors, were heavily motivated by the search for production and technological synergies. The consequence of related diversifications is the consolidation and centralization of corporate communication – and the pressure it places on the function to cohere internal communication in particular.

The idea that a well-designed strategy of related diversification could contribute to bottom-line financial performance depends very much on the company's ability to cohere relationships and communications across the corporate portfolio. The pragmatic implications for corporate communication have been:

■ a marked *centralization* of communication responsibilities in the headquarters office, and shift of control from the business-unit level to the corporate office;
■ the need for increased *coordination* within the headquarters office across the historically separate functions involved in communications, including advertising, public relations, and employee communications;
■ growing appreciation for the need for corporate communication – the importance of developing a reputation platform for the company as a whole;
■ increased interest in developing integrated solutions – the use of a global agency to present the company across audiences and channels.

Fostering competitiveness at the business level

Whereas corporate strategy examines the degree of diversification in the corporate portfolio and the search for synergies across business units, students of business strategy are concerned about the relative competitiveness of individual business units in that portfolio (Porter, 1980). They take an outside-in approach that places the marketplace, competition, and the customer as the starting point of strategy formulation. Academic research on competitive strategy has distinguished two principal competitive positions in most markets: (1) the pursuit of a low-cost strategy, and (2) the pursuit of a differentiation strategy. Both can be profitable, but each has different and compelling implications for internal structure and corporate communication.

Companies pursuing a *low-cost competitive strategy* are typically pushed to do so by intense rivalry in the industry, and the need to under-price rivals in order to attract customers. The low-cost strategy therefore calls for highly efficient line operations, minimum expenditures on staff activities, and increased commitment and reliance on an infrastructure that keeps costs low. A company that has successfully pursued a low-cost position in the computer industry is Dell. The role of corporate communication in implementing a low-cost position is to drive a single message (about the company's low costs and low prices) across channels, and to avoid burdening communication channels internally with advertising campaigns that over-inflate costs, thereby driving down competitiveness.

In contrast, companies competing through a strategy of *competitive differentiation* can only do so by implementing a more costly program of centralized corporate communication designed to build a reputation platform for the company that is consistent and distinctive from that of its rivals. The search for distinctiveness calls for more aligned employees, an ability to pull together behind a common vision that relies on internal creativity, enhanced coordination, and greater harmony of purpose. Differentiators spend more on communicating both internally and externally with their diverse audiences. Communication is more important to their strategic moves because it requires mobilized support from employees, localized responsiveness to customer demands, and a willingness to customize programs, communications, and initiatives to reinforce the company's competitive positioning. Inevitably it costs more, and significantly empowers the business unit.

Supporting the "core competence" of the whole organization

In contrast to the outside-in orientation of traditional corporate and business strategy research, a third stream takes an inside-out approach by emphasizing the role of "core competence" in driving a unified positioning for companies. Here, enduring competitive advantage comes from a company's ability to own a "core competence" that makes it distinctive, unique, and inimitable (Prahalad and Hamel, 1990; Albert and Whetten, 1985). A core competence can be any combination of applied knowledge, skills, and attitudes. In the long run, competitiveness derives from an ability to build and sustain core competences at a lower cost and more speedily than competitors. The real sources of competence are to be found in management's ability to consolidate corporate-wide technologies and production skills into competences, through which individual businesses can adapt quickly to changing circumstances.

The role of a business unit is to help to further develop the company's core competences, and the corporate center should not be just another layer of management, but must add value by articulating the strategic architecture that guides the process of competence building.

To qualify as a "core competence", a specific competency must fulfill two key conditions: (1) make a significant contribution to the benefits perceived by the customer, and (2) be difficult for competitors to imitate. Both are supported and strengthened by well executed corporate communication. On one hand, the communication system is responsible for ensuring that customer exposure to the company reinforces the benefits of the company's products. On the other, established relationships with stakeholders are themselves a key way of securing adequate resources for the company, of building a beachhead against rivals, and of making the company's position difficult to imitate.

Core competences are built through a process of continuous improvement and enhancement that fuels leadership in the design and development of a product class. It requires constant interaction between top management and business unit managers. The corporate communication system is therefore front and center in developing and sustaining a core competence. Corporate communication is also important in preventing core competences from developing into "core rigidities" – a form of internal inertia that can prevent the company from adapting quickly enough to changes in the environment (Miller, 1990). Successful companies are often built around core competences that can fuel their demise because they are locked into past choices that no longer reflect current circumstances. A crucial function of the communication system is therefore also to ensure that disconfirming data and research inconsistent with the company's operating paradigm also get heard at the top of the organization.

Inclusion in strategy formulation

If corporate communication is to operate in support of strategy implementation, the senior corporate communication officers should also be key participants in the strategy *formulation* process. That means reporting directly to the office of the chief executive, a seat on the strategic planning committee, and close involvement in the design of execution of outreach efforts targeted to customers, investors, and employees. Naturally this does not mean direct *responsibility* for all of these specialized functions. But it does point to the need for a skilled set of professionals capable of holding their own with senior line managers, and a degree of veto power over decisions that may be financially sound, but that do not make sense operationally for subtle reasons of alignment, image, identity, or reputation.

Building a strategic communication function

It is important to distinguish between communication as a "professional function" and the ongoing communications that are part of everyday activities in the company. We are concerned here with the professional communication function itself (Grunig and Grunig, 1989; Grunig, 1992; van Ruler and de Lange, 1995). The routine daily activities of the communication function include writing press releases, organizing press conferences, maintaining relationships with key stakeholder groups, organizing investor calls, writing speeches and creating corporate presentations for top managers to deliver, fundraising, managing trade shows, preparing institutional advertising, monitoring public opinion. Table 11.1 summarizes the key operational and strategic tasks that communication managers carry out in each of the five main specialty areas described in Chapter 8. Communication activities in each specialty area have a rich tradition and knowledge base of their own, and follow a long list of normative guidelines. There is a canon of accepted principles for producing annual reports, for running analyst calls, for handling media. The role of the senior officers of the communication function largely consists of ensuring, however, that they are grounded in a common denominator – the reputation platform and corporate story of the organization (Fombrun and van Riel, 2004).

Cranfield distinguishes between different phases in the "production" of a communication message: research, planning, coordination, administration, and finally the production. He also names a few other issues: community participation and advisory activities. Kitchen (1997) distinguishes between five roles in the communication function:

- *Communication technician*: a strong operational role that produces concrete communication messages;
- *Expert prescriber*: often an external consultant who helps determine the strategic course of action;
- *Facilitator*: intermediary role of a communication manager;
- *Bridge-builder* who can match people inside and outside the organization;
- *Problem-solving facilitator*: active solving of communication problems at strategic level.

A former head of corporate communications for major multinationals, Peter Knoers (2001) confirms these five roles, but also sees a more strategic role for the communication function in steering corporate communication policy. He explicitly points to the constant tug of war required to get attention for

Table 11.1 The principal activities of the communication function

Function	Execution	Strategy
Investor relations	Creating press releases, organizing roadshows, webcasts Organizing press conference Informal discussions with analysts Creating standard IR presentation	Planning the long-term direction concerning the style the organization chooses and how to engage in IR communication (in terms of contents, channels, and frequency) Determining measurable norms that can be used to determine the degree of success
Internal communication	Intranet House style Corporate presentations	Planning the long-term direction concerning the style the organization chooses and how to organize the IC-structure, contents, climate, and flow Determining measurable norms that can be used to determine the degree of success
Marketing communication	Preparing print and AV material Preparing and supporting trade shows Briefing ad-agencies Organizing media placements Sponsoring and fundraising	Planning the long-term direction concerning the positioning of the various PMCs related to the positioning of the corporate brand Determining measurable norms for communication at PMC level and for the relation between product and corporate levels
Public affairs	Informal discussion with governments Writing speeches Counseling top management (commissioning) research	Creating a long-term plan in which the most important relations with governments are listed and in which one explains what one wants to achieve Determining, who is to do this within the organization Determining measurable norms that can be used to determine the degree of success

continued

Table 11.1 continued

Function	Execution	Strategy
Issues management	Write speeches	Create a long-term plan in which it is made clear which issues can play a role and a direction is chosen to handle them
	Discussion with stakeholders	
	Press relations	
	Monitoring issues	Determining the responsibilities and who is responsible in measurable terms

communication themes at the strategic level. Another role he recognizes is as a private consultant to senior managers, acting almost like "corporate therapists" in listening to top managers and injecting appropriate comments that help them put things into perspective. Though seldom specified in job descriptions, these roles may be among the more important and rewarded activities of the communication function and its leadership.

In Table 11.2, we draw on van Ruler (2003) to contrast four dominant models for managing the communication function. Each model recognizes a more or less strategic role for the function. For the company as a whole, it is important to clarify the expectations held of the communication function. Only when expectations are clarified can we actually measure whether the communication function is delivering true economic value to the company.

In practice, the communication function is organized in many different ways across companies. In most cases, however, internal communication, investor relations, public affairs, and issues management are generally grouped together into a single staff function, whereas marketing communication is almost always embedded within business units and treated as a line function. In essence, the difference between line and staff managers can be described colloquially as the difference between "giving orders" and "giving advice". It suggests that the job of the communication function in most companies is primarily to advise and support line managers in the business units. This calls for a service orientation to staffing the communication function.

In most strategically oriented companies we have encountered, we have found that the head of the communication function almost always reports directly to the CEO. Reporting to the head of corporate communication are generally the specialists from media relations, internal communication, public affairs, and investor relations. To be effective, physical proximity to the CEO is also a useful integration mechanism. Business units in these large companies also generally have strong communication functions designed to cater to business-level stakeholders, further exacerbating the fragmentation problem. Figure 11.1 diagrams the typical structure of a communication function.

Table 11.2 Four models for managing corporate communication

Model	Information model	Persuasion model	Intermediary model	Reflective model
Variable				
Focus	Adequate spread of information	Adequate profiling of plans/decisions	Adequate support of the decision-making	Internal reflection on frames in the organizational openness
Intervention strategy	Announcing decisions	Persuade target audiences	Interaction between stakeholders and management	Monitoring and analysis of frames
Specialist's key tactic	Produce means	Control over all communication	Control of the dialogue in the strategic decision-making	Strategic advice for adequate response on the frames found
Indicator of success	Recognition/ media attention	Image of audiences	Trust of stakeholders	Public legitimacy

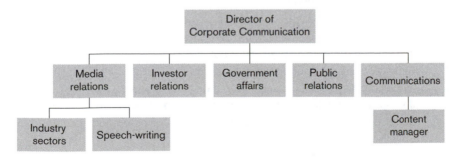

Figure 11.1 The structure of the typical communication function

Marketing communication is the only specialty communication function that falls outside the staff roles and typically gets treated as a line function. The ideal location for such a function depends in part on the nature and scope of the tasks the function is expected to fulfil.

Contributing to value creation

Communicators frequently bemoan their inability in making a "business case" for what they do, and in particular for reputation management (Fombrun and van Riel, 2004). This has been the holy grail of the communication function for some time – but has also proven elusive for the denizens of most staff functions, including corporate foundations, departments of community affairs, human resources, corporate libraries, and even of marketing and technology departments. Each one is increasingly tasked with creating a "business case" for itself to justify its budgets.

The business case for corporate communication is the same business case one would make for reputation management. It consists of three components. First, communication affects the operating performance of a company, and so its profitability. Second, profitability affects market perceptions of the company's future prospects – and so influences a company's market value. Third, the company's operating activities themselves contribute to building "reputation capital" – a shadow asset whose value encompasses the equity hidden in both a company's product brands and corporate brand, and that describes the positive regard in which it is held by all of the company's stakeholders (Fombrun and van Riel, 2004).

A study of 125 US manufacturing businesses compared the relative effects of industry structure, competitive strategy, and company-specific differences (Bharadwaj, 1995). The results confirmed the powerful effects of reputation on operating results. Factors associated with the industry's overall structure accounted for only a small percentage of observed variation in business performance. Competitive strategy variables such as product quality and sales force expenditures were not statistically significant in explaining variance in business performance, but company "market share" was. Finally, of all the company-specific variables, reputation, and brand equity of the business unit were found to be the best predictors of variation in business unit performance. Good reputation and high levels of brand equity come from effective corporate communication.

The higher levels of operating performance that result from having a good reputation virtually guarantee that a company will receive favorable endorsements from stakeholders and the media. As we described in Chapter 10, an early analysis of the *Fortune* AMAC ratings showed that reputational ratings are heavily influenced by a company's size, advertising, operating performance, market value, and media visibility – thereby confirming the idea that a company's operating performance, market value, and strategic behavior are heavily intertwined (Fombrun and Shanley, 1990).

The relationship is described in Figure 11.2 as the "Reputation Value Cycle". It illustrates how financial value and stakeholder support are dynamically intertwined: endorsements build value, and enable a company to expense funds on corporate activities such as advertising, philanthropy, and citizenship that generate media endorsements, attract investors, and add financial value. The net effect is a reinforcing loop through which communication, recognition, endorsement, and supportive behaviors from stakeholders create equity and financial value.

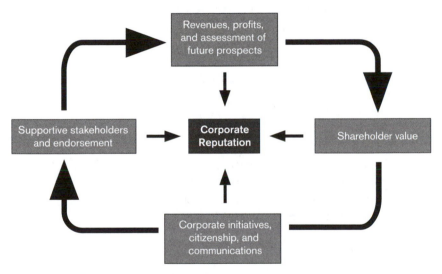

Figure 11.2 The reputation value cycle

A number of empirical studies have documented the fact that reputation and market value are intertwined:

▌ Research at the University of Virginia found a strong relationship between Fortune's measure of corporate reputation and the market values of those companies in the years 1984 through 1996 (Brown and Perry, 1997).

■ CoreBrand, a Connecticut-based communications consultancy, tracked "brand power" for 700 publicly traded companies using mailed surveys sent to business decision-makers. Taking advantage of a three-day period of unusually high US stock price volatility (October 24–28, 1997), they hypothesized that corporate reputation would act as a relative buffer for companies facing market volatility: companies with stronger reputations should experience less volatility and less market decline than those with weaker reputations. The study showed that all stocks fell significantly on Monday October 27, but by the close of the market on Tuesday October 28, the strongest brands had regained nearly all of their losses from the previous day. The weaker brands had not come close to recovering from Monday's precipitous drop. In addition, from Friday to Tuesday the strongest brands had actually gained a total of $7.09 billion in market capitalization, while the passive brands lost a total of $19.79 billion (Gregory, 1998).

■ A team of researchers compared ten groups of companies that had similar levels of risk and return, but different average reputation scores from Fortune's "most admired company" survey. They found that a 60 percent difference in reputation score was associated with a seven percent difference in market value. Since an average company in the study was valued at $3 billion, that meant a one-point difference in reputation score from six to seven on a ten-point scale would be worth an additional $51.5 million in market value (Srivastava et al., 1997).

■ Another team of researchers examined the relationship between market value, book value, profitability and reputation for all the firms rated in Fortune's "most admired company" survey between 1983 and 1997. They report that a one-point difference in reputation is worth about $500 million in market value. They concluded that, "our findings add support to existing research that internally generated intangibles not currently recognized as assets contribute to firm value and thus are viewed as assets by investors" (Black et al., 2000).

Clearly there is evidence of a close link between reputation and market value. The exact size of the effect is still in doubt, however, as is the actual value we can associate with "reputational capital" as such. But it is clear that a "business case" can be made for reputation management – and so for the portfolio of initiatives grouped under the corporate communication system.

Overcoming fragmentation and specialism

For the communication function, the problem lies therefore, not only in recognizing the existence of a business case for communication, but in the company's ability to exploit value-creation. As we recognized at the start of this book, the communication system that currently exists in most large companies is very fragmented and specialized. Fragmentation prevents the communication function from fulfilling its mission as the guardian of the company's strategic alignment and reputation.

Figure 11.3 outlines the value chain of corporate communication. It suggests that integration is the true challenge for the communication function, one that can only be met when the tactical activities of the specialty groups involved in corporate communication come together to fulfill the strategic objectives of the company, producing alignment, expressiveness, and reputation.

To facilitate integration, companies develop more or less complex administrative structures at the business-level (Lawrence and Lorsch, 1967; March and Simon, 1958). In business-units organized along functional lines, for instance, marketing communications bring together functional specialists who are responsible for product planning, advertising, and sales promotions. In business-units grouped by market, the company is typically organized around key client groups and marketing communications are customized to meet the needs of those clients. In business-units grouped around products, marketing communications are centred around product lines. Finally, in very dynamic environments, business-units often get organized into matrix structures, with different leaders for both markets and products (Galbraith, 1973). Marketing communications in these structures are developed and managed by specialists who report not only to the manager responsible for that market, but also to a brand manager or marketing manager responsible for the product side.

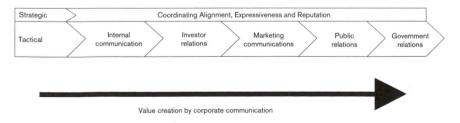

Figure 11.3   The value chain of corporate communication

Orchestration of communication can be achieved in different ways. Grant (1996) suggests four mechanisms that can be used to integrate specialized knowledge located in separate functional areas:

▪ *Rules and directives*: Consists of procedures, rules, standardised information, and communication systems;
▪ *Sequencing*: Involves organizing a process so that the input of a specialist is logically and sequentially linked to the inputs and outputs of other specialists;
▪ *Organizational routines*: The application of replicable actions automatically, making use of implicit mental scripts for handling situations;
▪ *Group problem-solving*: Personal interactions and communications customized to the situation.

Table 11.3 applied this scheme to the coordination of communication specialists. Group problem-solving is called for when a company is faced with high levels of uncertainty and complexity, and should be used sparingly.

Another tool for overcoming fragmentation is a *planning process* capable of coordinating a communication campaign. Viewed as a change process (Bennis *et al.*, 1976), it suggests the ideal order in which different phases of

Table 11.3 Mechanisms for orchestrating corporate communication

Rules of directives	Sequencing	Routines	Group problem solving
Common house style (parent visibility) Common starting points (content coordination) Guidelines for working with external agencies and internal budget responsibilities	Organization of communication function: tasks, responsibilities, budget Linking communication to commercial life cycle	Training and education of "protocol" to be used for press contacts, campaign presentations, and implementation, investor relations, etc.	Steering committee Annual/quarterly reviewing processes Ad hoc meetings

the information supply process should occur. The standard phases of the change process include diagnosis, formulation of objectives, strategy formulation, implementation, and evaluation. Each must meet a specific set of criteria (van Gent, 1973).

There has been remarkably little analysis of the execution of corporate communication campaigns. Some individual campaigns have been documented, but nothing has been produced showcasing how multiple campaigns are structured in practice – let alone the complex integration of corporate communication in a real company. Figure 11.4 illustrates how one might develop and represent an integrative planning process for a comprehensive communication system in a large company.

The process begins with collection of information from the external environment, and sorts it for relevance. An environmental scan results in a report which forms one of the inputs into the strategic business plan for the organization's communication strategy. The strategic business plan receives strategic inputs from the five core departments (marketing, production, human resources, finance, and information technology). Each of these departments makes demands on the company's communication system and should influence its strategy. The strategic business plan is translated into: (1) a set of plans for the five functional departments, and (2) a plan for organizational communication.

The operational plans of the five departments also have put pressure on the communication system, and gets outlined in individual department communication plans. To avoid producing a fragmented and even contradictory picture of the organization as a result of the overall communication plan and the departmental communication plans, the final plan must be internally coordinated, that is, within the departments and within the communication function. The reputation platform and corporate story can serve as "common starting points" by indicating the central values to use as a basis for clear and consistent communication across the company. When plans have been put on paper and tested against the reputation platform by all departments and by those responsible for concern communication, a coordinating group (preferably the communication function) can collate them and allocate budgets. In the final budget, resources should be allocated on the basis of three activities:

1. communication arising from the plans of the key departments;
2. communication arising from the organization's communication strategy;
3. communication at the corporate-level that cannot be anticipated but which will require action.

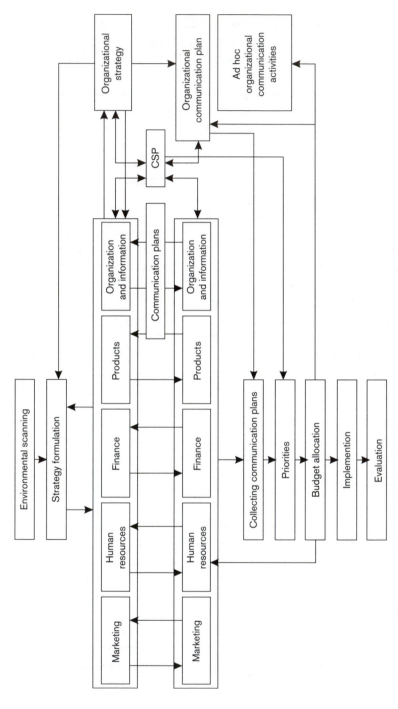

Figure 11.4   The process of communication planning

Ultimately, budgeting itself plays a crucial role in enabling and facilitating coordination because it plays a central role in setting priorities for the separately presented proposals across departments. There are seven methods for creating a communication budget (van Riel and van de Broek, 1992). Box 11.1 summarizes these budgeting approaches.

Box 11.1 Budgeting for corporate communication

Random allocation

Based on non-economic and non-psychological factors without any research. The means are distributed to the communication instruments without any concrete goal. The distribution generally takes place based on personal preference of the person responsible.

Percentage of sales (past year or projected)

The communication budget is determined by a certain percentage of the company's sales. This percentage is usually stable across years. This method gives the management the illusion of clarity and is financially quite safe because one knows that the total sum is always available. Competition is minimized because the participants base their budgets on market share. The mistake that is made here is that communication is seen as the result of and not the reason for sales. This method makes it easier to justify the budget to management and stockholders.

Return on investment

In this method, communications has to compete with other possible investments. Here the expected return of each investment is weighed with other possibilities in a certain term. The value of the expected future returns is calculated relative to the current situation. This gives the net current value. However, it is hard to predict this for communication budgets because there is little security about the size of the return and its spread in time. Furthermore, it is hard to tell which part of the return was caused by communication.

continued

Competitive parity

Here the communication budget is set equal to that of competitors in the same industry. The advantage is that the chance of an aggressive market war is minimized. Disadvantages are that there is no goal and one does not take the consumer into account. Furthermore, equal expenditures do not mean that one actually effectively uses the means.

All you can afford

Here the management spends as much as they can without bringing the financial liquidity in danger. All means that are left after a part of the results are reserved as profit, are spent on promotional communication. This method usually leads to under or over consumption.

Objective and task

Through this technique detailed goals are first drawn up and next the costs are calculated to realize these goals. Often a form of research or analysis is necessary to reach a clear formulation of the goals.

Historical extrapolation

Here the budget is based on that of the previous year. The board will be more likely to approve a budget that is equal to that of last year than one that is higher. A disadvantage of this method is that goals are not formulated again in order to determine the costs involved. In the long run this can lead to over consumption.

In the more complex and dynamic environments that companies increasingly operate in, formal structures, directives, planning, and budgeting are not enough, and companies draw on more complex forms of coordination involving group activities. A study by van Riel and Nedela (1988) showed that large American and European financial companies and institutions were relying on several different forms of team coordination to try to orchestrate their total communication output.

1. *Coordination by a steering committee* with representation of all communication departments, sometimes including line managers. Coordination is achieved by relying on guidelines developed from a common communication policy.

2. *Coordination by ad-hoc meetings*, organized to address situations where problems arise that must be solved collectively.
3. *Coordination by grouping communications managers together* in a single location, and "forcing" them to interact frequently, both privately and professionally.

Finally, cooperation among specialized communication departments can be achieved by relying on a "carousel" group. First, a coordinating group ("steering committee", "image-group", or "brand committee") is established, consisting of representatives of the most important communication departments (including both organizational communication and marketing communication), as well as senior management. The coordinating body acts like a rotating carousel at a fair – everyone has to work hard to resist the centripetal forces that threaten to throw them off. Active participation is more likely to result if senior management is present.

Two additional procedures can increase the carousel group effectiveness. For one, the carousel group should convene on a daily basis, with a minimum of three people participating regularly: a chairperson, a company secretary, and a member of the committee. Outside this "core", a wide variety of communication specialists can join in as regular participants in the group's deliberations. Naturally, only those people who play a central role in communication should be made full members. The chairperson needs to be somebody who could form a link in terms of authority and power between the board of directors and the CB.

The second requirement is to link explicitly the carousel group's operations with the different communication departments. Let us assume that in a certain company one needs to establish cooperation between organizational communication, the advertising department, and those responsible for sports sponsorship. In each case, each group must have a seat on the carousel group, to maintain the link between the group and their own department. As the chair of the group is by definition the link with the company's board of directors, a tighter bond will be created between the individual communication functions and senior management.

Contributors to the carousel group have to "prove" themselves by presenting brief outlines of the steps they believe should to be taken to implement corporate communication policy. Subsequently, the CB has a vital role to play in initiating and "controlling" the quality of the contribution that each communication function develops. A possible working process for such a carousel group is illustrate in Figure 11.5.

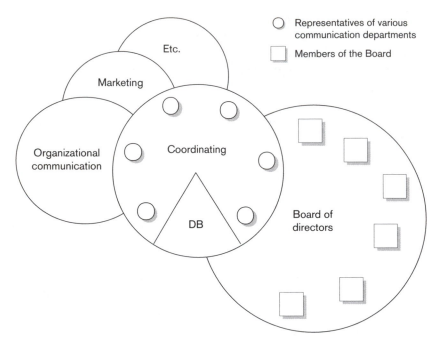

Figure 11.5   Coordinating corporate communication around the "carousel principle"

Conclusion: building a coherent communication system

Companies face significant challenges as they struggle to establish and maintain enduring competitive positions in the face of globalization, commoditization, and the rapid diffusion of information across markets. Among those challenges, the need to outdo rivals in attracting human, financial, and institutional resources remains the most daunting. It requires ever more sophisticated and coherent corporate communication throughout the company and with stakeholders.

To conclude this book, we call your attention to Figure 11.6. The diagram describes a series of models used by the Reputation Institute – the company we founded in 1997 – to help diagnose, strengthen, and empower corporate communication. The framework crystallizes the three domains that companies should pay attention to in order to enhance the effectiveness of their corporate communication. It describes the key diagnostic requirements of a coherent and effective corporate communication system.

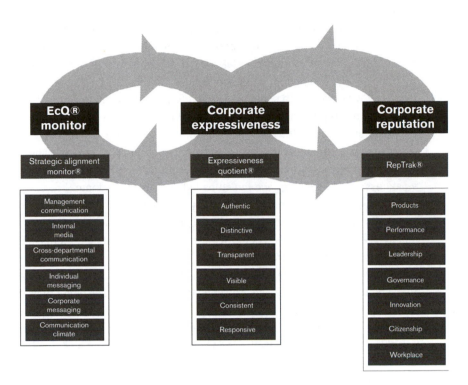

Figure 11.6 Building a coherent corporate communication system

Assessing the effectiveness of corporate communication begins with strategic alignment – an understanding that communication flows, communication content, and communication climate are the three principal drivers of employee support. Once employees are aligned in their awareness and understanding of the company's strategic objectives – and have the necessary abilities to deliver against those objectives – then they are more likely to act as ambassadors of the company. The EcQ® Strategic Alignment Monitor is a tool designed specifically to assess employee ambassadorship in companies.

Although mobilized employees are a necessary outcome of a coherent communication system, they are not sufficient. The company must also develop corporate communication that is expressive externally to its primary stakeholders. Expressiveness results from efforts to build coherence through the design of a reputation platform, consistent corporate story-telling, and a portfolio of related expressions carried out through branding and citizenship initiatives. If they are consistently expressed, distinctively conveyed, and transparent, the company is more likely to be well-regarded by outside audiences.

Finally, to be fully functioning, the corporate communication system must contribute to the company's reputational capital. The use of an instrument or set of instruments to measure stakeholder perceptions of the company is therefore a key component of the communication process – it closes the loop, as it were. Research sponsored by the Reputation Institute since 1999 suggests that reputations can be described in terms of a limited number of critical dimensions – the RepTrak® instrument uses seven dimensions and 23 attributes to profile corporate reputations. Application of the instrument typically produces diagnostic information about the relative strengths and weaknesses of companies, and the steps to take to address them.

Applying these tools can significantly enhance a company's ability to cohere its corporate communication. The tools are pragmatic – but they also summarize our understanding of the academic and practitioner literatures that have contributed to their creation.

In the coming decade, senior executives will require expert assistance from communications specialists. The knowledge they share can either remain "artistic", drawing primarily on intuition and experience, or can become more rigorous, scientific, and systematic. We believe the latter will prove increasingly valuable. For communications professionals, this means gaining a seat at the strategy-setting table. It also imposes demands on the training of professionals in corporate communication. Although sensitivity and skill in communication will remain a central requirement, the backgrounds required of professionals in this area must reflect an understanding of the business, an ability to speak the language of strategy, and fine-grained sensitivity to the value-creating role of corporate communication. We have drawn a distant line in the sand – hopefully our professional friends and colleagues will follow.

What motivated this book was our sense that managers have considerable difficulty looking at companies holistically. Integrative thinking is precluded because most managers are blinded by the artificial institutional walls that companies erect between functions and activities performed in separate parts of the company. As we end this book and our discussion about the organization of corporate communication, it is appropriate to recall John Godfrey Saxe's insightful poem "The Blind Men and the Elephant":

It was six men of Indostan
To learning much inclined,
Who went to see the Elephant – (Though all of them were blind),
That each by observation – Might satisfy his mind.

The First approached the Elephant,
And happening to fall
Against his broad and sturdy side, – At once began to bawl:
"God bless me! but the Elephant – Is very like a wall!"

The Second, feeling of the tusk,
Cried, "Ho! what have we here?
So very round and smooth and sharp? – To me "tis mighty clear
This wonder of an Elephant – Is very like a spear!"

The Third approached the animal,
And happening to take
The squirming trunk within his hands, – Thus boldly up and spake:
"I see," quoth he, "the Elephant – Is very like a snake!"

The Fourth reached out an eager hand,
And felt about the knee.
"What most this wondrous beast is like – Is mighty plain," quoth her;
"'Tis clear enough the Elephant – Is very like a tree!"

The Fifth who chanced to touch the ear,
Said: "E'en the blindest man
Can tell what this resembles most; – Deny the fact who can,
This marvel of an Elephant – Is very like a fan!"

The Sixth no sooner had begun
About the beast to grope,
Than, seizing on the swinging tail – That fell within his scope,
"I see," quoth he, "the Elephant – Is very like a rope!

And so these men of Indostan
Disputed loud and long,
Each in his own opinion – Exceeding stiff and strong,
Though each was partly in the right – And all were in the wrong!

Moral

So oft in theologic wars,
The disputants, I ween,
Rail on in utter ignorance
Of what each other mean,
And prate about an Elephant
Not one of them has seen!

BIBLIOGRAPHY

Aaker, D.A. (1996) "Measuring brand equity across products and markets", *California Management Review*, 38 (3): 102–121.

Aaker, D.A. (1999) *Building Strong Brands*, New York: Free Press.

Aaker, D.A. and Myers, J.G. (1991) *Advertising Management*, New York: Prentice-Hall.

Aaker, D.A. and Jacobson, R. (1994 July), "Study shows brand-building pays off for stockholders", *Advertising Age*, 65, 18.

Aaker, D.A. and R. Jacobson (1994) "The financial information content of perceived quality", *Journal of Marketing Research*, 31 (spring): 191–201.

Aaker, D.A. and Joachimstahler, E. (2002) *Brand Leadership*, New York: Free Press.

Aaker, J.L. (1997) "Dimensions of brand personality", *Journal of Marketing Research*, 34 (3): 347–357.

Abbott, L. (1955) *Quality and Competition*, New York: Columbia University Press.

Abrahamson, E. and Fombrun, C.J. (1992) "Forging the iron cage: interorganizational networks and the production of macro-culture", *Journal of Management Studies*, 29: 175–194.

Abratt, R. (1989) "A new approach to the corporate image management process", *Journal of Marketing Management*, 5 (1): 63–76.

Adema, R.L.A., Riel, C.B.M. van and Wierenga, B. (1993) *Kritische succesfactoren bij het management van corporate communication*, Delft: Eburon.

Albert, S. and Whetten, D. (1985) "Organizational Identity", in L.L. Cummings and B.M. Shaw (eds), *Research in Organizational Behavior*, pp. 263–295, Greenwich, CT: JAI Press.

Alhers, J.B.A. (1996) "De Brandasset™ Valuator als ondersteuning bij het ontwikkelen van strategie", *Tijdschrift voor Strategische Bedrijfscommunicatie*, 2 (3): 70–77.

Allen, F. (1984) "Reputation and product quality", *Rand Journal of Economics*, 15: 311–327.

Allen, R.K. (1977) *Organizational Management through Communication*, New York: Harper and Row.

Alvesson, M. (1990) "Organization: from substance to image?", *Organization Studies*, 11 (3): 373–394.

Ashforth, B.E. and Cummings, L.L. (1985) "Proactive feedback seeking: the instrumental use of the information environment", *Journal of Occupational Psychology*, 58: 67–79.

Ashforth, B.E. and Mael, F. (1989) "Social identity and the organization", *Academy of Management Review*, 14 (1): 20–39.

Ashforth, B. E. and Gibbs, B. W. (1990) "The double-edge of organizational legitimization", *Organization Science*, 1: 177–194.

Astley, G. and Fombrun, C. (1983) "Collective strategy: social ecology of organizational environments", *Academy of Management Review*, 8: 576–587.

Bagwell, K. (1992) "Pricing to signal product line quality", *Journal of Economics and Management Strategy*, 1: 151–174.

Baldinger, A.L. (1996) "Integrated communication and measurement: the case for multiple measures", in E. Thorson and J. Moore (eds), *Integrated Communications: Synergy of Persuasive Voices*, pp. 271–283, Mahwah, NJ: Lawrence Erlbaum Associates.

Balmer, J.M.T. (1997) *Corporate Identity: Past, Present and Future, International Centre for Corporate Identity Studies*, Working paper series 1997/4.

Balmer, J.M.T. and Wilson, A. (1998) "Corporate Identity: there is more to it than meets the eye", *International Studies of Management & Organization*, 28 (3): 12–31.

Balmer, J.M.T. and Greyser, S.A. (2002) "Managing the multiple identities of the corporation", *California Management Review*, 44: 72–86.

Barney, J.B. (1986) "Organizational culture: can it be a source of sustained competitive advantage?", *Academy of Management Review*, 11: 656–665.

Bauer, R. A. (1964) "The obstinate audience: the influence process from the point of view of social communication", *American Psychologist*, 19: 319–328.

Beijk, J. and Raaij, W.F., van (1989) *Schemata: Informatieverwerking: beïnvloedingsprocessen en reclame*, Amsterdam: VEA.

Bennis, W., Benne, K., Chin, R., and Corey, K. (1976) *The Planning of Change*, New York: Holt, Rhinehart & Winston.

Berens, G., Riel, C. B. M. van, and Bruggen, G. H. van (2005) "Corporate associations and consumer product responses: the moderating role of corporate brand dominance", *Journal of Marketing*, 69 (July): 35–48.

Bernstein, D. (1986) *Bedrijfsidentiteit – Sprookje en werkelijkheid*, Utrecht: L.J. Veen.

Bharadwaj, S.G. (1995) "Industry structure, competitive strategy, and firm-specific intangibles as determinants of business unit performance: towards an integrative model", Texas A&M University, Ph.D. dissertation, DAI-A 55/07.

Biel, Alexander L. (1992) "How brand image drives brand equity", *Journal of Advertising Research*, 32 (6): pRC-6-RC-12, 7p

Birkigt, K. and Stadler, M.M. (1986) *Corporate Identity, Grundlagen, Funktionen, Fallspielen, Verlag Moderne Industrie*, Landsberg am Lech.

Birkigt, K. and Stadler, M. (1988) "Corporate identity-Grundlagen", in: K. Birkigt and M. Stadler (eds), *Corporate Identity*, Landsberg am Lech: Verlag Moderne Industrie.

Black, E.L., Carnes, T.A. and Richardson, V.H. (2000) "The market valuation of corporate reputation", *Corporate Reputation Review*, 3 (1): 31–41.

Blauw, E. (1986) *Het corporate image: beeldvorming van de onderneming. Eén van de meest complexe managementvraagstukken*, Amsterdam: De Viergang.

Boer, D.J. den, Bouwman, H., Frissen, V., and Houben, M. (1984) *Methodologie en statistiek voor communicatie-onderzoek*, Houten: Bohn, Stafleu en van Loghum.

Boorstin, D. (1961) *The Image, or What Happened to the American Dream*, New York: Atheneum.

Boswell, W.R. and Boudreau, J.W. (2001) "How leading companies create, measure and achieve strategic results through 'line of sight'", *Management Decision*, 39 (10): 851–859.

Boush, David M. and Loken, B. (1991) "A process-tracing study of brand extension evaluation", *Journal of Marketing Research*, 28 (February): 16–28.

Brealy, R. and Myers, S. (1988) "*Principles of Corporate Finance*", New York: McGraw-Hill.

Bromley, D.B. (2000) "Psychological aspects of corporate identity, image, and reputation", *Corporate Reputation Review*, 3 (3): 240–252.

Bronn, C. (2002) "Organizational aspects of corporate communications", in: P. Simcic Bronn and R. Wiig (eds), *Corporate Communication: A Strategic Approach to Building Reputation*, Oslo: Gyldendal.

Bronn, P. S. and Bronn, C. (2002) "Issues management as a basis for strategic orientation", *Journal of Public Affairs*, 2 (4): 247–259.

Brounen, D., Cools, T.J.R., and Schweitzer, M. (2001) "Information transparancy pays: evidence from European property shares", *Real Estate Finance*.

Brown, B. (1998) "Do stock market investors reward companies with reputations for social performance?", *Corporate Reputation Review*, 1998, 1 (3): 271–280.

Brown, B. and Perry, S. (1994) "Removing the financial performance halo from Fortune's 'most admired' companies", *Academy of Management Journal*, 37 (5): 1347–1359.

Brown, S.R. (1986) "Q-technique and method", in: W. Berry and M. Lewis-Beck (eds), *New Tools for Social Scientists*, Newbury Park, CA: Sage.

Brown, T.J. (1998) "Corporate associations in marketing: antecedents and consequences", *Corporate Reputation Review*, 1 (3): 215–234.

Brown, T.J. and Dacin, P.A. (1997) "The company and the product: corporate associations and consumer product responses", *Journal of Marketing*, 61 (1): 68–84.

Caldwell, S.D., Herold, D.M., and Fedor, D.B. (2004) "Towards an understanding of the relationships between organizational change, individual differences, and changes in person–environment fit: a cross-level study", *Journal of Applied Psychology*, 89: 868–882.

Camerer, C. and Vepsalainen, A. (1988) "The economic efficiency of corporate culture", *Strategic Management Journal*, 9: 115–126.

Campbell, A. and Tawaday, K. (1990) *Mission and Business Philosophy: Winning Employee Commitment*, Oxford: Heinemann.

Campbell, A., Goold, M., and Alexander, M. (1995) "Corporate strategy: the quest for parenting advantage", *Harvard Business Review*, 73 (2): 120–132.

Carroll, C.E. and Riel, C.B.M., van (2001) *Organizational Identification and the Impact of Multiple Perceptions of Identity and Image in an International Policy-setting Organization*, Working paper, Rotterdam: Erasmus University, Corporate Communication Centre.

Carter, D.E. (1982) *Designing Corporate Identity Programs for Small Corporations*, New York: Art Direction Book Company.

Caves, R.E. and Porter, M.E. (1977) "From entry barriers to mobility barriers", *Quarterly Journal of Economics*, 91: 421–434.

Chajet, C. (1989) "The making of a new corporate image", *Journal of Business Strategy*, May–June: 18–20.

Chakravarthy, B. (1986) "Measuring strategic performance", *Strategic Management Journal*, 7: 437–458.

Chandler, A.D. (1962) *Strategy and Stucture*, Cambridge, MA: MIT.

Cheney, G. (1983) "The rhetoric of identification and the study of organizational communication", *Quarterly Journal of Speech*, 69: 143–158.

Cheney, G. (1991) *Rhetoric in an Organizational Society: Managing Multiple Identities*, Columbia: University of South Carolina Press.

Chernatony, L. de and McDonald, M.H.B. (1992) *Creating Powerful Brands: The Strategic Route to Success in Consumer, Industrial and Service Markets*, Oxford: Butterworth and Heinemann.

Choi, J.N. and Kim, M.U. (1999) "The organizational application of groupthink and its limitations in organizations", *Journal of Applied Psychology*, 84 (2): 297–306.

Chreim, S. (2002) "Influencing organizational identification during major change: a communication-based perspective", *Human Relations*, 55 (9): 117–137.

Cobb, B.W. and Elder, C.D. (1972) *Participation in American Politics: The Dynamics of Agenda Building*, Boston: Allyn & Becon.

Cobb-Walgren, C., Ruble, C., and Donthu, N. (1995) "Brand equity, brand preference, and purchase intent", *Journal of Advertising*, 24 (3): 25–40.

Cock, G. de, Bouwen, R., de Wilde, K., and de Visch, J. (1984) *Organisatieklimaat en -cultuur: Theorie en praktische toepassing van de Organisatie klimaat index voor Profit Organisaties (vokipo)*, Amersfoort: Acco Leuven.

Collins, J.C. and Porras, J.I. (1994) *Build to Last: Successful Habits of Visionary Companies*, New York: Harper Business.

CoreBrand (2004) *Directory of Brand Equity, Q3–Q4 2004*.

Corley K.G. and Gioia, A. D. (2000) "The rankings game: managing business school reputations", *Corporate Reputation Review*, 3 (3): 319–333.

Corley, K.G. and Gioia, D.A. (2004) "Identity ambiguity and change in the wake of a corporate spin-off", *Administrative Science Quarterly*, 49: 173–208.

Cornelissen, J. (2000) "Corporate image: an audience centered model", *Corporate Communications*, 5 (2): 119.

Cramer, S. and Ruefli, T. (1994) "Corporate reputation dynamics: reputation inertia, reputation risk, and reputation prospect", Conference paper, presented at the National Academy of Management meetings, Dallas.

Cutlip, S.M., Center, A.H., and Broom, G.M. (1994) *Effective Public Relations*, Englewood Cliffs: Prentice-Hall.

Davidson, D. (1990) "The structure and content of truth", *Journal of Philosophy*, 87 (6): 279–328.

Davies, G., Chun, R., Da Silva, R.V., and Roper, S. (2003) *Corporate Reputation and Competitiveness*, London: Routledge.

Deng, Z. and Lev, B. (1997) *Flash-Then-Flush: The valuation of Acquired R&D in Process*, Working paper, New York University.

Dichter, E. (1964) *Handbook of Consumer Motivation*, New York: McGraw-Hill.

Diefenbach, J. (1987) "Design considerations", in: M. Simpson (ed.), *Corporate Identity: Name, Image and Perception*, highlights of a conference, Report no. 989, Washington: The Conference Board.

DiMaggio, P.J. and Powell, W.W. (1983) "The iron cage revisited: institutional isomorphism and collective rationality in organization field", *American Sociological Review*, 48: 147–160.

Dobson, J. (1989) "Corporate reputation: a free market solution to unethical behavior", *Business and Society*, 28 (1): 1–5.

Doidge, C., Karolyi, A. and Stulz, R.M. (2005) *Why Do Countries Matter So Much For Corporate Governance?*, Working paper, University of Toronto.

Schultz, D.E., Tannenbaum, S., and Lauterborn, R.F. (1993) *Integrated Marketing Communications*, Lincolnwood, IL: NTC Business Books.

Dowling, G.R. (1986) "Managing your corporate images", *Industrial Marketing Management*, 15: 109–115.

Dowling, G.R. (1994) *Corporate Reputations: Strategies for Developing the Corporate Brand*, London: Kogan Page.

Dowling, G.R. and Roberts, P.W. (2002) "Corporate reputation and sustained superior financial performance", *Strategic Management Journal*, 23: 1077–1093.

Downs, C.W. (1988) *Communication Audits*, Scott Foreman.

Downs, C.W. and M.D. Hazen (1977) "A factor analytic study of communication satisfaction", *Journal of Business Communication*, 14 (3): 63–73.

Dreman, D. (2001) "Inefficient market", *Forbes*, 168.

Dutton, J. and Ottensmeyer, E. (1987) "Strategic issue management systems: forums, function and context", *Academy of Management Review*, 12: 355–365.

Dutton, J.E. and Dukerich, J.M. (1991) "Keeping an eye on the mirror: image and identity in organizational adaptation", *Academy of Management Journal*, 34: 517–554.

Dutton, J. and Penner, W. (1992) "The importance of organizational identity for strategic agenda building", in J. Hendry and G. Johnson (eds), *Strategic Thinking and the Management of Change*, New York: Wiley.

Dutton, J.E., Dukerich, J.M. and Harquail, V.V. (1994) "Organizational images and member identification", *Administrative Science Quarterly*, 39 (2): 229–263.

Edell, J. A. (1993) "Advertising interactions: a route to understanding brand equity", in A. A. Mitchell (ed.), *Advertising Exposure, Memory, and Choice*, pp. 195–208, Hillsdale, NJ: Lawrence Erlbaum Associates.

Edell, J.A. and Staelin, (1983) "The information processing of picture in print advertisements", *Journal of Consumer Research*, 10 (1): 45–61.

Edmondson, A.C. (2003) "Speaking up in the operation room: how team leaders promote learning in interdisciplinary action teams", *Journal of Management Studies*, 40 (6): 1419–1452.

Eisenberg, E.M. (1984) "Ambiguity as strategy in organizational communication", *Communication Monographs*, 51: 227–242.

Engel, J.F., Blackwell, R.D., and Miniard, P.W. (1990) *Consumer Behavior*, Chicago: Dryden Press.

Falcione, R.L., Sussman, L., and Herden, R.P. (1987) "Communication climate in organizations", in F.M. Jablin, *et al.* (eds), *Handbook of Organizational Communication*, Newbury Park, CA: Sage.

Farmer, B.A., Slater, J.W., and Wright, K.S. (1998) "The role of communication in achieving shared vision under new organizational leadership", *Journal of Public Relations Research*, 10 (4): 219–235.

Farquhar, P.H. (1989) "Managing brand equity", *Marketing Research*, 1 (September): 24–33.

Fenkart, P. and Widmer, H. (1987) "Corporate identity: Leitbild, Erschienungsbild", *Kommunikation*, Zürich: Orell Fuessli.

Fiol, C.M. (2002) "Capitalizing on paradox: the role of language in transforming organizational identities", *Organizational Science*, 13 (6): 653–666.

Fishbein, M. and Ajzen, I. (1975) *Belief, attitude, intention and behavior: an introduction to theory and research*, Reading, MA: Addison-Wesley.

Fombrun, C.J. (1982), "Strategies for network research in organizations", *Academy of Management Review*, 7 (2): 280–291.

Fombrun, C.J. (1996) *Reputation: Realizing Value from the Corporate Image*, Boston: Harvard Business School Press.

Fombrun, C.J. and Zajac, E.J. (1987) "Structural and perceptual influences on intra-industry stratification", *Academy of Management Journal*, 30: 33–50.

Fombrun, C.J. and Shanley, M. (1990) "What's in a name? Reputation building and corporate strategy", *Academy of Management Journal*, 33 (2): 233–258.

Fombrun, C.J. and Riel, C. van (1997) "The reputational landscape", *Corporate Reputation Review*, 1 (1 and 2): 5–13.

Fombrun, C.J. and Riel, C.B.M. van (2004) *Fame and Fortune: How the World's Top Companies Develop Winning Reputations*, New York: Pearson Publishing and the Financial Times.

Fombrun, C.J., Tichy, N.M., and Devanna, M.A. (1984) *Strategic Human Resource Management*, New York: John Wiley.

Fombrun, C.J., Gardberg, N.A., and Sever, J.M. (2000) "The reputation quotient: a multi-stakeholder measure of corporate reputation", *Journal of Brand Management*, 7 (4): 241–255.

Foreman, P. and Whetten, D.A. (1994) "An identity theory perspective on multiple expectations in organizations", Conference paper, presented at the Academy of Management Meetings.

Foreman, P.O. and Whetten, D.A. (1997) *An Identity Theory Perspective on Multiple Expectations in Organizations*, Working paper, University of Illinois.

Frank, A. and Brownell, J. (1989) *Organizational Communication and Behavior: Communicating to Improve Performance*, New York: Holt, Rinehart & Winston.

Franzen, G. (1984) *Mensen, produkten en reclame*, Alphen a/d Rijn: Samsom.

Freeman, R.E. (1984) *Strategic Management: A Stakeholder Approach*, Boston: Pitman Press.

Fryxell, G.E. and Wang, J. (1994) "The Fortune's corporate 'reputation' index: reputation of what?", *Journal of Management*, 20 (1): 1–14.

Gagliardi, P. (ed.) (1990) *Symbols and Artifacts: Views of the Corporate Landscape*, New York: Aldine de Gruyter.

Gagnon, M. and Michael, J. (2003) "Employee strategic alignment at a wood manufacturer: an exploratory analysis using lean manufacturing", *Forest Products Journal*, 53 (10): 24–29.

Galbraith, J. (1973) *Designing Complex Organizations*, Reading, MA: Addison-Wesley.

Gardberg, N.A. (2006) "Repuration, reputazione, reputatie, ruf: a cross-cultural qualitative analysis of construct and scale equivalence", *Corporate Reputation Review*, 9 (2): 1–23.

Gent, V. van (1973) *Andragologie en voorlichtingskunde*, Meppel: Boom.

Ginzel, L.E., Kramer, R.M., *et al.* (1993) "Organizational impression management as a reciprocal influence process: the neglected role of the organizational audience", in L.I. Cummings and B.W. Staw (eds), *Research in Organizational Behavior*, Greenwich, CI: JAI Press.

Gioia, D.A. and Thomas, J.B. (1996) "Identity, image, and issue interpretation: sensemaking during strategic change in academia", *Administrative Science Quarterly*, 41 (3): 370–404.

Gioia, D.A., Schultz, M., and Corley, K.G. (2000) "Organizational identity, image and adaptive instability", *Academy of Management Review*, 25 (1): 63–81.

Glynn, M.A. (2000) "When cymbals become symbols: conflict over organizational identity within a symphony orchestra", *Organizational Science*, 11: 285–295.

Goldhaber, G. and Rogers, V. (1979) *Auditing Organizational Communication Systems: The ICA Communication Audit*, Dubuque: Brown Publishers.

Granovetter, M. (1985) "Economic action and social structure: the problem of embeddedness", *American Journal of Sociology*, 91: 481–510.

Grant, R.M. (1996) "Toward a knowledge-based theory of the firm", *Strategic Management Journal*, 17: 109–122.

Gray, E.R. and Balmer, J.M.T. (1998) *Managing Corporate Image and Corporate Reputation*, London: Long Range Planning.

Green, D. and Loveluck, V. (1994) "Understanding a corporate symbol", *Applied Cognitive Psychology*, 8: 37–47.

Greenbaum, H.H., Clampitt, P., and Willihnganz, S. (1988) "Organizational communication: an examination of four instruments", *Management Communication Quarterly*, 2 (2): 245–252.

Greenley, G.E. and Foxall, G.R. (1997) "Multiple stakeholder orientation in UK companies and the implications for company performance", *Journal of Management Studies*, 34 (2): 259–284.

Gregory, J. (1998) "Does corporate reputation provide a cushion to companies facing market volatility? Some supportive evidence", *Corporate Reputation Review*, 1 (3): 288–290.

Grossman, S. and Stiglitz, J. (1980) "On the impossibility of informationally efficient markets", *American Economic Review*, 70: 393–408.

Grunig, J.E. (ed.) (1992) *Excellence in Public Relations and Communication Management*, Hillsdale, NJ: Lawrence Erlbaum Associates.

Grunig, J.E. and Hunt, T. (1984) *Managing Public Relations*, New York: Holt, Rinehart and Winston.

Grunig, J.E. and Grunig, L.A. (1989) "Toward a theory of the public relations behavior of organizations: review of a program of research", *Public Relations Research Annual*, 1, 27–63.

Guildford, J.P. (1954) *Persönlichkeit*, Weinheim.

Gusseklo, W.G. (1985) "Reclameplanning", in: *Handboek Reclame, 1984–85*, Deventer: Kluwer.

Gustafson, L.T. and Reger, R.K. (1995) "Using organizational identity to achieve stability and change in high velocity environments", *Academy of Management Journal*, Best papers proceedings.

Guzly, R.M. (1992) "Organizational climate and communication climate: predictors of commitment to the organization", *Management Communication Quarterly*, 5 (4): 379–402.

Hamel, G. and Prahalad, C.K. (1996) *Competing for the Future*, Boston, MA: Harvard Business School Press.

Handy, C. (1992) "Balancing corporate power: a new federalist paper", *Harvard Business Review*, November–December: 59–71.

Harris, P. and Moss, D. (2001) "Understanding public affairs", *Journal of Public Affairs*, 1 (1): 6–8.

Hatch, M.J. (2003) "The Jazz metaphor in reputation management research", Presentation at the Seventh Reputation Institute Conference, Manchester.

Hatch, M.J. and Schultz, M. (2000) "Scaling the tower of Babel: relational differences between identity, image, and culture in organizations", in: M. Schultz, M.H. Hatch, and M.H. Larsen (eds), *The Expressive Organizations: Linking Identity, Reputation and the Corporate Brand*, pp.11–35, New York: Oxford University Press.

Hedlin, P. (1999) "The internet as a vehicle for investor relations: the Swedish case", *European Accounting Review*, 8 (2): 373–381.

Henderson, P.W. and Cote, J.A. (1998) "Guidelines for selecting or modifying logos", *Journal of Marketing*, 62 (2): 14–30.

Herr, P.M. and Fazio, R.H. (1993) "The attitude-to behavior process: implications for consumer behavior", in: A.A. Mitchell (ed.), *Advertising Exposure, Memory and Choice*, pp. 119–140, Hillsdale, NJ: Erlbaum.

Heugens, P.P.M.A.R., Bosch, F.A.J. van den and Riel, C.B.M. van (2002) "Stakeholder integration: building mutually enforcing relationships", *Business and Society*, 41 (1): 37–61.

Heugens, P.P.M.A.R., Riel, C.B.M. van, and Bosch, F.A.J. van den (2004) "Reputation management capabilities as decision rules", *Journal of Management Studies*, 41 (8): 1349–1377.

Higgins, R.B. and Diffenbach, J. (1989) "Communicating corporate strategy: the payoffs and the risks", *Long Range Planning*, 12 (3): 133–139.

Hinterhuber, H.H. (1989) *Der Stand der corporate-identity-politik in der Bundesrepublik Deutschland und West-Berlin, in Österreich und der Schweiz, eine Untersuchung über die strategische Bedeutung von Corporate Identity in Industrieunternehmen,* Munich: Dr. Höfner Management Software Gmbh.

Holzhauer, F.F.O. (1991) "Corporate image en brand image", in C.B.M. van Riel and W.H. Nijhof (eds), *Handboek corporate communication,* Deventer: van Loghum Slaterus.

Jablin, F.M. and Putnam, L.L. (eds) (2001) *The New Handbook of Organizational Communication: Advances in Theory, Research, and Methods,* Thousand Oaks, CA: Sage.

Jackson, P. (1987) *Corporate Communication for Managers,* London: Pitman.

Jefkins, F. (1983) *Dictionary of Marketing, Advertising and Public Relations,* London: International Textbook Company.

Jemison, D.B. and Sitkin, S.B. (1986) "Corporate acquisitions: a process perspective", *Academy of Management Review,* 11: 145–163.

Johannsen, U. (1971) *Das Marken- und Firmenimage: Theorie, Methodik,* Berlin: Praxis, Dumcker und Humbult.

Johansson, J.K. and Nebenzahl, I.D. (1986) "Multinational production: effect on brand value", *Journal of International Business Studies,* 17 (3): 101–126.

Johnson, G. and Scholes, K (1989) *Exploring Corporate Strategy,* New York: Prentice-Hall.

Johnson, J.D., Donohue, W.A., and Atkin, C.K. (1994) "Differences between formal and informal communication channels", *Journal of Business Communications,* 31 (2): 111–122.

Jones, G.H. (2000) "Reputation as reservoir", *Corporate Reputation Review,* 3 (1): 21–29.

Kammerer, J. (1988) *Beitrag der Produktpolitik zur Corporate Identity,* GBI-Verlag, Munich.

Kapferer, J.N. (1992) *Strategic Brand Management,* London: Kogan Page.

Kapferer, J.N. (2002) "Is there really no hope for local brands?", *Journal of Brand Management,* 9 (3): 163–170.

Kapferer, J.N. and Laurent, G. (1993) "Further evidence on the Consumer Involvement Profile: five antecedents of involvement", *Psychology & Marketing,* 10 (4): 347–356.

Katz, H. and Lendrevie, J. (1996) "In search of the holy grail: first steps in measuring total exposures of an integrated communications program", in: E. Thorson and J. Moore (eds), *Integrated Communications: Synergy of Persuasive Voices,* pp. 259–270, Mahwah, NJ: Lawrence Erlbaum Associates.

Keller, K.L. (1991) *Conceptualizing, Measuring, and Managing Customer-based Brand Equity,* Cambridge, MA: Marketing Science Institute.

Keller, K.L. (1993) "Conceptualising, measuring, and managing customer based brand equity", *Journal of Marketing,* 57: 1–22.

Keller, K.L. (1996) "Brand equity and integrated communication", in: E. Thorson and J. Moore (eds), *Integrated Communications: Synergy of Persuasive Voices,* pp. 103–132, Mahwah, NJ: Lawrence Erlbaum Associates.

Keller, K.L. and Aaker, D.A. (1998) "Corporate-level marketing: the impact of credibility on a company's brand extensions", *Corporate Reputation Review,* 1(4): 356–378.

Kennedy, S.H. (1977) "Nurturing corporate images: total communication or ego trip?", *European Journal of Marketing,* 11 (I): 120–164.

Kitchen, P.J. (1997) *Public Relations: Principles and Practices*, London: Thomson Business Park.

Kitchen, P.J. (1999) *Marketing Communications: Principles and Practice*, London: International Thomson Business Press.

Kleijneijenhuis, J. (2001) "Organisatiereputatie en publiciteit", in: C.B.M. van Riel (ed.), *Corporate Communication: Het Managen van reputatie*, pp. 131–155, Deventer: Kluwer.

Knapper, W. (1987) "De VEA op het Vinketouw I en II", *Onderzoeksverslag*, Amsterdam: BvA and vea.

Knecht, J. (1986) "Zin en onzin over images en reclame, Toespraak tijdens corporate image/identity symposium", georganiseerd door esprit/motivaction, Amsterdam: Amstel Hotel.

Knecht, J. (1989) *Geïntegreerde communicatie*, BvA and VEA, Amsterdam.

Knecht, J. and Stoelinga, B. (1988) *Commmunicatie begrippenlijst*, Deventer: Kluwer Bedrijfswetenschappen.

Knoers, P. (2003) "Organisatie van de communicatie", in: C. van Riel (ed.), *Corporate Communication. Het managen van reputatie*, pp. 383–407, Deventer: Kluwer.

Korsgaard, M.A., Brodt, S.E., and Whitener, E.M. (2002) "Trust in the face of conflict: the role of managerial trustworthy behavior and organizational context", *Journal of Applied Psychology*, 87 (2): 312–319.

Kotha, S., Rindova, V., and Rothaermel, F. (2001) "Assets and actions: firm-specific factors in the internationalization of US Internet firms", *Journal of International Business Studies*, 32: 769–792.

Kotler, P. (1988) *Marketing Management, Analysis, Planning, Implementation and Control*, Englewood Cliffs: Prentice-Hall International.

Krone, K., Jablin, F.M., and Putnam, L.L. (1987) "Communication theory and organizational communication: multiple perspectives", in: F.M. Jablin *et al.* (eds), *Handbook of Organizational Communication*, pp. 18–69, Newbury Park, CA: Sage Publications.

Kundera, M. (1990) *Onsterfelijkheid*, Baarn: Ambo.

Kuylen, T.A.A. and Verhallen, Th. M.M. (1988) "Natural grouping of banks", paper presented at Esomar Seminar on Research for Financial Services, Research International Netherlands.

Lancaster, K.M. and Katz, H.E. (1989) *Strategic Media Planning*, Lincoln Woods: MTC Business Books.

Lang, M.H., Lins, K.V., and Miller, D.P. (2002) *Do Analysis Matter Most When Investors are Protected Least? International Evidence*, Working paper, University of North Carolina, University of Utah, and Indiana University.

Larçon, J.P. and Reitter, R. (1979) *Structures de Pouvoir et Identité de l'entreprise*, Paris: Editions Nathan.

Larçon, J.P. and Reitter, R. (1984) "Corporate imagery and corporate identity", in: M. Kets de Vries (ed.), *The Irrational Executive: Psychoanalytic Explorations in Management*, pp. 344–355, New York: International University Press.

Larsen, D. (2003) "The role of financial communication in the relationship between corporate reputation and financial performance", Master of Corporate Communication thesis, Rotterdam: Erasmus University, Corporate Communication Centre.

Larsen, M.H. (2000) "Managing the corporate story", in: M. Schultz, M.J. Hatch, and M.H. Larsen (eds), *The Expressive Organization: Linking Identity, Reputation and the Corporate Brand*, New York: Oxford University Press.

Lawrence, P.R. and Lorsch, J.W. (1967) *Organization and Environment*, Cambridge, MA: Harvard University Press.

Lev, B. and Sougiannis, T. (1996) "The capitalization, amortization and value-relevance of R&D", *Journal of Accounting and Economics*, 21: 107–138.

Leyer, J. (1986) *Corporate communicatie in de strategie van ondernemingen in beweging*, Amsterdam: BVA.

Lilli, W. (1983) "Perzeption, Kognition, Image", in: M. Irle, and W. Bussman (eds), *Handbuch der Psychologie*, 12. Band, 1, Göttingen: Verlag für Psychologie.

Littlejohn, S.W. (1989) *Theories of Human Communication*, Belmont, CA: Wadsworth.

London Stock Exchange (2001) *Practical Guide to Investor Relations*, p. 8.

Luscuere, C. (1993) "Organisatiekunde en corporate communication", in: C.B.M. van Riel (ed.), *Corporate Communcation: Het managen van reputatie*, Alpen aan den Rijn: Kluwer.

Lux, P.G.C. (1986) "Zur Durchführung von Corporate Identity Programmen", in: K. Birkigt and M. Stadler, *Corporate Identity*, pp. 515–537, Landsberg/Lech.

Maanen, J. van (1988) *Tales of the Field: On Writing Ethnography*, Chicago: Chigaco University Press.

Maathuis, O.J.M., Riel, C.B.M. van, and Bruggen, G.H. van (1998) "Using the corporate brand to communicate identity: the value of corporate associations to customers", abstract of paper presented at Second International Conference on Corporate Reputation, Identity and Competitiveness, January 16–17, Amsterdam.

McCauley, D.P. and Kuhnert, K.W. (1992) "A theoretical review and empirical investigation of employee trust in management", *Public Administration Quarterly*, 16 (2): 265–284.

McGuire, J.B., Sundgren, A., and Schneeweiss, T. (1988) "Corporate social responsibility and financial performance", *Academy of Management Journal*, 31 (4): 854–872.

McKeown, B. and Thomas, D. (1988) *Q-methodology: Quantitative Applications in the Social Sciences*, Newbury Park, CA: Sage.

Mackiewicz, A. (1993) *The Economist Intelligence Unit Guide to Building a Global Image*, New York: McGraw-Hill.

McLeod, J.M. and Chaffee, S.H. (1973) "Interpersonal approaches to communication research", *American Behavioral Scientist*, 16: 469–500.

McNaughton, L. (2004) "The power of brand equity", presentation at Vuepoint Forum.

Mael, F. and Ashforth, B.E. (1992) "Alumni and their alma mater: a partial test of the reformulated model of organizational identification", *Journal of Organizational Behavior*, 13: 103–123.

March, J.G. and Simon, H.A. (1958) *Organizations*, New York: John Wiley.

Marcus, B.W. and Wallace, S.L. (1997) *New Dimensions in Investor Relations: Competing for Capital in the 21st century*, New York: John Wiley.

Margulies, W. (1977) "Make the most of your corporate identity", *Harvard Business Review*, July–August, pp. 66–72.

Merkle, W. (1992) *Corporate Identity für Handelsbetriebe, Theoretische Grundlagen und Realiserungskonzeptes*, Göttinger Handelswissenschaftliche Schriften eV, Göttingen.

Meyer, A. (1982) "Adapting to environmental jolts", *Administrative Science Quarterly*, 27: 515–537.

Miles, R. and Cameron, K. (1982) *Coffin Nails and Corporate Strategies*, New York: Prentice-Hall.

Milgrom, P. and Roberts, J. (1986) "Relying on the information of interested parties", *Rand Journal of Economics*, 17: 18–32.

Miller, D. (1990) *The Icarus Paradox: How Excellent Companies Can Bring about Their Own Downfall*, New York: Harper Business.

Minekus, G. (1989) "Geintegreerde communicatie", *Reclame & Onderzoek*, 1: 3–14.

Mitchell, R.K., Agle, B.R., and Wood, D.J. (1997) "Towards a theory of stakeholder identification and salience: defining the principle of who and what really counts", *Academy of Management Review*, 22 (4): 853–886.

Moore, J. and Thorson, E. (1996) "Strategic planning for integrated marketing communications programs: an approach to moving from chaotic toward systematic", in E. Thorson and J. Moore (eds), *Integrated Communications: Synergy of Persuasive Voices*, pp. 135–152, Mahwah, NJ: Lawrence Erlbaum Associates.

Muir, N. (1987) *Rebuilding Equity. The Standard Oil Company, Corporate Identity: Name, Image and Perception*, Washington: The Conference Board.

Myers, S. and Majluf, N. (1984) "Corporate financing and investment decisions when firms have information investors do not have", *Journal of Financial Economics*, 13 (2): 187–221.

Nagashima, A. (1977) "A comparative 'made in' product image survey among Japanese businessmen", *Journal of Marketing*, 41 (3): 95–100.

Napoles, V. (1988) *Corporate Identity Design*, New York: van Hostrand Reinhold Company.

Nayyar, P.R. (1990) "Information asymmetries: a source of competitive advantage for diversified service firms", *Strategic Management Journal*, 11: 513–519.

Noble, C.H. (1999) "Building the strategy implementation", 42 (November–December): 19–28.

Nowak, G.J. and Phelps, V. (1995) "Geïntegreerde marketingcommunicatie", *Tijdschrift voor Stategische Bedrijfscommunicatie*, Jrg.1, nr. 2, 4–29.

Olins, W. (1978) *The Corporate Personality*, London: Thames & Hudson.

Olins, W. (1989) *Corporate Identity: Making Business Strategy Visible through Design*, London: Thames & Hudson.

Olins, W. (1990) *The Wolff Olins Guide to Corporate Identity*, London: The Design Council.

Orlitzky, M., Schmidt, F., and Rynes, S. (2003) "Corporate social and financial performance: a meta-analysis", *Organization Studies*, 24: 403–441

Park, C.W., Jaworski, B.J., and MacInnis, D.J. (1986) "Strategic brand concept/image management", *Journal of Marketing*, 50 (October): 135–145.

Percy, L. and Rossiter, J.R. (2000) "Building and managing brands with traditional marketing communication", in: Franz-Rudolf Esch (ed.), *Moderne Markenfuhrum*, pp. 493–508, Germany: Gables.

Petty, R.E. and Cacioppo, J.T. (1986) *Communication and Persuasion: Central and Peripheral Routes to Attitude Change*, New York: Springer Verlag.

Pfeffer, J. and Salancik, G.R. (1978) *The External Control of Organizations: A Resource Dependence Perspective*, New York: Harper Row.

Pincus, J.D., Robert, A.P.R., Rayfield, A.P.R., and DeBonis, J.N. (1991) "Transforming ceos into chief communications officers", *Public Relations Journal*, 47 (11): 22–27.

Pine, B.J. and Gilmore, J.H. (1999) *The Experience Economy: Work Is Theatre and Every Business a Stage*, Boston: Harvard Business School Press.

Poiesz, T.B.C. (1988) "The image concept: its place in consumer psychology and its potential for other psychological areas", Conference paper, presented at the 24th International Psychological Congress, Sydney, Australia.

Porac, J.F. and Thomas, H. (1990) "Taxonomic mental models in competitor definition", *Academy of Management Review*, 15: 224–240.

Porter, M.E. (1980) *Competitive Strategy: Techniques for Analyzing Industries and Competitors*, New York: Free Press.

Prahalad, C.K. and Hamel, G. (1990) "The core competence of the corporation", *Harvard Business Review*, May–June: 79–91.

Pratt, M.G. (1998) "To be or not to be? Central questions in organizational identification", in: D.A. Whetten and P.C. Godfrey (eds), *Identities in Organizations: Building Theory through Conversations*, pp. 170–207, Thousand Oaks, CA: Sage Publications.

Pratt, M.G. and Rafaeli, A. (1997) "Organizational dress as a symbol of multilayered social identities", *Academy of Management Journal*, 40 (4): 862–898.

Pratt, M.G. and Foreman, P.O. (2000) "Classifying managerial responses to multiple organizational identities", *Academy of Management Review*, 25 (1): 18–42.

Pruyn, A.Th.H. (1990) "Imago: een analytische benadering van het begrip en de implicaties daarvan voor onderzoek", in: C.B.M. van Riel and W.H. Nijhof (eds), *Handboek Corporate Communicatie*, Deventer: van Loghum Slaterus.

Quinn, J.B., Mintzberg, H., and James, R.M. (1988) *The Strategy Process: Concepts and Cases*, London: Prentice-Hall.

Raaij, W.F. van and Verhallen, Th.M.M. (1990) "Domein-specifieke marktsegmentatie", *Tijdschrift voor Marketing*, April: 6–15.

Ramanantsoa, B. (1988) *Strategor, Strategie, Structure, Décision, Identité: politique générale d'enterprise*, Paris: InterEditions.

Ravasi, D. and Rekom, J. van (2003) "Key issues in organizational identity and identification theory", *Corporate Reputation Review*, 6 (2): 118–132.

Ray, M.L. (1982) *Advertising and Communication Management*, Englewood Cliffs: Prentice-Hall.

Redding, W.C. (1972) *Communication within the Organization: An Interpretive Review of Theory and Research*, New York: Industrial Communication Council.

Reinsch, N.L. and Beswick, R.W. (1990) "Participation and productivity: an empirical study", *Industrial and Labor Relations Review*, 33 (3): 355–367.

Rekom, J. van (1992) "Corporate identity, Ontwikkeling van concept en meetinstrument", in:

C.B.M van Riel and W.H. Nijhof (eds), *Handboek Corporate Communication*, Deventer: van Loghum Slaterus.

Rekom, J., van (1997) "Deriving an operational measure of corporate identity", *European Journal of Marketing*, 31 (5/6): 410–422.

Rekom, J. van and Riel, C.B.M. van (2000) "Operational measures of organizational identity: a review of existing methods", *Corporate Reputation Review*, 3 (4): 334–350.

Rekom, J. van, Riel, C.B.M. van, and Wierenga, B. (1991) *Corporate Identity: van vraag concept naar hard feitenmateriaal*, Working paper, Corporate Communication Centre, Rotterdam.

Rekom, J. van, Riel, C.B.M. van and, Wierenga, B (2006) "A methodology for assessing organizational core values", *Journal of Management Studies*, 42 (2): 175–201.

Reynolds, T.J. and Gutman, J. (1984) "Advertising is image management", *Journal of Advertising Research*, 24: 27–37.

Riel, C.B.M. van (1992) *Identiteit en imago: Een inleiding in de corporate communication*, Schoonhoven: Academic Service, 1st edn.

Riel, C.B.M. van (1994) "Balanceren tussen variëteit en uniformiteit in het corporate communication beleid", Inaugurele lecture, Erasmus University, Rotterdam, Houten: Bohn Stafleu van Loghum.

Riel, C.B.M. van (1995) *Principles of Corporate Communication*, London: Prentice Hall.

Riel, C.B.M. van (2000) "Corporate communication orchestrated by a sustainable corporate story", in: Mary-Jo Hatch Majken Schultz and Mogens Holten Larsen (eds), *The Expressive Organization: Linking Identity, Reputation and the Corporate Brand*, pp. 157–181, Oxford: Oxford University Press.

Riel, C.B.M. van (2001) "Sustaining the corporate story", in: M. Schultz, M.J. Hatch, and M.H. Larsen (eds), *The Expressive Organization*, pp. 157–181, Oxford: Oxford University Press.

Riel, C.B.M. van and Nedela, J. (1989) *Profiles in Corporate Communication in Financial Institutions*, Delft: Eburon.

Riel, C.B.M. van and Broek, M. van de (1992) "Besluitvorming over concerncommunicatie-budgetten", *Massacommunicatie*, 4: 267–286.

Riel, C.B.M. van and Ban, A. van den (2000) "The added value of corporate logos: an empirical study", *European Journal of Marketing*, 35 (3): 428–440.

Riel, C.B.M. van and Bosch, F.A.J., van den (2000) "Professioneel reputatiemanagement bij strategische issues – Greenpeace versus Shell rondom de Brent Spar case", in: E. Denig and A. Weisnk (eds), *Uitdagingen voor Communicatie*, BvC, Alphen aan den Rijn: Samson.

Riel, C.B.M. van and Berens, G. (2001) "Balancing corporate branding policies in multi-business companies", in: P.J. Kitchen and D.E. Schultz (eds), *Raising the Corporate Umbrella: Corporate Communications in the 21st century*, New York: Palgrave.

Riel, C.B.M. van and Bruggen, G.H., van (2002) "Incorporating business unit managers' perspectives in corporate branding strategy decision making", *Corporate Reputation Review*, 5 (2/3): 241–251.

Riel, C.B.M. van, Smidts, A., and Pruyn, A.Th. H. (1994) *ROIT: Rotterdam Organizational Identification Test*, Working paper, First Corporate Identity Conference, Department of Marketing, Strathclyde University, Glasgow.

Riel, C.B.M. van, Stroeker, N.E., and Maathuis, O.J.M. (1998) "Measuring corporate image, corporate reputation,' *Corporate Reputation Review*, 1 (4): 1–13.

Riel, C.B.M. van, Berens, G., and Dijkstra, M. (2005) *Creating Strategic Business Alignment through Information and Dialogues*, ERIM Working paper, Erasmus University.

Ries, A. and Ries, L. (2002) *The Fall of Advertising and the Rise of PR*, London: Harper-Collins.

Rieves, R.A. and Lefebvre, J. (2002) *Investor Relations for the Emerging Company*, New York: John Wiley.

Rindova, V. (1997) "The image cascade and the dynamics of coporate reputations", *Corporate Reputation Review*, 1 (2): 188–194.

Rindova, V. (1999) "What corporate boards have to do with strategy: a cognitive perspective", *Journal of Management Studies*, 36 (7): 953.

Rindova, V., and Fombrun, C.J. (1999) "Constructing competitive advantage: the role of firm-constituent interactions", *Strategic Management Journal*, 20 (8): 691–710.

Rinnooy Kan, E.A. (1988) *Syllabus middelen planning*, Amsterdam: SRM.

Roberts, K.H. and O'Reilly, C.A. (1973) "Some problems in measuring organizational communication", Paper prepared for US Office of Naval Research, US Department of Commerce.

Rosenberg, R.D. and Rosenstein, E. (1980) "Participation and productivity: an empirical study", *Industrial and Labor Relations Review*, 33 (3): 355–367.

Ross, S.A. (1977) "The determination of financial structure: the incentive-signaling approach", *Bell Journal of Economics*, 8 (1): 23–40.

Rossiter, J. and Percy, L. (1987) *Advertising and Promotion Management*, New York: McGraw-Hill, 2nd edn 1999.

Rossiter, J.R. and Percy, L. (1997) *Advertising Communications & Promotion Management*, New York: McGraw-Hill.

Roth, G. and Kleiner, A. (1998) "Developing organizational memory through learning histories", *Organizational Dynamics*, Fall: 43–60.

Ruler, A.A. van (2003) "Communicatiemanagement: van kwantiteit naar kwaliteit, over het managen van organisationele communicatie", Inaugural lecture, Twente, Enschede.

Ruler, B. van and Lange, R. de (1995) "Trendonderzoek Public Relations 1995", Faculteit Sociale Wetenschappen, Universiteit Utrecht, *Isor Onderwijsreeks*, 95-06, Utrecht.

Rumelt, R.P. (1974) *Strategy, Structure, and Economic Performance*, Cambridge, MA: Harvard University Press.

Russell, D.A. and Starman, D.L. (1990) "Measuring the emotional response to advertising: BBDO's emotional measurment system and emotional photo deck", *Reclame en onderzoek*, 1, pp. 15–26.

Schendelen, M.P.C.M., van (ed.) (1993) *National Public and Private EC Lobbying*, Aldershot: Dartmouth.

Schendelen, R., van (2002) "The ideal profile of the PA expert at the EU level", *Journal of Public Affairs*, 2 (2): 85–89.

Scheutze, W. (1993) "What is an asset?", *Accounting Horizons*, 7.

Scholten, H.N. (2002) *Een ervaring rijker; experience als stuwende kracht achter mens en organisatie*, DST Experience Communicatie.

Scholten, H.N. and Kranendonk, B. (2003) "'Concerning': het Huis van COR, de marketing van het nieuwe millennium", *DST Conceptancy*, May 1.

Scholten, M. (1993) "The meaning of choice alternatives: attitudes and images", Dissertation, Katholieke Universiteit Brabant, January 15.

Schultz, D. (1993) "Just what are we integrating?", *Marketing News*, 27 (11): 10–11.

Schultz, D., and Barnes, Beth E. (1995) *Strategic Advertising Campaigns*, Lincolnwood, IL: NTC Business Books, 4th edn.

Schultz, D., Tannenbaum, S.I., and Lauterborn, R.F. (1993) *Integrated Marketing Communications: Pulling It Together and Making it Work*, Lincolnwood, IL: NTC Business Books.

Schultz, M., Hatch, M.J. and Larsen, M.H. (2000) *The Expressive Organization: Linking Identity, Reputation, and the Corporate Brand*, New York: Oxford University Press.

Schultz, T.P. (1994) "Human capital, family planning and their effects on population control", *American Economic Review*, 83: 255–260.

Schweiger, D.M. and Denisi, A.S. (1991) "Communication with employees following a merger: a longitudinal field experiment", *Academy of Management Journal*, 34 (1): 110–135.

Selame, E. and Selame, J. (1975) *Developing a Corporate Identity: How to Stand Out in the Crowd*, New York: John Wiley.

Selznick, P. (1957) *Leadership in Administration: A Sociological Approach*, Evanston: Row, Peterson and Company.

Senge, P.M. (1994) *The Fifth Discipline: The Art and Practice of the Learning Organization*, New York: Currency Doubleday.

Shapiro, C. (1983) "Premiums for high-quality products as returns to reputations", *Quarterly Journal of Economics*, 98: 659–681.

Shapiro, S.P. (1987) "The social control of impersonal trust", *American Journal of Sociology*, 93: 623–658.

Shrum, W. and Wuthnow, R. (1988) "Reputational status of organizations in technical systems", *American Journal of Sociology*, 93: 882–912.

Sikkel, D. (1991) *Natural Grouping*, Rotterdam: Computer programma Research International Netherlands.

Simon, H.A. (1997) *Administrative Behavior: A Study of Decision-making Processes in Administrative Organizations*, New York: Free Press.

Smidts, A., Pruyn, A.Th.H., and Riel, C.B.M., van (2001) "The impact of employee communication and perceived external prestige on organizational identification", *Academy of Management Journal*, 44 (5): 1051–1062.

Sobol, M.G. and Farrelly, G. (1989) "Corporate reputation: a function of relative size or financial performance?", *Review of Business & Economic Research*, 24: 45–59.

Spiegel, B. (1961) *Die Structur der Meinungsverteilung im sozialen Feld*, Stuttgart: Verlag Hans Huber.

Srivastava, R.K., McInish, T.H., Wood, R.A. and Capraro, A.J. (1997) "The value of corporate reputation: evidence from the equity markets", *Corporate Reputation Review*, 1: 62–68.

Stigler, G.J. (1962) "Information in the labor market", *Journal of Political Economy*, 70: 49–73.

Stiglitz, J. (1989) "Imperfect information in the product market", in: R. Schmalensee and R. Willig (eds), *Handbook of Industrial Organization*, pp. 769–847, Amsterdam: Noord-Holland Pers.

Strahle, W.M., Spiro, R.L. and Acito, F. (1996) "Marketing and sales: strategic alignment and functional implementation", *Journal of Personal Selling and Sales Management*, 16 (winter): 1–20.

Sullivan, M. (1990) "Measuring image spillovers in umbrella-branded products", *Journal of Business*, 63 (3): 309–329.

Tafertshofer, A. (1982) "Corporate identity: Das Grundgesetz des Unternehmensideologie", *Die Unternehmung*, 36 (1): 11–25.

Tajfel, H. (1981) *Human Groups and Social Categories: Studies in Social Psychology*, New York: Cambridge University Press.

Tanneberger, A. (1987) "Corporate identity. Studie zur theoretischen Fundierung und Präzisierung der Begriffe Unternehmenspersönlichkeit und Unternehmens–identität", Dissertation, Universität Freibourg, Schweiz.

Thönissen, C.E.G. (2003) *De beklimming van "Mount Trust": Do's and don't in Investor Relations*, Rotterdam: Erasmus University, Corporate Communication Centre.

Tichy, N.M. and Fombrun, C. (1979) "Network analysis in organizational settings", *Human Relations*, 11: 923–965.

Topalian, A. (1984) "Corporate identity: beyond the visual overstatements", *International Journal of Advertising*, 3 (1): 55–62.

Trombetta, J.J. and Rogers, D.P. (1988) "Communication climate, job satisfaction, and organizational commitment", *Management Communication Quarterly*, 4 (1): 494–514.

Turner, J.C. (1987) *Rediscovering the Social Group: A Self-Categorization Theory*, New York: Basil Blackwell.

Varona, F. (1996) "Relationship between communication satisfactions and organizational commitment in three Guatemalan organizations", *Journal of Business Communications*, 33 (2): 111–140.

Verbeke, W., Mosmans, A.P., and Verhulp, M. (1988) *Communicatiebeleid binnen Nederlandse Ondernemingen*, Rotterdam: Erasmus University.

Verhallen, Th. M.M. (1988) "Psychologisch marktonderzoek", Inaugural lecture, October 7, Katholieke Universiteit Brabant, Tilburg, Netherlands.

Wartick, S.L. (1992) "The relationship between intense media exposure and change in corporate reputation", *Business & Society*, 31: 33–49.

Wathen, M. (1986) "Logomotion, corporate identity makes its move into the realm of strategic planning", *Public Relations Journal*, May 24–29.

Weick, K. (1995) *Sensemaking in Organizations*, Thousand Oaks, CA: Sage.

Weigelt, K. and Camerer, C. (1988) "Reputation and corporate strategy: a review of recent theory and applications", *Strategic Management Journal*, 9: 443–454.

Westendorp, P.H., van and Herberg, L.J., van der (1984) "The KS technique: more value from image research for less money", *Esomar Congress Proceedings*, Esomar, Amsterdam.

White, C.H. (1981) "Where do markets come from?", *American Journal of Sociology*, 87: 517–547.

Wiedmann, K.P. (1988) "Corporate Identity als Unternehmensstrategie", *Wist*, 5: 236–242.

Wierenga, B. and Raaij, W.F. van (1987) *Consumentengedrag, theorie, analyse en toepassingen*, Leiden: Stenfert Kroese.

Wiio, O.A. and Helsila, M. (1974) "Auditing communication in organizations: a standard survey, LTT communication audits", *Finnish Journal of Business Economics*, 4: 305–315.

Wilson, R. (1985) "Reputations in games and markets", in: A.E. Roth (ed.), *Game-theoretic Models of Bargaining*, Cambridge: Cambridge University Press.

World Advertising Trends (2003) Oxford: NTC.

Zimmermann, S., Davenport, S.B., and Haas, J.W. (1996) "Communication meta myths in the workplace: the assumption that more is better", *Journal of Business Communication*, 33 (2): 185–203.

INDEX

3M 114, 133-134
4P's 28

AAA Model 154–156
Accenture 126–127
Accountability 34
  Coordinated 34
  Overall 34
  Specialist 34
AC²ID Model 72
Act-Up 2
ADMOD Model 176
Advertising Research Foundation's Model
    (ARF) 7
Ahold 187
Akzo Nobel 63
Altria Group 46, 107–108
Amazon.com 137
American Association of Advertising
    Agencies (AAAA) 19
American Chemistry Council 128
Applied research programs
    230–232
  BrandDynamics Pyramid 237–238
  CoreBrand's "Brand Power" 230,
    243–245
  EVA rating 234
  Fortune's "America's Most Admired
    Companies" (AMAC) 230,
    246–248
  Harris-Fombrun's "Reputation
    Quotient" (RQ)
    230, 248–252

  Harris Interactive's "Equitrend" 230,
    239, 242–243
  Power Grid 233–235
  Reputation Institute's "RepTrak®
    System" 230
  WPP's "BrandZ" 230, 237–239
  Young & Rubicam's Brand Asset
    Valuator (BAV) 230,
    232–236
Associations
  Organizational 118
  Product 118
  Dimensions of 119
  Corporate ability 119
  Social responsibility 119
  Relationships between various 120
AT&T 3
Attitude scales 222
Authenticity 62

Bank Slaski 109
Basel II 109
Boeing 4–5
BP 133
BrandEconomics 234
BrandDynamics Pyramid, *see* Applied
    research programs
Brand 4, 39, 107
  Drivers of corporate 110–111
  Equity 7–8, 242
  Generating value from the corporate
    117
  Image 7

The purpose of a 4
    typology 121
Brief, see also Copy platform 170
British Airways 126, 219
British American Tobacco 3
British Telecom 63

Card-sorting 221
Carrousel principle 279–280
Chanel 27
Climate Index (SOCIPO) 92–95
Coca Cola 243
Communication 1, 9
    Budgets 277–278
    Carousel principle 279–280
    audits 97
    Core competences
        264
    Designing effective 161
    Effective 7–8
    Fostering competitiveness through
        263
    Four perspectives on 33
    Integrated 3, 8, 9–10
    Management 14, 15–17
    Marketing 14, 17–19
    Organizational aspects of 260
    Organizational 14, 20–21
    system 2, 9, 280–282
    Structuring corporate 261
    Success criteria for 34–36
    Types of 14
    Value chain of 273
Communication Audit Survey (CAS),
        see ICA Audit
Communication function
    Principal activities 267
    Typical structure 269
    Five roles in communication function
        266
    Four mechanisms for integration 274
Communication Planning System (CPS)
    30
Consensus Profile 82–84
Construed identities 62
Content analysis 90
Coordinating teams 30
Co-orientation Model 168–169
Copy platform, see Brief
CoreBrand, see Applied research
    programs

CoreBrand's "Brand Power", see Applied
    research programs
Core competence, see also
    Communication 264
Corporate brand, see Brand
Corporate Communication, see also
    Communication
    Definitions 25
    Key tasks for 23–24
    Perspectives on 22
    Tools 27
Corporate Communication Centre 115
Corporate image, see Image
Corporate personality 40, 68
    scale 40–42
    profile 84
Corporate reputation, see Reputation
Corporate Reputation Review 21, 43
Communication Satisfaction (CS) 97,
        99–100
Corporate story 136
    Building blocks 144
    Creating a 149
    Unique elements 145
    Unique plots 145
    Unique presentation 146
Country-of-origin effects 45
Customer Relations 193–194
    Experience Marketing 194

DaimlerChrysler 31, 73, 112–113, 262
Dell 264
DHL 109
Domino Effect 167–168
DuPont 137
Dutch Association for Investor Relations
    (NEVIR) 184

EcQ®-The Strategic Alignment Monitor
    209–210, 281
Elaboration Likelihood Model (ELM) 53
Employee Relations (ER) 188
    Climate 192
    Content 191–192
    Flow 191
    Roles ER specialists 188
    Structure 190
European Marketing Confederation
    (EMC) 19
EVA ratings, see Applied research
    programs

Evoked set 47
Experience Marketing, *see* Customer
    Relations 194
Expressiveness 212, 281
    Reputation IMPACT Model 179
Expressiveness Profile 90–91
ExxonMobil 133

Federal Drug Administration (FDA) 197
FedEx 243
FHV/BBDO 218
Ford Motor Company 113, 262
Fortune's "America's Most Admired
    Companies" (AMAC), *see* Applied
    research programs
Fragmented identity syndrome 74
    Aggregation 74
    Compartmentalization 74
    Deletion 74
    Integration 74

Gallup 207
Game theory 53
General Electric (GE) 107, 133, 173, 183
General Motors 112–113, 195, 228, 263
GlaxoSmithKline 2, 109
Google 243
Government Relations 196–199
    Lobbying 196–197
    Public Affairs 196
Graphic Audits 103–105
Greenpeace 2, 170, 204

Harley-Davidson 27
Harris Interactive 202, 230, 248
Harris Interactive's "Equitrend", *see*
    Applied research programs
Harris-Fombrun's "Reputation Quotient"
    (RQ), *see* Applied research
    programs
Hewlett Packard 133–134
Hierarchical Value Map (HVM) 88
HSBC 172
Human memory
    Long-term memory 52
    Sensory memory 52
    Short-term memory 52

ICA Audit, *see also* Communication audit
    survey 97, 100
IBM 133

Identification 75
    Employee 115–116
Identity
    Applied 70, 88–89
    Definitions 66
    Desired 70, 82–85
    Ideal 70
    cobweb 82–83
    Measurement approaches 80, 82
    mix 62, 67–69, 92
    rooted in design 63
    rooted in corporate culture 64
    rooted in communication 65
    scales 86–87
    Multiple 73–74
    Perceived 70, 85–87
    Process of management 78–79
    Projected 70, 89–91
    Selecting elements of 69–70
    Three approaches 63
IDU Method 155, 161
IKEA 137, 140–142
IMPACT Model 177–178
    Reputational IMPACT Model, *see also*
        Expressiveness 179
Image spillover effect 117
Image, *see also* Corporate Image 26, 39
ING Group 109, 162
Information processing
    Individual 49, 51–53
    Levels of 46
International Association of Business
        Communications (IABC) 19
International Communication Association
        (ICA) 97
Interpublic 262
INVE 134, 139, 142–144
Invention of tradition 132
Investor Relations (IR) 183
    External audiences 185–187
    Internal audiences 184–185
Issues Management, *see* Public Relations

J.D. Power & Associates 228
Johnson & Johnson 137, 173–174,
    243

Knowledge, Attitude and Behavior Model
    (KAB Model) 31, 35–36
Kodak 133
Kelly Repertory Grid 88, 215

Laddering 88
LEGO 146–148, 194
Lobbying, *see* Government Relations
LTT Communication Audit Questionnaire,
    see also Organizational
    Communication Audit
    Questionnaire (OCA) 97

MacDonalds 52, 133
Marketing communication, *see also*
    communication
  Integrated 28–29
  5 stages of 29
Marks & Spencer 70–71, 239, 241
MECCAS Model 174–175
Media
  mix 175
  balloon 176
MEDICA Model 176
Memory, *see* Human memory
Merck 2, 109
Messaging Profile 89
Microsoft 31–32, 45, 133

Natural Grouping 216
Nestlé 109
Nike 27, 52, 133, 163
Nomenclatures 132
  Steps driving 135
Nokia 133–134
Novartis 109
NSS Market Research 221

Omnicom 262
Organizational Communication Audit
    Questionnaire (OCA), *see* Applied
    research programs
Organizational Communication
    Instrument (OC), *see* Applied
    research programs

Parenting advantage 108
Personality Profile, *see* Corporate
    personality
Pfizer 2, 109, 128, 133–134, 137
Pharmaceutical Research and
    Manufacturers of America
    (PhRMA) 197
Philips 109, 133, 173
Photo-sort 218
Port-Authority Study 76

Power Grid, *see* Applied research
    programs
PPT Model 171
Press agentry, *see also* Propaganda 34
PriceWaterhouseCoopers 125
Process of communication planning 276
Propaganda, *see* Press agentry
Public information 34
Public Relations (PR) 200–206
  Issues Management 203–206
Publicity 18
PUL Model 164–165, 167

Q-sort 217

Rabobank 145
Rebranding 125
Renault 63
RepTrak® 230, 253–256
  analysis 256, 258–259
  instrument 282
  scorecard 253
  system 253–256
Repsol 63
Reputational capital 59
Reputational ratings, *see* reputation
Reputation 38, 40, 43–44
  Applied research programs, *see*
      Applied research programs
  Approaches to management 213
  Building 36, 46
  Decision-making 224–225
  Measurement options 211,
      226–227
  Ratings 207–208
  The importance of 47–48
  Value Cycle 271
Reputation Institute (RI) 21, 43, 202,
    230, 248, 250, 253, 280
Reputation Institute's "RepTrak®
    System", *see* Applied research
    programs
Reputation Platform 131–132, 136
  Activity theme 136
  Benefits theme 136
  Emotional theme 137
Reputation Quotient (RQ) 43,
    248–252
Revised Basel Framework, *see* Basel II
Rotterdam Organizational Identification
    Test (ROIT) 95–97

Sarbanes-Oxley Act 109
Scope 114
Securities & Exchange Commission
        (SEC) 197
Shell 2, 31, 170, 171, 204
Sir Richard Branson 137–138
Southwest Airlines 137
Stakeholder
   Perceptions 38
Starbucks 52, 107, 195
Steinway 27, 52
Stakeholder Linkage Model 163,
        182
Strategic alignment 209, 281
Strategy-Identity-Brand Triangle
        (SIB Triangle) 35
Symbols 101–103

Two-way asymmetric communication
        34
Two-way symmetric communication
        34
Typology of corporate brands

Olins' branding strategies 121
Kammerer's action types
        121–122
Van Riel's typology 122–125

Unilever 114
UPS 243

Virgin Group 137–139
Visual identity systems 27
Volkswagen 195
Volvo 137

Wal-Mart 205
WPP 262
WPP's "BrandZ", see Applied research
        programs

Xerox 133

Young & Rubicam's Brand Asset
        Valuator, see Applied research
        programs